Theatre and Cultural Interaction

Theatre and Cultural Interaction

Maria Shevtsova

SYDNEY STUDIES

Theatre and Cultural Interaction

Sydney Studies in Society and Culture 9

Published by the Sydney Association
for Studies in Society and Culture
The University of Sydney
NSW 2006

and distributed by
Sydney Studies
PO Box 575, Leichhardt
NSW 2040
Australia

ISBN 0 949405 08 6
ISSN 0192 6402

Printed in Australia by Berget Pty Ltd

Published with the assistance of
the University of Sydney

CONTENTS

PREFACE

The essays collected here reflect some of my main concerns during the past ten years and belong to the sociology of the theatre as I have understood and developed it until now. The areas of my research that I have chosen for the purposes of this volume are productions, audiences and performers. These are essential components of the theatre which, while distinguishing it from literature, dramatic and otherwise, place the theatre firmly in the realm of what in French is exquisitely called *les arts du spectacle*, "performing arts" in English not quite capturing the precision of the French phrase. Even so, the term *spectacle* is not monosemantic and thus not crystal clear: it incorporates a wide range of shows (variety and circuses, for example, are *spectacles*) that leave the term and, with it, the very notion of art, open to debate.

My essays do not dwell on problems of definition. Their focus, whether viewed from the perspective of spectators, performers or directors (as happens in the second essay, Universal Theatre/Universal Culture? and again when Jean-Pierre Mignon discusses his staging of *Peer Gynt*), is on performance works in which dialogue plays a considerable part. Their centre of interest, then, is what is known in Italy as *teatro di prosa*, which most usefully distinguishes play performance (or "performance of plays") from other types of play or performance. Two of the essays devoted to productions - *Peer Gynt* by Patrice Chéreau and another stage version of the same play by Jean-Pierre Mignon - show that the "theatre" at issue here involves play performance and not other kinds of *teatro* or *spectacle* or performance, nor - least of all - the relatively new genre going under the name of "performance art". The latter cannot, of course, be confused with the plural "performance arts". The third essay, which gives an account of a bilingual *Three Sisters*, in French and Russian and directed by Nika Kossenkova and Pascal Larue, stays within the definition of the theatre as outlined here.

Even these brief words suggest that I have not taken a monocultural or monolingual approach to the subject at hand. The approach may be generally described as "European" insofar as European directors/thinkers have nurtured my own reflections. Nevertheless, however appropriate, if unstable, the adjective "European" may be today in a federated Europe - so far of twelve countries - it is not the European aspect of the chosen directors/thinkers that is of most importance to these essays. Nor, consequently, am I proposing a Eurocentric or western view, or whatever other definition is used, favourably *or* pejoratively.

In other words, notwithstanding the fundamental role played by a broadly European social and cultural context in the elaboration of their ideas and practice, a role to which I certainly pay attention, what takes precedence in these essays is the *theoretical* value to be gained from the directors/thinkers cited. Consequently, the works of Mikhaïl Bakhtin and Pierre Bourdieu, on the one hand, and, on the other, the principles guiding the theatre practice of Peter Brook, Jerzy Grotowski and Eugenio Barba provide major theoretical categories as well as points of reference for the hypotheses, proposals and arguments running through this book.

The fourth area, then, in which I have been working and which is included in the present collection involves theory. It was logical to call my first section "Theoretical Considerations" precisely because, although I regard theory as an area of the discipline of the sociology of the theatre (as is, for example, the rubric of "spectators", it seems to me to be impossible to deal with the empirical reality of the theatre without some kind of conceptual framework. Theories provide us with something on which to hang our ideas, feelings, images and sensations, and a means of constructing them and pulling them together so that they make sense.

No one would contest the fact that we do or make theatre, which is why it is a practice in the truest sense of the word. And few would disagree that it is an art. Many, however, have been slow to recognize that theatre art is generated by social agents in a social context and that, as a socialized and socializing action, it is full of *social* as well as aesthetic meaning. We could put this differently by saying that everything we think of as being art in the theatre is not purely aesthetic: what belongs to art comes out of a society, and is caught up in a tangled network of activities to which are given such names as "economics", "politics", "education" and "culture". The accumulation of these and more activities in time, and the changes wrought upon them by women and men over the course of time, give us "history", from which the theatre, like all other practices, is inseparable. The theatre builds its own history in relation to this larger history. But no matter where it is constructed, the theatre vibrates with the movements of its society.

These points are at the heart of the sociology of the theatre and must reappear, as they do in various guises, throughout this book. Nevertheless, what I emphasize here is one particular point or, rather, focus of interest that the sociology of the theatre would do well to develop. This concerns culture. The theatre, by being a social activity through and through, and consequently a collective one, is also a cultural practice. In other words, it is created out of the behaviours, emotions and values that are invested in the images and symbols appropriate to a particular social group. Once again, I do not concentrate on matters of definition, this time of the term "culture". This term, like every other one that I have used so far, refers to complex phenomena and its very complexity assures its multiple meanings.

Suffice it to say that I draw on two main blocs of meaning: on "culture", when it refers to the behaviours, values, customs and assumptions manifested in everyday life, and on "culture", when it means the arts and related constructions of the imagination, feelings and mind. Clearly, the two blocs of meaning must be interconnected in some way. The theatre is culture as defined within the second bloc. Hence such descriptions as "high" or "learned" or "intellectual" culture. However, since the theatre does not, and cannot, spin in a rarefied atmosphere (this would be the arcane sphere of Art) but, on the contrary, has its feet firmly planted on the ground (irrespective of how ethereal or magical its effects), it is "culture" according to the first bloc. That is to say, it is part of the everyday organization of values, customs, and so on, by which this or that group of people lives, and is influenced, if not moulded, by that very organization. "Culture" irrevocably calls upon "society", and vice versa. It would be hard to imagine a society without a culture (more likely cultures) or a culture that has not been elaborated by a collectivity - "society" - of some sort.

The intricacies of culture, of values, mentalities and perceptions, which are integral to societal interaction, permeate my research on theatre spectators. Since the research is ongoing, I have deliberately kept the "in progress" quality of my essays on spectators.

This having been said, these essays are nevertheless a significant contribution to the study of audiences - particularly because of their emphasis on a *qualitative* approach. Their qualitative dimension is highlighted by their emphasis on the culture of spectators, which culture includes the latter's value-systems, evaluative skills vis-à-vis the theatre, expectations of the theatre, and the roles/purposes/values attributed by spectators to it. Despite the growing number of audience studies available, it is still most unusual to find the kind of culturally-focused, qualitatively-centred perspective that seeks to bring out the interactive relationship between spectators and performance and that is characteristic of my work.

ACKNOWLEDGEMENTS

I am indebted to the Australian Research Council for awarding me a grant under the Large Grants Scheme and which enabled me to carry out a good deal of the work recorded in this volume, particularly on theatre spectators. I wish to thank my Research Assistants, Roberta Burke and Racheline Barda; and Wendy Cobcroft who helped me to see the material through to publication and helped in so many ways that words of gratitude pale into insignificance. I owe to Anne Daniel, Michael Bittman and Michael Pusey, all in the Department of Sociology at the University of New South Wales, illuminating commentaries on the definitions of the occupational categories provided by the Australian Bureau of Statistics. Neville Shulman, President of the British chapter of the International Theatre Institute, generously sent me information he thought I might find useful. David Williams at the University of Western Australia, Perth, has always given me his unfailing support.

On the Paris side of my research, I wish to thank warmly for their many kindnesses my colleagues Martine Burgos, Brigitte Navelet and Jacques Leenhardt at the Ecole des Hautes Etudes en Sciences Sociales, and Patrice Pavis, Professor in the Département d'Etudes Théâtrales, Université de Paris VIII.

"Minority/Dominant Culture in the Theatre" is a revised version of a paper presented in 1991 at "Theatre and the Discourses of Power", a conference sponsored by the Department of Drama at the University of Exeter.

"Social and Cultural Elites" is a revised version of a text for the annual conference of the Australasian Drama Studies Association held in 1991 at the University of New South Wales.

The material in my essay on audiences for *Phedra*, the tragedy by Racine staged by Michael Gow, was first used for a paper delivered at Melbourne University in 1991. The occasion was a conference of the

Melbourne Performance Research Group entitled "Performance and its Discourses".

"Cultural Values and the Purposes of the Theatre" was first given in an abridged form and with a slightly different emphasis at "The Arts in the Media Age", a conference of the Research Committee 37 "Sociology of the Arts" of the International Sociological Association held at the University of Trento in 1992.

PART I

THEORETICAL CONSIDERATIONS

1

MINORITY/DOMINANT CULTURE IN THE THEATRE (WITH SPECIAL REFERENCE TO BAKHTIN AND BOURDIEU)

Theatre theory encompasses a diverse range of interests and perspectives which cannot be neatly captured in a few words. Nevertheless, we fall back on convenient phrases - take, for example, "from Aristotle to Brook" - because we assume that what has been left unsaid will be understood. Not so long ago the line would probably have stopped at Brecht. Today it extends to semiotics as well as to various theories of postmodernism, or what are described as postmodernist, this new contribution coming out of universities rather than from theatre artists themselves. The way in which the academy has become the major source of theorizing about the theatre indicates an important slide (or perhaps even shift of power?) away from the site of theatre practice to institutions whose experts do not necessarily have a working expertise in the theatre or a special sensitivity towards it as a living, breathing art. It seems that, until relatively recently, theatre practitioners - Brecht and Brook certainly among them - would have towered over any survey of theatre theory.

The purpose, of course, of any overview, wherever it may begin or end, is to point out that a canon is available for our edification. Pierre Bourdieu, in a different context, calls it a "scholarly culture" which, he argues, both consolidates and legitimates the standing of dominant social groups.[1] In other words, scholarly culture - and it is by no means confined to academics - is especially useful for preserving the status quo. What, though, has happened to our theoretical canon and particularly to its reputed classics, modern "classics" included? Irrespective of whether or not they constitute an established culture, which, in Bourdieu's terms, is exclusive to elites, they have retreated into the shadows, only appearing now and again in cameo parts to remind us of their existence.

Meanwhile, the new culture, which theatre semiotics may be said to represent, has claimed the limelight. This has to do with fashions, trends, and the like. Yet fashions catch on in a given time and place, mediating the socioeconomic structures, institutions and criss-cross of values from which they climb to prominence. Theories, then, although conceptual constructions, do not transcend the pressures of empirical reality. Bourdieu would here say that theories, and specifically the theorists developing or annexing them, play for high stakes, for the symbolic power invested in knowledge and which is conferred on those who have knowledge perceived to be at the top of current intellectual priorities.[2] In addition, still following Bourdieu, symbolic power is never more prestigious than when real power - economic, social or political - is well and truly out of reach. The notion of power as regards knowledge, referred to here, has to do with much more than the notion of "cultural competence" on which Bourdieu relies in order to explain how certain theorists rise to the top and succeed in maintaining their position of strength against contenders. That is to say, insistence on one's own competence (which bestows authority on the claimant) implies a lack of competence and even sheer incompetence on the part of those who are deemed to be out of the running for the symbolic power in question. If nothing succeeds like success, nothing succeeds in "scholarly culture" - here providing further interpretation of Bourdieu - like brash confidence, especially when technical and other instrumentalist ideas of learning and implementation thereof are called upon to legitimize the activity. Nothing succeeds today like justification in the name of use-value, whether scientific and technological, or purely commercial.

The ascent of semiotics is related to the great value accorded to the technological sciences in the second half of the twentieth century. The sociological intricacies involved need not concern us unduly, but what should at least be noted is the impact of semiotic theory on so-called traditional notions of theatre art. In other words, the ideas integral to aesthetics, from which the very terms "playtexts" and "stage productions" draw their meaning, have taken on a scientific character where the laws of sign systems, and the models, schemas and diagrams illustrating them, abound. Never before have works of the theatre been subjected to such strict analytical procedures, nor been so tightly bound by the rules purportedly governing them. Nor have dramatists, actors, directors and all other participants in theatrical activity, audiences included, ever been so completely removed from sight. Clearly, a theory that can do all this is nothing if not efficient.[3]

Now, these remarks do not call into question the internal coherence of the theory as such. Theatre semiotics is certainly rigorous and consistent. Major problems arise, however, when factors considered to be external to it enter onto the scene. Theatre semiotics has relegated categories external to its framework to other approaches: "art" to aesthetics, "society" to sociology, "culture" to anthropology, and the list could go on, each item ensuring a plurality of methodologies applicable to the study of theatre. The whole thing looks like an equitable division of labour, but is, in fact, an exercise in fragmentation from which theatre emerges impoverished. The step from impoverishment to disempowerment is very small indeed.

The separation between approaches in the name of pluralism probably has less to do with the open-minded tolerance advocated by it and more to do with the decidedly non-pluralistic supposition that different approaches are mutually exclusive. Yet theatre would be far better served if we looked for connecting links between them. This does not imply borrowing pieces from here and there in the hope that they will fit together. It entails a search for mutually inclusive principles. These would allow us to cross barriers imposed artificially beforehand by theoretical fiat. They may resist attempts to bind them into a fully coherent theory. So be it, for if they illuminate theatre practice, which is precisely what theatre is, they will have fulfilled their purpose. And, in any event, even the most complete theories are not self-sufficient, self-regulating entities. They are designed to help us understand and explain the empirical, concrete world - in our case, theatre. Put differently, this means that theories cannot rely solely on their internal organization. They are always at the beck and call of something external to them. If they fail to respond, they have to be rethought.

And here is the crux of the matter. Theatre practice, though involving creativity, fantasy, imagination - in a word, art - is the action of those who do it. Whether professionals or amateurs, their work takes place in nameable societies which, despite the all-embracing term "society", are neither unified nor homogeneous. Societies, wherever they are geographically, are composed of groups differentiated by gender, ethnic identity, religion, occupation, salary and other sociodemographic features, some of them common to several groups. Although the criteria for defining them vary, social groups form strata, castes, classes, sub-classes or sets, the number and kind of larger groupings depending on the present circumstances as well as the historical antecedents of a particular society. The individuals who combine into groups, small or large, are social beings, whether they like it, admit it, or deny it because they feel they are unique. A unique one is no less social for being distinctive from many.

The individuals coming together to mount a stage production, this entailing a variety of preparatory processes, are no less social because they are directors, actors and so on, that is, distinguished by their role in creative enterprise. Try as we might, then, we cannot cut society out of theatre. For this reason alone, an activity belonging to the conceptual framework of aesthetics belongs, at the same time, to a sociological framework.

A series of objections could be raised at this point, going roughly as follows. The interconnection described applies to people's activities on the job, but is irrelevant to the final outcome of their efforts, namely, the works or products produced by them. Plays and play productions are compositions. They are forms, genres, styles - everything that is specific to art. A given tragedy, for instance, conforms more or less to the genre, which is why it cannot be confused with other types of plays. When it is staged it becomes a performance, and this relies on numerous interpretative skills: vocal projection, gesture and movement, taking only the bare minimum from a whole array displayed by performers. Then there are props, costumes, music, lighting, and the like. These are integral to the stage composition and to its overall style. Then there is the director, or her/his equivalent, whose aesthetic vision is intrinsic to the aesthetic of the production itself. All this is the final product to which the specialized discourse known as aesthetics refers. Since society is extrinsic to the former, talk of societal principles in relation to the principles of aesthetics is misplaced.

As the argument very briefly outlined draws to a close, it becomes apparent that the purely formalistic view of plays and productions around which it revolves means they are bound to be treated as things, as objects identified by their properties. But this is the aestheticized counterpart of the scientific endeavour of semiotics, genres and related concepts replacing sign systems. We are left with little choice. Either we adopt the idea that theatre works are things and proceed accordingly. Or else we persist in believing that theatre is practice. The second commits us to the idea that works not only embody someone's actions, but are also actions in their own right. In other words, they are charged through and through by the dynamic process of creation generated by their creators.

With this in mind, let us return to the notion that signs constitute the systems which, in another language, are called "works". Does defining works as actions mean abandoning the very concept of the sign? I think not, provided it is taken out of the static, mechanistic sphere of systems and put into the dynamic and changing sphere of practice. When this is done, we can talk about sign processes that activate works of the theatre instead of sign systems that control them. It also helps us to understand why theatre signs are social signs.

Here we must turn to Bakhtin for whom signs, if not social, can be nothing at all. Bakhtin, it must be remembered, does not discuss the theatre. Which does not mean his ideas are irrelevant to it. Moreover, although he is essentially concerned with verbal signs, he occasionally extrapolates from them so as to cover signs in general. Thus his observations are applicable to facial, gestural and visual signs, among many more, which, besides the verbal signs rendering dialogue and prompting its inflections, intonations and rhythms, give sense and meaning to stage productions. These, because of the network of signs overlaying each other simultaneously, are extremely complex aesthetic compositions put together in the very moment of creation by performers, the creativity of non-performers (for instance, of the director, set, lighting and costume designers) welded into their performance.

Bakhtin's theory is based on the premise that signs are brought about by people as they interact with each other. Speech, although crucial for their social interaction, is but one of numerous activities in which they are engaged during the course of their lives. Since people are not amorphous, the signs they make are specific to their social groupings, some signs becoming strong markers of this or that social class as a whole. We could say, for example, following Bakhtin's train of thought, that lawyers do not speak, dress or gesticulate in the same way as street cleaners. The differences in sign production, then, have to do with social relations; in addition, with the social values attached to signs by those making them and those to whom they are conveyed. The values in question are not necessarily exactly the same for each partner in the exchange of signs taking place.

The idea of exchange alluded to here is at the heart of Bakhtin's argument that meanings of some sort are always communicated through the ongoing flow of signs between social beings as they construct their world. Signs are the very substance of communicated meanings which are specific to the situations in a determined space and place where communication occurs. Meanings are understood best when signs and, therefore, the evaluations made through them are shared. They are poorly communicated, or miscommunicated altogether, when words, tones, images, movements, and so forth, are too closely bound to the "jargons" of their users. (I am using "jargons" for non-verbal as well as verbal signs for want of a better term.) Bakhtin maintains that the meanings in and of signs are constantly involved in processes of exchange between people. Thus, although they are specific to social groupings and to the situations relevant to these groupings, they are circulated across the board; and precisely because they are circulated throughout society in general, sign-meanings can be appropriated by a singular or collective someone else for their own purposes. It must be noted that the concept of appropriation developed by Bakhtin is not the same as those of co-option or annexation with which it is sometimes confused.

What must now be added to my interpretation of Bakhtin's theory is his idea that signs are made intentionally. That is to say, they depend on the volition, intentions, decisions and goals of people at a given historical time. Hence his emphasis on their irreducibly social character.

Several more points are worth making. A theory of culture is implicit in Bakhtin's observations, particularly on discourses in the novel, the art form of special interest to him. However, his focus on the social sources, communicative powers and capacities for the interchange of signs can be widened to include their cultural significance. If we develop Bakhtin's argument in this way, signs can be understood to be sociocultural signs.

The following considerations now need to be taken into account. Cultures, like societies, are heterogeneous. A whole host of different cultures exist in one country and within its national culture. We speak of "regional", "folk", "popular" and "high-brow" cultures, among possible descriptions. Bourdieu, as was noted earlier, speaks of the culture of the elite, this category intertwined with a series of categories designating what he generally calls a dominant culture. Whichever term is used to distinguish one type of culture from the next, its applicability depends on the momentum of a society as well as on the groups, castes, classes, or whatever is peculiar to it. This is why Bourdieu, when referring to the phenomenon he identifies as dominant culture, must also refer to the dominant classes or class fractions whose culture predominates. According to Bourdieu, these classes or class fractions wield such enormous power through the institutions they have inherited from their forebears, and which they continue to reproduce, that social mobility is virtually impossible. Furthermore, they impress upon subaltern classes the view that their own cultural tastes, vis-à-vis works of art in particular, are the most valid tastes to be had and, consequently, are to be desired above all others. This view is imparted so effectively through all the institutional channels monopolized by the ruling minority that the subaltern classes absorb it, thereby bending their will to the dictates of an oligarchy whose tentacular culture is, in any case, inaccessible to them. Their attempts to generate an autonomous culture are thwarted at every turn.

Given his vision of what can only be called social blockage, where art-culture, too, is obstructive and obstructed, Bourdieu has no alternative but to conclude that popular culture or a people's culture is sheer myth.[4] It may once have been viable (presumably when powers of coercion were not quite so ruthless - here surmising from Bourdieu's omissions regarding this subject) but is out of the question for a highly rationalized France which Bourdieu seems to take to be representative of "advanced", "post-industrial" or "postmodernist" societies, the choice of adjective not changing in the slightest an irreversible state of affairs. The situation delineated by Bourdieu simply cannot accommodate a people's theatre, a minority theatre (as opposed to the "majority" theatre of the establishment), or any other theatre that does not conform to the canonical expectations, aspirations and tastes of the ruling elite.

Bourdieu's conclusion needs to be critically reassessed, as do a number of the steps by which he reaches it. However, I have referred to him in order to stress that notions to do with culture call upon those to do with society, and vice versa. How this necessary linkage between the two is dealt with is of consequence, as is clear from Bourdieu, to the role and status of works of art for those who make them, those who enjoy them and those who are excluded from them. The penalty of exclusion, Bourdieu maintains, is dispossession, not least in respect of works of art which, by the force of circumstances, are transformed into cultural goods. Bourdieu, of course, concentrates on the processes by which these goods are distributed unevenly. And, although perfectly aware of the impact of signs (arguing, for instance, that cultural capital is a sign of distinction for those who have it, and is interpreted accordingly by those who do not), he is not concerned with the sign processes constituting art works as such.

Here we may return to Bakhtin, whose theory of signs - or more accurately of sign processes - allows us to understand how and why stage productions purposefully communicate something to someone. The "something" at issue refers to multiple meanings and the "someone" refers to spectators who, although united for the duration of a performance, are far from being a single social unit. This by no means repeats the idea that spectators are an anonymous body, an abstraction to whom the performance must nevertheless play in order to be a performance in any sense of the word at all. Nor does it resuscitate the old idea, let us call it the fourth wall syndrome, which places performers on one side of a barricade and spectators on the other, thereby turning spectators into mere onlookers or, worse still, into voyeurs poking in the dark. More recent variations on the theme of onlookers give us spectators who are receivers of art objects or, as Bourdieu puts it, of cultural goods. Reception theory embellishes the theme but, despite enhancing the role of spectators, essentially leaves them on the receiving end of the transaction. That is to say, the artefact comes first and its reception follows. What might be called functionalist approaches cast spectators in the role of consumers. Thus the stage production is the product packaged on the assembly line, while the consumer is the buyer who closes the production-consumption circuit. But, although the image has changed from lines to circuits (walls also being lines), the buyer, who legitimates the input of labour into the commodity, is outside the productive force itself.[5]

None of these holds when we take a Bakhtinian perspective on the relationship between performers, performances and spectators, a relationship acknowledged by theatre studies to be crucial but which, all things considered, has not had the attention it deserves. What Bakhtin offers us is a number of interlocking concepts with which to grasp this relationship as one composite process (thereby also allowing us to see how theoretical discourse can be adequate to theatre practice, an issue raised earlier). The composite process in question re-positions spectators, who are no longer outsiders looking in - and the reverse holds for performers, that is, they are no longer insiders looking out - but who, *together* with performers, make the meanings of performances. Meanings, as Bakhtin's principles indicate, are neither univocal nor monolithic. Nor, again, do they turn inwards, as if on an axis unique to the stage processes at hand. They come from outside that plethora of sign activities which are materialized by and through social beings in the complex, diversified and contradictory place and space of society. They are borrowed and interpreted by performers for the intentions of a particular performance, these intentions not always conscious, deliberate or even transparent. And they are interpreted by spectators who, since they share the experience of the performance and share, however unequally, the social space encompassing the theatre, recognize the signs that come to them and go back to the stage in the form of sighs, tears, laughter, applause or any other form of responsive return. The communication taking place on multiple interpretative levels can only occur because the "outside" world is inside the theatre. Thus, how a performer speaks, moves, gesticulates, and so on, draws on the speech, movements, gestures, and so on, that spectators also know, feel and can imagine precisely because they, too, produce similar signs in their daily interaction. Nothing in the theatre is plucked out of pure nothing.

Now, just because communication occurs in variegated tones and colours does not mean that spectators will interact in directly corresponding fashion, tone for tone. As was indicated earlier, spectators, albeit temporarily united, are anything but a homogeneous mass. They are anything but united as one. Their differences, by whichever criteria are brought into play (gender, ethnic origin, ethnic self-definition, class background, aspirations to class ascent, and more again), help explain why certain sign processes in performance have a special resonance, a special spring and bounce for some members of the audience, and evoke perhaps little more than a token gesture of recognition from their neighbours.

Spectators, although differentiated, do not have absolute liberty to interpret as they will. A very subtle, moderately discreet or sometimes blatant guide is right there in the aesthetic vision mediating the performance's content or substance. It guides the spectators' entry into the dialogue which is presupposed from the outset for any kind of communication to happen at all. Dialogue fails to take place when certain spectators experience exclusion. However, exclusion, just like inclusion, is relational, that is, with respect to its implied antinomies, however ambivalent or opaque they may be. And this means that, when exclusion is experienced, a limited form of communication has occurred, a negative communication which relies on the great range of sign-actions and sign-meanings circulating, as Bakhtin describes it, throughout a given society. In other words, while the sign processes going back and forth between performers and spectators are group-specific or even group-centred, they break out in kaleidoscopic fashion, refracting (another Bakhtinian trope) the multiple social relations without which they simply could not exist.

All this suggests that everything Bakhtin says about social signs is just as relevant for what I have called sociocultural signs. Let us take the distinctions between classical high-art theatre, which belongs to the canon, and "popular" theatre which, in being non-canonical by design (until such time as it is co-opted!), either has a lower position in the hierarchy (thus "low-art") or is outside the vertical structure altogether, decentred, so to speak, and delineating margins of its own. A production of, say, Shakespeare, Racine or Chekhov, whether performed in their national culture or transferred across cultures, targets audiences who are equipped with a certain "cultural baggage" or, at least, are presumed to be capable of acquiring the requisite trappings for understanding it. The production may not be oriented to very specific, perhaps even well-seasoned, theatregoers. It may be attempting to reach a "wider audience", this phrase often referring euphemistically to economically disadvantaged groups. In which case, it will anticipate the capacities for interpretation on the part of the potential or explicitly identified spectators who, to boot, may well be totally new to the theatre. As Bakhtin reminds us, sign-makers always seek out other sign-makers by their very actions. If this were not so, we would only talk or gesticulate to ourselves. Even then, Bakhtin argues, we are engaged in interior dialogue, in the necessarily dialogical relationship between self and other that is contingent upon the use of signs. In the case of interior dialogue, we might be said to be communicating with a number of split selves in our persona, all of which refract our interface with numerous others filling our world. The issue of the "other" (someone who is not-I) is rooted, in Bakhtin, in his completely materialist conception of social relations. It does not, in other words, stem from psychoanalytical considerations on the self or on alterity to self, many of which have fed postmodernist theories of one kind and another.

My hypothetical production, then, not only builds shared knowledge, experience, emotions and expectations into its structure in order to have this or that special resonance for a collectivity, whatever its size. It also appeals to the cultural predilections of its real or imputed spectators. In being part of a theatre culture, whether exclusive to an elite (as Bourdieu would say) or open to purposeful appropriation beyond an elite (as Bakhtin would say), the production's entire aesthetic is constructed from the sociocultural signs at its disposal. A play by Shakespeare performed, for instance, by the Comédie Française, not only reprocesses linguistic signs, but, in doing so, finds the vocal registers, physical images and spatial dispositions that are bound to strike some chord appropriate to the culture of its spectators. "Culture" here has two main meanings. The first refers to culture in the broadest sense of the term, which gives us "French" as distinct from "English" culture. The second has the narrower meaning denoted by such terms as class culture or group culture. The play performed by a different company based in the working-class suburbs of Paris (or, for that matter, of regional cities) is sure to keep an eye on its known or imagined audiences, communicating to them somewhat differently from the modes adopted by the Republic's (formerly the King's) consecrated players.

Well, the second instance may be an example of Shakespeare brought to the people, as the expression goes. Indeed, the issue of whether, today, a classical heritage can or should be "brought" to the people is vast. It involves, inter alia, debates on the educative value of theatre. It is as vast as the issue of whether and how non-privileged communities, which by the catch-all "people" are distinguished from privileged ones, should develop their own theatre, with or without the classics. Even to begin to tackle these issues would take me much further afield than is possible in the present context. However, the very least that may be suggested is this in the form of questions. If Shakespeare is confined to the hallowed halls of culture, which halls, as scholars have argued, have expropriated him from the people, are societies doomed to the impasse analyzed by Bourdieu? Will established theatre remain, to all intents and purposes, the theatre of the establishment, all alternative theatrical forms meanwhile pushed to the periphery where they will be little more than curiosities, minor cultures with little hope of matching the culture of a minority?

Further. If the subaltern classes do develop their own theatre, let us say *without* Shakespeare (or Racine, or any canonical figure), does the ensuing empowerment, culturally speaking, bring about a contradictory situation, namely: they are empowered in the delimited sphere of culture which is justly their own, but remain disempowered in respect of a far bigger conglomeration that, while no longer dominating them completely, confines them to ghettos? I have used "subaltern classes" for the sake of terminological consistency vis-à-vis my references to Bourdieu. However, it should be noted at this particular juncture that I am including in the category, as in the generalized "people" cited earlier, the now unfashionable working classes, rural workers and peasants, as well as the urban and rural poor who elude precise classification. By the same token, I am also including the now fashionable groups who, although certainly no less important for being discursively *à la mode*, go under the general rubric of ethnic minorities and women.

So, having inelegantly left you with the questions, let me come back to the spectators who, dignified by a sociocultural perspective derived from Bakhtin, resist being defined as the pawns of systems. For, as soon as theoretical reasoning aided by empirical observation acknowledges them to be empowered, albeit to varying degrees in dissimilar social conditions, spectators can no longer be put in the abject position of recipients on whom graces are bestowed. Furthermore, the whole notion of production-performance takes on an entirely different dimension when spectators are understood to be active partners in it. It is imperative to remember this in an era where talk of the "theatre industry" assails our ears. The pre-emptive idea of industry, with its goods and products replacing art and creativity imposes the view that spectators are incapable of asking the theatre to speak to their lives. The assumption behind the rule of commerce is that their lives are a matter of behaviourism, of the right stimuli triggering the right mechanical responses.

On the assumption that the dominion of markets has not crushed the vitality of cultures, the threads of my argument must converge on the issue of multiculturalism. The social heterogeneity of spectators is intertwined with the fact that multiple kinds of productions can be mounted in any one society at any one time. But this heterogeneity can be primarily defined, as it tends to be in Bakhtin, in terms of group-and-class cultures. (A group culture could be, for example, the culture of a certain profession - say that of doctors - which has a world-view, practical approach to life, method for dealing with it, jargon for articulating it, and so on, that gives it a particular character and distinguishes it from other group cultures.) What needs to be taken into account, especially in our time, is the *ethnic* heterogeneity to be found in one social structure, and which problematizes the very notion of a national culture, national theatre included. Awareness of ethnic heterogeneity and, consequently, of the cleavages between "minority" and "majority" cultures, has led to attempts to come to grips with the phenomenon, without necessarily relinquishing the principles on which modern nation-states were founded.

How does this affect the theatre, not to mention theories of the theatre? The question, when posed in relation to the points briefly mentioned here, is difficult enough, but is compounded when we consider the work of Peter Brook with the CICT. As is well known, Brook's performers come from a range of disparate races and cultures. Their collective purpose is to create productions which, when performed to heterogeneous audiences, will mean something to everybody. The aim of maximized communicability reflects Brook's conception of "popular" theatre. It also endorses his goal of a universal theatre which, in cutting across ethnic, linguistic and value differences, will traverse cultural boundaries, closing the gaps that divide race from race, class from class and whatever else sets divisions in motion. *The Mahabharata* is, to date, the most eloquent example in the theatre of multiculturalism conceived in terms of the multi-cultures making up what is known as the "world community". True to its vocation, it travelled across the planet before returning to its cultural source in India.

The Mahabharata amply demonstrates how a production anticipates widely differentiated audiences whose very diversity is both physically and symbolically represented by the cast. (There are performers from India, Senegal, Vietnam, Japan and Iran, as well as from Europe and North America.) In the process, it shows how an entire production interprets signs so that they may be interpreted with the greatest flexibility by spectators. This is done in an intentionally contradictory manner. Verbal signs are simplified to the maximum so that a maximum number of spectators, whoever they may be in precise sociocultural terms, can follow what is said. All other signs are *synthesized* to the maximum so that a maximum number of sociocultural inferences may be drawn from them. For example, the war between the Bharatas, which is the third and last part of the nine-hour performance, synthesizes steps, positions, movements, and more again, to be found in Chinese martial arts and acrobatics, Japanese martial arts and dance, Indian classical dance (notably

Kathakali), classical ballet, and folk and tribal dances - the whole giving an infinitely suggestive choreography where words, sounds and music are also choreographed rather than delivered or played. This, as Brook sees it, is exactly how spectators can be empowered to the maximum: for, by drawing on whatever is familiar to them, even subliminally, they can take hold of worlds that are foreign to them. A proper valorization of cultural difference - difference or "otherness" being inseparable from dignity - accompanies the realization brought about by performers and spectators of their common humanity. Humanity, past and present, is the core of the production. As such, it reflects what performers and spectators are meant to have achieved together, this fusion mirroring Brook's conception of the theatre as a binding force. What emerges from *The Mahabharata*, besides its extraordinary aesthetic achievement, is Brook's vision of the theatre's social role and power. Words to this effect are to be found in his essays which, although not claiming to be theoretical, have the generalizing thrust of theory.[6]

Brook's work with the CICT suggests how multiple cultures may be appropriated, in Bakhtin's sense of the term, in order to create a theatre that is "popular" insofar as it draws on the resources of the folk arts and seeks to redefine canonical theatre through them. It is also "popular" in that it aims to reach the widest audience possible, not through mere touring but because, when appearing on the international stage, it intends to be accessible to the common people. Yet here Brook's enterprise is ensnared in a web of difficulties, starting with the fact that the common people may not have the cash for costly tickets. Furthermore, official discourses vis-à-vis the arts in general hold such sway over perception, projecting an image of the arts as the property of a select few, that the very idea of attending performances valued by perceived elites may well be unthinkable.

This is not to say that the theatre, by definition, is doomed to Bourdieu's paradigm for culture. What these remarks suggest is that the cleavages between "minority" and "majority" cultures alluded to earlier, and which are at the heart of Brook's endeavour to blend disparate forces, reappear every time socioeconomic inequalities enter the picture. Nor can they be willed away in the name of race or, worse still, through a mystique of race. In other words, when talk of ethnic diversity is obfuscated in this way, "minority" cultures of one kind or another either become colourful ornaments or pose a mysterious threat. In both cases, the divisions set up on all fronts by very real, and not purely symbolic, inequalities are reinforced. This is especially relevant when intra-ethnic diversity in one society is at issue, though is not immaterial to the inter-ethnic diversity of the kind called upon by Brook. The second, because on a global scale, can be distanced. Or else, as happens in Brook's theatre, it can be absorbed more easily into a humanistic and humanitarian perspective.

It is worth recalling that Bourdieu, when making the distinction between minority and dominant cultures, relegates the former to the working classes, popular classes or lower classes, each term belonging to a concatenation of terms signifying the opposite of the elite. Bourdieu identifies various elites, which are distinguished by the relative edge they have on their coevals. Thus they are economic, social, political, intellectual or cultural elites. An economic elite, for example, does not necessarily coincide on all points of the graph with an intellectual elite. Nevertheless, the elites form a dominant bloc which stultifies movement. Ethnic minorities which, after all, belong to all classes and class fractions across the board, virtually disappear from Bourdieu's schema. Perhaps this is so because they are subsumed under his general "minority". And yet, when minority culture is invoked, they surely need to be particularized. If not, the whole notion of minority culture risks becoming a metaphor. Whereas the numerous disadvantages ushered in by economic dispossession are exacerbated when dispossession by ethnicity is added to them.

The issue is enormous. However, it has to be kept somewhere in sight when discourses of power in respect of the theatre - and, ipso facto, in respect of society - are at issue. It is incipient in the very fact that multiple cultures exist, which the theatre respects or usurps. Above all, it cannot be shelved when multiculturalism, in a more focused, more precise sense than can be attributed to Brook's theatre, enters the fray. Multiculturalism, as it is known today, may be said to be the expression, by ethnic minorities, of their desire and right to develop their languages, arts, crafts, values and particular way of life (the latter giving us "culture" in the broadest anthropological sense of the word). Since it is inseparable from the economic conditions that splinter ethnic minorities, multiculturalism may also be said to be a popular phenomenon, that is, not generated by the middle classes of these minorities. Multicultural theatre, then, when understood in the terms outlined, is a form of its own.

Several closing remarks are now in order. They concern Italo-Australian bilingual theatre, the type of multicultural theatre with which I am most familiar. This bilingual theatre essentially comprises the Sydney-based FILEF Theatre Group, and Adelaide's Doppio Teatro whose justly celebrated *Ricordi* travelled to the Mayhem Festival in Leeds in 1990. Both groups began their work in the early eighties as part of the community theatre movement whose antecedents may be traced back to the late sixties. They shared with the community movement in general the idea that "ordinary people" in suburban and regional zones had not had direct access to the theatre; further, that these people could make theatre together with the professional artists in their midst. The professionals engaged in the work, besides providing artistic inspiration and guidance, doubled as animators whose principal task was to galvanize communities through their own creative efforts. Community theatre in the seventies serviced a non-specified "community" in that, solely in English, it was geared to monolingual, monocultural audiences. However, the areas in which theatrical events took place were populated by large groups whose origins were anything but Anglo/Celtic. Many of them were far from fluent in English.

The FILEF Theatre Group and Doppio Teatro were formed in order to remedy a situation which, by distorting social reality, continued to isolate non-Anglo/Celtic immigrants from national life. They explicitly targeted Italians who had emigrated, especially from southern Italy, in the late forties, during the fifties, and still in the sixties and who, on arrival, swelled the ranks of the industrial, construction and farm workers required for Australia's economic expansion. The forties-fifties was a period of mass immigration into Australia by a labour force which, apart from Italy, came from Greece, Macedonia, Central Europe, Eastern Europe and, also, from the United Kingdom. Italians or those of Italian descent constitute approximately 5% of Australia's total population of 17 million and are the second-largest minority group in the country. (About 4 million are of non-English-speaking background; recent immigrants are mainly from Asia and the Middle East.)

The two companies cited have common objectives: tackle material of relevance to immigrant communities but which mainstream theatre still ignores; show that the issues raised concern the whole of Australian society and not merely its ethnic enclaves; validate the history of immigrants, Italian immigrants in particular, by bringing to light the role they have played in the history of Australia; make theatre accessible to the Italian-born who for economic, linguistic and related sociocultural reasons not only do not go to mainstream or even "alternative" theatre, but have been marginalized in other respects as well; reach their children, namely the second and third generation of Italo-Australians who may have been more or less assimilated into the dominant Anglo/Celtic culture but who, on the other hand, are losing or have lost touch with their language and culture of origin; evaluate positively a cultural legacy that had been virtually driven underground by the immigrants in question and derided by their adoptive country. The purpose, then, of working in two languages was to foreground all these difficulties and help alleviate them. The dialogue and songs of productions move from Italian to English while expository passages delivered by narrators, who also play characters, usually summarize in English preceding scenes performed in Italian.

Both companies cull stories from Italian families, associations (which group people from specific regions in Italy) and clubs. Oral history is then transformed into productions functioning to all intents and purposes like living documents. The FILEF Theatre Group has used dozens of grandparents, parents and children in performances combining the dynamics of religious processions with the humour of fables, puppetry and commedia dell'arte. Doppio Teatro, by contrast, rarely uses amateurs. Its productions, to date, have been elliptical, poetic. The masks, robes and legends of southern Italian popular culture intercept, as in a montage, scenes from the present, the whole reminding spectators of a cultural heritage, which is above all a *popular* heritage, that has been fragmented and dissipated by immigration. The power of memory is an important motif in Doppio productions. So, too, is cultural identity. These motifs are linked so as to highlight the difficulties of integration, where incomprehension, resistance or outright rejection appear on both sides, Anglo/Celts urging conformity with their norms, Italians meanwhile fearing to let go of the very thing, "identity", that had assured their survival in an alien society.

My research on audiences of the FILEF Theatre Group shows that they clearly understand the aims of Italo-Australian theatre, Italians being particularly appreciative of its focus on their history past and present. This not only vindicates, in their eyes, the painful experiences they have undergone, but also encourages them to feel pride in the contribution they have made to the country.

Their children, most of whom were born in Australia, recognize in the productions the dilemma of living within two cultures, the old impinging on the new without necessarily being fully accepted by them; and yet the new does not fully accept them. Spectators from other minority groups comment on the pertinence to their own situation of the scenes presented. Spectators of Anglo/Celtic origin generally show that they are aware of the problems, some of them explicitly referring to details of Italian immigration to indicate support, while others suggest that they are leaving the performances with a new insight into another culture and its importance for the overall culture. Some of them say they feel excluded because of the use of Italian.

Perhaps one of the most striking things to emerge from spectators' observations, whatever their ethnicity, is their feeling that this type of theatre can play a significant role in changing perceptions and attitudes, and in fostering greater understanding of social and cultural mix. Irrespective of differences of emphasis and stylistic approaches, the whole point of ethnically-oriented, interventionist theatre in a multicultural society is to empower minorities, allowing them at least the beginnings of a real social input that supersedes the logic of economic exploitation. Multiculturalism is not unique to Australia. It is the condition of our post-imperial or, perhaps more accurately, deimperializing epoch, each variant of it a particular case, but all of them together radically altering the shape of the world. Theatre, an intrinsic part of culture, cannot help but be affected, affecting in turn the myriad of societies to which it is indissolubly bound. Thus, what is pertinent to multicultural theatre in Australia will be pertinent, albeit differently, elsewhere.

Several shifts have occurred during my exposition. We have moved from the grand art of Peter Brook to the small, though by no means insignificant, art of Italo-Australian theatre; from institutionalized great theatre to impermanent, localized theatre; from a fusion of cultures to contradiction and tension between cultures. And we have moved away from the controlled world of Bourdieu to a world where intervention and change are possible. Brook's form of intervention has a utopian quality insofar as it projects an ideal to be attained. Yet the harmonious universe imaged in Brook's theatre is fractured when transferred to the theatre of ethnic minorities. Bakhtin's vision of open-ended, ongoing processes, with which Brook's practice has a good deal in common, is open to minorities only when they become protagonists of their own destiny. Theatre is the art of the possible. As social practice it is as strong as the societies, however large or small, major or minor, where it is generated, performers and spectators interchanging roles in order to make the possible real. Discourses on the theatre, to return to my point of departure, either attempt to come to grips with this social practice, or else risk a canonization that will see them frozen in time - suspended, abstracted icons of their own image.

NOTES

1. For what might be termed a summary of some of Bourdieu's main theses, see "Artistic Taste and Cultural Capital". *Culture and Society: Contemporary Debates*. Jeffrey C. Alexander and Steven Seidman, eds. Cambridge: Cambridge University Press, 1990, pp. 205-15. However, this paper draws on the whole corpus of Bourdieu's work and, notably, on *Les Héritiers* (with J-C. Passeron). Paris: Les Editions de Minuit, 1964; *L'Amour de l'art* (with Alain Darbel and Dominique Schnapper). Paris: Les Editions de Minuit, 1969; *La Reproduction* (with J-C. Passeron). Paris: Les Editions de Minuit, 1971; *La Distinction: critique sociale du jugement*. Paris: Les Editions de Minuit, 1979.

2. The linkage between knowledge and symbolic power appears in all the works cited above. It is specifically related to the question of whether and how contemporary French intellectuals define educational institutions and are, in turn, defined by them, this being the principal subject of *Homo academicus*. Paris: Les Editions de Minuit, 1984.

3. For a relatively detailed critical account of theatre semiotics, see my article "The Sociology of the Theatre, Part Three: Performance". *New Theatre Quarterly* V, 19 (August 1989), pp. 282-300.

4. As expressed in an interview with Didier Eribon regarding the pessimistic view expounded in *La Distinction*. See Pierre Bourdieu, *Questions de sociologie*. Paris: Les Editions de Minuit, 1980, p. 15.

5. I am here generalizing, as regards functionalist methods, and so on, from the assumptions more or less implicit in such books as Anne Ubersfeld, *L'Ecole du spectateur*. Paris: Les Editions Sociales, 1981 and Patrice Pavis, *Voix et images de la scène: pour une sémiologie de la réception*. Lille: Presses Universitaires de Lille, 1985. Pavis, it would not be wrong to say, draws on the *Rezeptionsästhetik* of the Konstanz school as exemplified by Hans Robert Jauss in *Toward an Aesthetic of Reception*. Translated from the German by Timothy Bahti, with an introduction by Paul de Man. Minneapolis: University of Minnesota Press, 1982. For an example of functionalist approaches to literature, which are absorbed by semiotic studies of reception, see Robert Escarpit, *Introduction à la sociologie de la littérature*. Paris: Presses Universitaires de France, 1958 and Robert Escarpit, ed. *Le Littéraire et le social*, Paris: Flammarion, 1970.

6. For a detailed study of *The Mahabharata* from the point of view very briefly outlined here, see my "Interaction-Interpretation: *The Mahabharata* from a Socio-Cultural Perspective". *Peter Brook and The Mahabharata: Critical Perspectives*. David Williams, ed. London: Routledge, Chapman and Hall, 1991, pp. 206-27. For Brook's reflections on his work, notably with the CICT, see *The Shifting Point*. New York: Harper & Row, 1987. See also Brook's foreword to his English translation of Jean-Claude Carrière, *The Mahabharata*. New York: Harper & Row, 1987, pp. xiii-xvi.

2

UNIVERSAL THEATRE/UNIVERSAL CULTURE? BROOK, GROTOWSKI, BARBA

The Sociology of Stage Productions: Science and Art

The sociology of the theatre is still beleaguered by problems of status, even though an increasing number of scholars are working in the field or in closely related areas not claiming the title as such.

The standing of the discipline depends on how it is assessed from within the social sciences where it properly belongs. It must belong to this vast domain, in which sociology on its own is vast enough, because the sociology *of* the theatre targets all aspects of theatre in society. It therefore understands theatre to be a specific collective activity involved in a network of economic, political and other activities, all designated differently, that are brought about by social agents.

The discipline is also based on the premise that theatre is permeated through and through with social meaning. Meaning may be generalized, that is, recognized as being appropriate for the whole of a historically bounded and geographically delimited society. Or it may be precise, that is, confined to discernible social groups, what it communicates extending little, or not at all, beyond them. However, when meaning is localized and narrowed down in this way, it can nevertheless be situated back in, and be seen to be part of, the given whole described as m society in n place at s time.

Thus collective action and societal meaning are two fundamental principles of the sociology of the theatre which this discipline shares with the social sciences in general. On the other hand, its standing as a discipline also depends on how it is related to the broad field of theatre studies (or even to performance studies, arguably a different area from the former) in which it also belongs. The fact that the sociology of the theatre has not yet become an integral part of theatre studies has as much to do with its hitherto limited scope (a paradox, seeing that its terrain of *society* is virtually inexhaustible) as with how "theatre studies" has been traditionally defined. The history of the theatre, for example, has been an incontestable component of theatre studies, as have directors' writings on method or biographies of directors and actors. A good deal of information concerning a given society informs any theatre history or biography worthy of the name. Yet this information is usually considered to be of subsidiary importance, like the *basso continuo* of a piece highlighting soloists. Leaving this musical metaphor behind, we could say that the societal material used in these sorts of works is not sociologized: it is neither foregrounded nor treated through the concepts and categories, as well as methods - both theoretical and practical - pertinent to sociology.

In addition, when theatre studies takes on board structuralism and semiotics or encounters anthropology (this meeting being decisive for performance studies), it generally does so by adapting familiar features and leaving unfamiliar ones alone. The great caution with which it first greeted structuralism and semiotics is revealing in this respect because both deal with dramatic texts and/or productions. They deal, in other words, with material acknowledged to be central to theatre studies. The resistance towards them expressed by conservative theatre specialists was not caused by their objects of study but by their supposedly scientific methods. "Structure", "system" and "sign", among a whole gamut of terms and techniques whose goal was absolute "scientific" objectivity, threatened the concepts of art, creation and individual imagination which distinguished a theatrical work as an "art" work. Furthermore, the same methods, with their predilection for anonymous - scientific and objective rather than personalized and subjective - "things" without authors, called into question the very notion of *artists*, whether playwright, actor, director or any other individuated participant in the making of theatre.[1]

Structuralism and semiotics put together have given rise to theatre semiotics. Whether the latter actually succeeds in analyzing textual and performance compositions or, on the contrary, establishes models which are parallel to them and function autonomously as models per se is not the issue being addressed here. I have broached this issue elsewhere and now refer to it merely in a sub-textual manner.[2] My principal point is that theatre semiotics, whatever opposition it has received because of its methods, has been incorporated into theatre studies without great difficulty. Assimilation was possible because its purported objects of study did not question the subject matter considered to be fundamental to theatre.

The spectre of science conjured up by theatre semiotics may be compared to the negative impact made by the notion of "society" on theatre studies. "Society", when invoked, was usually separated from theatre "art" for all analytical purposes. At best it provided a descriptive background for "art". At worst it was extraneous, simply extra-artistic, since dramatic texts and stage productions were presumed to have intrinsic formal value. These premises continued to reinforce the division between aesthetics and sociology.

In the light of such habits, for which there are sociological-historical explanations, it is not surprising that theatre studies has been slow to validate the sociology of the theatre in general and the sociology of theatre works, written or performed, in particular. This recalcitrance is evidenced by the discipline's absence from the programmes of theatre schools, departments of theatre studies in tertiary institutions, and so on.

What we have is a contradictory situation, for "theatre" goes hand in glove with the sociology of the theatre. However, the contradiction has not been generated solely by theatre studies. Here we must return to the point noted earlier, namely, the restricted range of the sociology of the theatre until now. The discipline has acquired some theoretical bases. It has produced empirical studies of audience composition, the rate of attendance by audiences at certain theatres, elements of what is known as "spectator response" and issues to do with cultural policy. Many of these studies have amalgamated theatre with all the other arts.[3] But the discipline has been singularly remiss in dealing with performed works conceived simultaneously as performance art and social process. Numerous problems are involved in this curious state of affairs and help to explain the neglect regarding performed works. Let us take several of the fundamental problems which have general rather than particular significance.

First of all, there is the old problem of just how scientific any sociology - and, therefore, the sociology of the theatre - is or can be. Whether, how and why sociology is a science has been debated on a theoretical level so often (leading all too frequently to a dead end) that there is little sense in going over the issues again. Suffice it to note that Lucien Goldmann in *Sciences humaines et philosophie* has indicated how the whole question of science in the social sciences should be reformulated.[4] We should note, by the same token, that the theoretical debate has had important consequences for sociological practice. It has spawned methodologies that have privileged facts, figures, graphs and case studies - in short, techniques and material belonging to a rampant empiricism which has heavily influenced the sociology of the theatre itself and perhaps even blocked its growth.

None of this is to say that empirical investigation is unnecessary for the study of social life, theatre included. What these remarks do suggest (apart from the difference between empiricism and empirically-based research) is that sociology's preoccupation with scientific principles has led to its insecurity (and also insensitivity) vis-à-vis art. Our second problem, then, is related to the ambiguous view of art - and ipso facto of theatre works - held by sociology, a reputed science. The sociology of the theatre thus replicates the dilemma besetting theatre studies, this time by inverting it: in other words, by placing science and society above art (instead of *art* above science and society) in the hierarchy of priorities established. When faced with the conditions generic to sociology, how indeed does the sociology of stage productions, the area at issue here, deal with the creativity, fictitiousness and subjectivity involved in theatre art?

This question overlaps with a third problem, that of finding a methodological solution to the question posed. Stage productions may be quantified for specific reasons - for instance, how frequently, when, where and why productions are performed. Even so, the question "Why are they performed?" draws on matters to do with sociocultural values. It no longer assumes a purely quantitative approach but introduces a qualitative dimension into the discussion. However, just because values have entered the fray does not mean that analyses of the stage processes constituting productions will automatically follow. This step, although logical, has not been taken, if only because the very idea that a production is made up of different components (movement, colour, light, and so on) has been relegated historically to aesthetics.

And yet the sociology of the theatre cannot avoid referring to aesthetic concepts. Even the most seemingly anodyne of them (take the concept of form, for example) leads us to a fourth problem among the general problems raised here, namely, that of expanding the discipline's horizons beyond the confines of sociometric studies. The sociology of the theatre has two explicit frames of reference: the study of society and the study of theatre. These, as was indicated earlier, are not in a dualistic relation to each other, but are contained in each other. Therefore, what is necessary for the one is also necessary for the other. This means that the resources customarily reserved for theatre studies need to be used by the sociology of the theatre.

The fact that the sociology of the theatre must go beyond the boundaries hitherto drawn for it by sociology as such has enormous consequences. What this means, where the sociology of stage productions is concerned, is learning to handle the tools used by theatre studies for studying performed works so as to show that works-in-performance are also works-in-society. Aesthetics is one of the main pieces of equipment held by theatre studies. Theatre semiotics, though recently acquired, is another. Caution, however, is required. Useful machinery cannot be transported to a sociological field without undergoing modification. For instance, its voltage (keeping my trope) might require adjustment. Such is the case of the concept of sign which is crucial to theatre semiotics, but where it is conceived and exercised in a strictly formal and profoundly asocial way. Consequently, this particular view of signs is not appropriate for sociological analyses of stage productions. Yet its inadequacy does not rule out the usefulness of an alternative, sociologically adequate, concept of sign.

The alternative at issue is the concept of *social* sign. Since this redefinition is radical, more than adaptation and adjustment is at stake. The result, from our perspective, may be letting go altogether of theatre semiotics as it exists today.

It is not my intention to repeat here the theoretical foundations of a redefined concept of sign as social sign. The briefest of outlines will remind my reader of the nodal points to be kept in mind, as follows. Social signs are brought into existence by social agents interacting and communicating with each other in specific sociocultural circumstances. These agents are not spread out indiscriminately, even though they cannot always be precisely identified sociologically. Signs mean and change according to their makers. As such, they are not things. Nor are stage works predetermined, fixed objects, "aesthetic" or "scientific". They are social actions made for spectators who are themselves social actors.[5]

It is now time to record a fifth problem of importance for sociological analyses of stage productions. It concerns the contribution of theatre companies and directors which, precisely because productions require producers, is at the core of our subject.

The contribution referred to is multiple. There is the performed work, which is an ensemble of stage processes presented and communicated to audiences by actors, director, stage designer, costume designer and related participants. Movement, gesture, voice, light and colour are just some of the processes integral to any work.

Then there is a whole host of preparations behind the scenes. Several will have been clearly structured into the public presentation. Others will have left traces not necessarily visible to spectators. For instance, certain movements originating from exercises during rehearsals may have survived in a residual way in the production. Audiences will not realize that they are looking at imprints left behind by something else.[6] Or economic imperatives will have left either bold or barely discernible marks, as happens, say, when costumes envisaged for the sense of a work in its entirety are replaced by a less expensive, perhaps less elaborate, version of the original idea. Concessions of this kind are usually made within acceptable limits so as not to betray the artistic objectives set for the work. Spectators, however, will not be aware that the costumes in front of them are not exactly what was desired. They have to go on what they see. In other words, the production's meaning is prescribed by what is actually performed, and is communicated and interpreted accordingly.

The third contribution of relevance to this discussion concerns the intentions of the director. The question of intentions is complex. For our purposes, "intentions" refers to the ideas and feelings guiding a director's work with her/his collaborators. Thus it refers to the director's vision of theatre-making with others, the results of which bear her/his creative stamp and distinguish them as the work of b rather than c director. A director's vision is not hermetically sealed off from all the social forces affecting her/him daily. Vision is neither isolated nor asocial just because it is individual. Furthermore, its individuality depends on the input of the socioprofessional groups - actors, dramatists, dramaturges, managers, and so on - with whom the director interchanges experience. Vision emerges from, and shapes, shared practice.

As well as the intentions-vision incarnated in a production, the term "intentions" includes the director's words, oral or written, about her/his work. This body of statements (credo, method, testimony, theory, or what you will) is part and parcel of the thought processes involved in the vision that is materialized in performance. Spectators may not worry about whether the stage work corresponds with its director's pronouncements, especially not when they are watching a performance. For them, "intentions" are what the production is doing to them - how it affects them emotionally and how and why they react as they do. The director, on the other hand, may well be wondering whether what is happening is how she/he had conceived it; and may develop, from these reflections, new ideas to be tested in practice and written down for public distribution.

Preparatory periods and theoretical underpinnings are relevant to sociological analyses of stage productions, even though the performed work is their focus. Analysis is inseparable from interpretation, which continues after the performance event. Sociological analyses are derived from heterogeneous factors: what a network of social signs was communicating at the time of viewing; what it suggests later on when layer upon layer of sign processes have been sifted out by the analyst and put together again, memory of the performance also playing a role in how the analysis is done; how the sign processes project given social perspectives as well as evaluate them; for which social groups and classes these perspectives have the most significance; why these groups and classes rather than some others are the production's explicitly or implicitly targeted audiences. All these points, and more not listed, are crucial for understanding that a production is an identifiable, penetrable and dynamic entity having collective resonance and impact.

Although the entity is a completed work, it is not self-explanatory. Whatever clarifies an interpretation or puts it to the test cannot be cast aside on the grounds that it is extrinsic to the production. Sociologists, when interpreting, ask sociological questions. If they argue that a director's oral or written point of view is connected to theatre theory but not to sociological research, they are making a sociological error. Where else, if not in a society, does a director formulate her/his ideas? What generates these ideas, if not society in some sense of the word? Theatre practitioners, not least directors, construct the social practice of theatre. What they say may be as telling from a sociological point of view as what they do. To deny this is tantamount to sending selected aspects of the theatre back to theatre studies, thereby reaffirming the dualism - theatre art in opposition to society - discussed earlier.

All in all, then, sociological analyses of productions should be capable of drawing on the stated intentions (or theory) of theatre workers. A sociologist's procedures for a particular production may not depend on this or that director's conceptual framework. However, when these procedures are not checked against the frames of reference developed by the theatre (and which change continually through practice), the sociologist runs the risk of losing touch with reality. Or else sociologists would have no alternative but to be confined to itemizing, tabulating, classifying and fragmenting productions. The energy of stage works, that momentum which comes from the powerhouse of change and renewal in theatre and society simultaneously, would be lost to inadaptable, sterile methods.

Brook, Grotowski, Barba

It should be clear from the preceding paragraphs that the sociology of productions, a fundamental component of the sociology of the theatre as a whole, must rely on principles that bring out what is particular to productions in a delimited time, place and culture - in short, in a living, active and finite space for which we use the term "society". A society cannot exist without the people who make it, any more than can the theatre. And the people at issue are to be differentiated according to the world they make, whether on a large scale (as is implied when "nation" is synonymous with "society") or on a micro-level (as is implied by such adjectives as, for example, "local", "village" or "neighbourhood" when added to "society" or "culture"). The thrust, then, of the preceding pages, is that productions for and in performance are specific, unique and even idiosyncratic in respect of the specific, unique and even idiosyncratic world where they are made.

This view runs counter to the thesis that, since human beings everywhere belong to the same species, what they make in the theatre springs from a universal fount of meaning. In other words, when theatre is performed it comes from, and speaks to, universally shared and universally understood signs, the signs of our common humanity. In the context of what might be termed a debate between the particular and universal conceptions of the theatre, each of which is underpinned by a corresponding conception of society and culture, I have chosen to look briefly at Peter Brook, Jerzy Grotowski and Eugenio Barba, each of whom enriches this debate, but none of whom succeeds in resolving its difficulties.

These three directors are to be placed closer to the universal side of the argument insofar as they share, to varying degrees, what may be broadly termed an anthropological conception of theatre. Barba's "theatre anthropology" is probably its most succinct expression. "Theatre anthropology", when understood to be referring principally to an innate humanness binding human beings together, is probably the antithesis of the sociology of the theatre. Taken generally, this anthropological conception poses a number of problems for the concept of social sign which, as I indicated earlier, is indispensable for analyzing stage productions sociologically.

Words, tones, cadences, postures, bearing, and so forth, are social signs. They are made, used and exchanged by groups of individuals who are linked by gender, affectivity, profession or family - to name only a few of the ties that bind people together, allowing sociologists, after the event, to differentiate between groups. Groups may be very closely knit, shutting off their idiosyncratic signs from the outside world (as occurs, for example, in certain religious sects). Or they may grow outwards and proliferate, giving rise to class fractions or whole classes as they do so. Where socioprofessional groups are concerned, lawyers, for example, do not communicate through exactly the same signs as doctors. Where class distinctions are concerned, lawyers do not speak, dress or gesticulate in the same way as plumbers. The differences in sign production have to do, though not exclusively, with the social values attached to signs by those bringing them about.

Signs are also culturally specific. Culture may be designated according to countries. Hence we speak of French, Italian, Chinese culture, and so forth. It is also differentiated by activities. Thus we speak of political culture or theatre culture. And it is differentiated by the behaviours, attitudes and customs of specific groups, which means that culture in this sense is related to class. From here comes the category of class culture on which various sociologists depend. Or else, when the concept of class is considered outmoded, a whole host of terms is invented to mark out the hierarchical differences between groups and the particular character of their way of life ("culture" in the most flexible sense of the word as anthropologists might use it). Social signs are therefore always cultural signs in some sense of the word "culture".

Now, the major problem posed by the anthropological conception of theatre that I have alluded to is its presupposition that human beings have signs in common due to their species. Signs are neither culture-specific nor culture-bounded but diffused throughout the world. This is possible because of underlying psychobiological characteristics making human kind one.

Here we should distinguish between an older, early twentieth-century anthropology which has been absorbed both by theatre studies and the sociology of the theatre, and the assumptions connecting Brook, Grotowski and Barba; and these three directors are linked despite the special anthropological hallmark of each one of them.

Let us start with the older variety. Its stress is on ceremonies, rites and rituals, all aspects of the religious life studied by Durkheim, Frazer (notably in *The Golden Bough*) and others inspired by them. It has been fertile ground for theses on the theatre as a quasi-sacred phenomenon galvanizing communities, a mass spectacle celebrating the life-force of societies and a symbolic representation of the social order, as well as a means of maintaining the status quo. There is no doubt about the central importance of this kind of anthropology to Jean Duvignaud's theory of the theatre.[7] Since Duvignaud owes a great deal to Durkheim, it is understandable how Durkheimian sociology and Durkheimian anthropology - the one almost a shadow of the other - merged to provide the foundations for Duvignaud's sociology of the theatre.

Residues of ritual-oriented anthropology survive in the historically more recent view which is of principal interest to our discussion. Brook's notion of "holy theatre" invokes the idea of sacredness cherished by early anthropology;[8] and the hushed ceremonial opening and close of his tremendous epic production *The Mahabharata* (also "epic" in its duration of nine hours) could not illustrate more clearly the awesome heights on which theatre as sacred rite can be placed. However, Brook does not stay on a single line of thought. He glides from an indeterminately "religious" viewpoint (that is, not tied to a particular dogma) to a humanistic one devoted to the search for universal signs that have been freed from cultural constraints. If we are to judge by interviews with Brook in the late 1980s as well as by *The Shifting Point*, his most recent publication, cultural frames of reference, when explicit (or over-explicit), are obstacles to the purity which the theatre endeavours to create. What must be added here is that Brook's wariness of cultural signs, especially in their strongest manifestations, is closely bound up with his aim of *blending* cultural signs so that the synthesis emerging from them is extremely finely textured. This fine synthesis is a prerequisite for a theatre that, in superseding this or that cultural sign system, comes closer to being a veritable universal theatre which also projects an image of a universal rather than a particular culture.[9]

Brook's ideal of a "holy theatre", to which, through its aspirations to purity, his "universal" theatre also belongs, has some features in common with Grotowski's far more single-minded quest for a similar goal. Grotowski's trajectory appears to be fraught with unexpected turns. Yet his steps from "poor theatre" to paratheatre and then to "objective theatre" are sustained by an overriding conviction that multiple expressive capabilities are secreted by the human body and that these are not dependent upon social and cultural parameters. The body is its own source of inspiration. Heartbeat, breathing patterns, certain sounds and pitches, rhythms and movements - among a wide range of physical actions - constitute a universal psychophysiological system from which can spring a universal performative system. We could call it a transcultural system.

Consequently, the actor's craft renders in a superlatively concrete way all that is elemental and archetypal in human behaviour. Put differently, this means that the actor's technique is neither learned nor taught. It wells up out of innate organic and psychic resources and, so to speak, taps them at the fountainhead. Culture does not intervene in the displays of Grotowski's "holy" actor.

The religious or, better still, mystical dimension of Grotowski's work with actors is derived from a vocation no longer conceived primarily in professional terms. The vocation is for a way of life. Paradoxically, the actor's journey inwards towards a heightened inner state is repeated publicly in performance. Productions like *Apocalypsis Cum Figuris* might accurately be described as internal apocalypsis figured externally. Although theatre, in that it is publicly performed, the production could just as easily have stayed in the paratheatrical temple where actors work day and night without the obligation to perform in front of and for audiences.

Not for nothing, moreover, did Grotowski choose the title of "laboratory" for the arduous labour carried out behind closed doors and which, when opened, showed actors whose aura of privacy was so intense that spectators might as well have been intruders. Stanislavsky's "fourth wall" is nothing when compared to this barrier. By the same token - we are once again in the realm of paradoxes - it could be that intense intrapsychic fusion occurs between performers and spectators because of the deeply contained, inward-bound strength momentarily made public by the performers. In which case, Grotowski and his company will have realized Artaud's dream of non-cognitive, non-rationalized and non-rational communion through performance. Artaud, it is worth remembering, looked to oriental civilization, principally Balinese dance and trance-in-performance, for models for western civilization. The anthropology of the first decades of the century nourished his discovery of the East.

Brook, when viewed beside the Polish director, proves to be committed to an open and down-to-earth communication between performers and spectators. In Brook, the great discoveries made in the theatre are intended to further the ordinary, everyday communication presumed to have been lost in everyday life. More differences between Brook and Grotowski emerge. Where Grotowski seeks universal principles which are stored in the innermost recesses of the actor's body, Brook seeks a universal means of communication. For Brook, unlike Grotowski, universality does not reside within. It is to be found in the social world and achieved through merging aspects of that world. It can be reached through theatre because it exists outside theatre. Performance processes have the power to communicate with spectators whoever and wherever they are for this very reason. The sense and meaning of productions transcend different cultures for the same reason.

In short, Brook explores performative skills, though not for the ends of a universal performative system. Skills are developed by his actors in relation to anticipated audiences. Whatever actors find within themselves is ipso facto oriented towards the universal dialogue envisaged and which, as appears from his productions and writings, Brook believes is the primary role of the theatre. His idea of universal dialogue is predicated on the assumption that a world community exists whose powers of unification and harmony are far greater than any that may be attributed to a particular society.

Barba, in this respect, is closer to Brook than to Grotowski. In fact, he surpasses Brook on ideas to do with how the theatre encapsulates a world community. Barba's relation to Brook on this point only highlights, strangely enough, his kinship with Grotowski with whom, after all, he had spent a number of years. Like Grotowski, Barba seeks to uncover the inner mystery of human kind. In Barba's view, divisions between civilizations (for Barba principally between "eastern" and "western" civilizations) have obscured this discoverable mystery. Consequently, his work with performers from a variety of western and eastern cultures is an attempt to distil, drop by drop, the essence of humanity. The performance situation is the most favourable site for this extraction in which the principles of human behaviour and those of the theatre are inseparable. Herein lies the full meaning of Barba's "theatre anthropology". In his words:

> Theatre anthropology does not seek principles which are universally *true*, but rather directions which are useful. . . . Originally, the term anthropology was understood as the study of man's behaviours not only on the socio-cultural level, but also on the physiological level. Theatre anthropology consequently studies the socio-cultural and physiological behaviour of man in a performance situation.[10]

It is quite clear, especially from Barba's last sentence, that the "behaviour of man" (my "essence of humanity") is to further the cause of *theatre*, not that of anthropology. Yet what are we to make of Barba's reference to the "socio-cultural level"? Barba's argument suggests that the purpose of sounding the depths of sociocultural behaviour (or what could be called its manifestation through sociocultural signs) across different cultures is to devise something of universal significance from this behaviour. The aim, in Barba's words, is to find "the basic principles which [one theatre] has in common with other theatres. . . . Theatre anthropology seeks to study these principles: not the profound and hypothetical reasons which might explain why they resemble each other, but their possible uses".

We should note, in passing, that seeking "reasons which might explain why" would indeed bring a sociocultural dimension to bear on the enterprise. However, the main point to be underlined is that Barba's emphasis on "uses" indicates that the "basic principles" are to be used for theatre, indeed for a performative science not unlike Grotowski's proposed "objective theatre". Is it possible that, for this particular part of his quest, Grotowski was inspired by Barba?

Barba's statement of intention could hardly be clearer: sociocultural differences are to be assembled and crystallized in order to form what might be called an Ur-theatre. Given this objective, the name of *Odin Teatret* for Barba's celebrated group - *one* theatre rather than many theatres - is extremely eloquent. It is also significant that Barba should have set up an organization for international research in ISTA (International School for Theatre Anthropology). An Ur-theatre transcends, by definition, the culture-specific components which it appropriates, and must appropriate deeply, for its very existence.

Barba does not reject the idea of cultural identity. Nor does he deny that there are performative styles specific to cultures. Kathakali is Indian. Noh is Japanese (besides being aristocratic, as distinct from middle-class Kabuki). However, it is not his purpose to seek either the societal impetus behind them or their precise sociocultural meaning within a defined culture - national culture, caste culture, sub-culture, or what have you. Doing so would involve working with sociological principles (starting with the principle of explaining *why* p is different from q), rather than relying on an anthropological notion of "humanness" or human "essence". Furthermore, if an anthropological framework were indeed to be the main point of reference, then it would at least have to be of the kind used by many contemporary anthropologists whose methods are permeated through and through with sociological principles. The close relationship today between sociology and social and cultural anthropology cannot be denied; and has resulted, in fact, in overlapping areas of study and methodological approach (for example, in studies by anthropologists of the composition and behaviour of urban communities - city "apaches", ethnic groups, groups defined by gender and/or sexuality, groups of youths, and so on).

In Barba's case, the kinds of sociological principles alluded to here are probably out of the picture altogether insofar as he can be said to be striving for an *archaeology* of theatre knowledge. An *archaeology* of knowledge cannot be confused with sociology, as Michel Foucault demonstrated possibly unintentionally but quite brilliantly. Nor, therefore, can it be confused with the societally explainable knowledge produced by sociology. The main task of archaeology, as Foucault understands it, is to trace a given phenomenon diachronically, marking its patterns of sameness and repetition across time and space. The phenomenon can be madness, the penal system, or the structure of discourse itself.[11] But what is important is its manifestations as such - how it is, and not where it comes from or why. Barba's search for resemblances rather than particularity and difference, combined with his negation of "hypothetical reasons which might explain why they resemble each other" (see the second quotation from Barba above), certainly suggests his intellectual kinship with Foucault; and suggests that, in his view, sociological principles, at whose core is the principle of explaining why, cannot be brought into play in any truly significant manner in understanding the processes of performance.

Perhaps, in fact, it is not so much understanding the processes of performance "in a performance situation" as *observing* them that interests Barba most. And his interest in the performer, which is at the heart of his theatre anthropology, has led Barba to make a fascinating distinction between an "*incultured* body", then "incultured performers", and "*accultured* performers". Thus:

> Each one of us is an *incultured* body. We use a daily body technique which derives from the culture in which we have been born, from our family environments, from our work. This inculturation, which is organically absorbed from the first hours of life and continues to develop through one's personal history, constitutes our "spontaneity" - that is, a net of conditioned reflexes or of unconscious automatisms.
>
> Some performers develop this "spontaneity", exploiting the potential richness of their own inculturation. Others move away from it: they pass through a process of physical *acculturation* which introduces them to an extra-daily body technique.
>
> One can also speak of *incultured* performers or of *accultured* performers. This distinction has been reinforced for a long time in the West, with the very strange hallucination that "dance" is different from "theatre".[12]

Further on in the same text, Barba speaks of the performer who passes from "an incultured spontaneity to an accultured spontaneity", thereby acquiring a "second nature" and becoming a "body-in-life". In this situation, the performer's "technique" or her/his "body-instrument" are irrelevant concepts. So too, it seems, is the culture in which the performer was born, physical acculturation, as Barba understands it, transcending (and effacing?) what had initially been organically absorbed from that culture. Does this mean that theatre art, when at its summit, has a life of its own, surpassing social life? And must we now speak of the *performer's* culture per se, which not only cuts across national-geographical boundaries but also the frontiers between theatrical genres? Barba suggests that the answer would be in the affirmative when, in giving examples of the "accultured performer", he cites "Balinese or ballet dancer, Kathakali actor or mime, opera singer, *joruri* or *dalang*", all in one breath.[13]

There can be no doubt that the impact of Brook, Grotowski and Barba on theatre throughout the world has been tremendous, whether on companies with established reputations and luminaries of their own or on amateur groups. Workshops held in numerous countries and, as in the case of Barba's ISTA, at regular intervals, have guided and inspired theatre practitioners of one kind and another. Extensive touring, particularly in the case of Brook's CICT (Centre International de Créations Théâtrales), has meant that thousands upon thousands of spectators in Europe, the Anglo-American countries and parts of Asia, notably India and Japan, have had access to a way of conceiving and performing productions that has surely had a profound effect on their perception, affective as well as cognitive, of the theatre. The question to be asked is whether, and to what extent, internationalization actually helps establish the phenomenon propagated by each company in its own way (say, Barba's transcendental performance or Brook's transcultural theatre, each being a different facet of the idea of universal culture at its base).

The respective visions of our directors can be studied sociologically - why and how each one of them has been shaped by the time and place and, therefore, by the social and artistic-cultural conditions and expectations of their immediate working environment: Poland in the 1960s for Grotowski, for example, and France in the 1970s for Brook. Whatever else may have been decisive, there is a sociological basis to why Brook's work had found a "captive" audience in Paris in the seventies, which audience has continued to expand up to the present day. His work gave replies to some of the main sociocultural questions - and dreams - of the time (for instance, how to democratize the arts and make them more accessible to more people; how to simplify their trappings in the process of making them less elitist; the dream of recovering personal and collective freedom, which the events of May '68 had promised but which subsequent events had disappointed; the desire for escape into another, even "exotic", world). Then there is the role played by the French Ministry of Culture in helping to finance the CICT. The Ministry's support is interconnected with the French Government's sociocultural and political programs in which notions of State patronage, national prestige and international clout go hand in glove with what might be termed faith in art.

Other sociological considerations are relevant. Why, for instance, is Brook's enterprise backed by important international organizations? Why, as his productions travel, do they generate such enthusiasm in places where the cultural touchstones are not the same as those pertinent to Parisian audiences? Also relevant is the question of how international touring creates audiences, who are perhaps increasingly similar in kind. (For a start, they are increasingly exposed to the same works.) Just as important is the issue of international political and economic currents, how they criss-cross and create turbulences, and how they flow from institutions in one society to another, thereby affecting the changes already taking place in the direction of that flow.

Changes, whether evident or hidden, are not to the advantage of all social groups and classes at the same time. The effects of international relations on local conditions shift the balance of interests locally. Theatregoers, not least spectators of imported performances, are hardly immune to this complex play of forces. They are influenced or simply attracted by foreign theatre companies when the conditions in their society facilitate this influence or appeal or whatever other interaction occurs between visitor and visited. And even if we assume that the audiences for foreign companies are predominantly drawn from the educated and/or cultivated sectors of the middle class, their receptivity is connected in some way with the sociocultural circumstances affecting them in their daily lives. If this were not so, we would never see a certain company's failure to please one year and then meet with resounding success several years later. Nor would we have the phenomenon known as "fashion".

Influence cannot be exercised when it is met with silence, confusion or downright opposition. It is mitigated when it encounters resistance. What is true for individuals is just as true for social groups, which are groupings of specific kinds of individuals. The same holds for theatre practitioners. Grotowski's influence on Brook and Barba and then, later, Barba's on Grotowski was not merely a matter of personal taste. It occurred when a number of very important social transformations converged, opening and channelling the receptivity necessary for that influence to be felt. Grotowski's impact on the theatre, first of all in America from where the impact radiated globally, is inseparable from the counter-cultural and grass-roots movements of the sixties in the United States and the libertarian and radical politics that went with them (anti-Vietnam and civil rights demonstrations rubbing shoulders with spiritualism, flower power, drop-out culture, drug culture, and so on). This was Grotowski as high priest, master and guru all in one. His *artistic* influence takes its full sense from the historical context in which it flourished. Brook's wish or need as an *artist* to participate in Grotowski's workshops occurred at this time. The European version of America's great period of iconoclasm, known aphoristically as May '68, nurtured artistic and other drives, needs as well as tastes that went far beyond any individual's expression of them. We should probably consider seriously the hypothesis that the three variants of "universal" culture at issue here were well and truly the children of the sixties. Maybe only the sixties could have spawned such transcendental and/or mystical notions, the sky being the limit. Similarly, maybe only the sixties could have propagated with such fervour and in such a widespread manner the "sacred" East, which was appropriated ruthlessly, albeit in "soft" guise, in the West (for example, in the insignia and rites of hippies). Barba's ideal of merging "eastern" and "western" performance is sure to be bound up with the sociohistorical momentum outlined.

These various considerations complicate, on the one hand, Brook's goal of universal communication and, on the other, the issue of Grotowski and Barba's universal performative "laboratory" (Grotowski) or "body" (Barba). They also oblige us to return once again to the problems posed for the notion of social-cultural sign by ideas claiming that the sign processes constituting productions are beyond cultural constraints - that is, universal.

Now, studies of the practice of directors cannot ignore their own views of their intentions, which intentions are (ideally) made concrete in performance. Do our directors, by their very rejection of cultural and historical specificity, compel us to review the whole notion of social sign? Are we, then, to conclude that signs are general rather than particular, the latter meaning that they are socioculturally *constrained*? Brook's *Mahabharata* is a challenging case. It amalgamates sign processes from such diverse provenances as Indian classical dance (by no means a homogeneous bloc), Chinese martial arts and Chinese and broadly European acrobatic traditions, among many examples. It can be argued that *The Mahabharata* belongs to a totally new theatrical genre created drop by drop over ten years and more by Brook and the CICT. Since this new genre does not have one, definite social source, must we abandon all hope of the social sign and approach Brook's productions through his own guidelines, particularly those on what I have called the transcendent sign?

The situation, in Brook's case, is perhaps not as drastic as it first appears insofar as each different sign process used in *The Mahabharata* has culturally specific origins. For example, movements and gestures recalling Kathakali invoke Kathakali: there is no mistaking their source. Chinese acrobatic tumbles which blend with other kinds of tumbles nevertheless show the culture that had inspired them. Thus each sign process in the production comes from a precise cultural location. It is not initially conceived of as an indeterminate, amorphous, general sign. However, it is *generalized* through the way it is used for performative ends, its merger with comparable sign processes (for example, Chinese Opera tumbles with "western" circus tumbles) contributing significantly to the generalizing power of all the signs-in-action throughout the performance.

Brook's art of blending presupposes that a production can be understood by a whole range of people from disparate cultures. The universalizing power of a work may be said to lie in its diverse spectators' capacity to recognize, appreciate and even accurately place what the work is doing. Brook's supposition is perfectly justified in that art works have been disseminated across countries for centuries. There is, in other words, a historical precedent for the strong international distribution of art works in our time. What needs to be considered is the fact that this "world heritage" of art which, precisely because it is said to be *of* the world, is supposed to belong to no one in particular, is fundamentally the culture of an elite. This elite is defined in the first instance in relation to its own national context. When it becomes international, it is defined in relation to elites across the board. Elites, then, are the first to enjoy the fruits of the world heritage. And here begins the problematical relationship between an elite's "high" culture and the so-called "low" cultures of subaltern groups in which, somewhere, lies the commercial monster known as mass culture.

The issue is a very difficult one, bringing into play the questions of access to, and the accessibility of, art works to social groups who have neither made them nor necessarily have the keys - or the desire - for an understanding of them. Brook takes seriously the notion of maximum access to art irrespective of social barriers. Hence his hypothesis that universal *communication* is possible is not a mere abstraction. The difficulty, then, is not to be found here. It lies, rather, in our understanding whether, how and why performative processes, whose capacity for communication partly relies on the theatre culture accumulated by spectators (which accumulation already defines them as belonging to an elite), communicate to spectators who have *not* acquired the same culture and may not even have *any* theatre culture at their disposal.

There is, in addition, the great problem of cultural domination or, when neo-colonialism is at issue, of cultural imperialism. Spectators in a colonial or neo-colonial situation will not necessarily see with the eyes of a colonizing elite, not, that is, unless they are in complicity with that elite whose culture, for all its apparent "civilizing" purposes, operates objectively as an instrument of oppression. When these sorts of points are taken into account, the question of the sociocultural specificity and historicity of signs reappears with renewed vigour, forcing us to look closely, once again, at the nuances of meaning introduced by universalists of one kind and another. It is also necessary to ask whether the theories of a given director are strong enough to undermine the concept of social-cultural sign, particularly as regards productions that manifestly do not share her/his ambitions.

Let us now take the psychobiologism inherent in Grotowski and Barba's perspectives. The argument that we have breathing patterns in common because of the way the human organism is structured is hardly alarming. That these patterns can be explored for the sake of developing performative processes is simply an aestheticized variant of a biological "fact". However, this naturalism, where "natural" bodily functions are pushed to the extreme to create artifice that does not look artificial, presupposes that whatever mediation occurs on the part of the performer occurs in a pure state: that is, mediation can never come from outside the "natural" body, which, since it is always in its natural, pure state can be nothing other than an elemental, primitive or primeval organism. In other words, no matter how sophisticated, supervised and controlled the breathing patterns of the performer have become (taking only this example), they are supposed to stay within the orbit of the body. Putting it aphoristically: nature is not transformed into culture; nature is returned more than ever to itself.

The banal example of eating - perhaps the next step after breathing - may be taken as another case in point. Eating is a biological necessity. But how we eat what we eat is socioculturally motivated. Signs made during the act of eating reverberate with sociocultural denotations and connotations. In other words, the passage from nature to culture is mediated by social intervention. Barba's "theatre anthropology", on the one hand, and Grotowski's "science" of natural (if subliminal) behaviour, on the other, appear to be founded on the idea that natural behaviour is transformed into culture precisely because it is transformed into performance. The idea seems to be all the more persuasive because behaviour in a "performance situation" (Barba) is not presented as merely a replica of natural behaviour in its crude state. The missing link, however, in this conceptual-practical schema is the mediation through social intervention which is part and parcel of "behaviour" and without which behaviour would be reduced to snorts and grunts and other reflex actions. It is precisely because this intervention occurs that we have *performance* and not random activity; and a plurality of theatres instead of one grand syncretic fusion of many.

The upshot of all this is that the concept of social-cultural sign must also enter this particular, biologistic picture. Signs are processes of reprocessing sounds, gestures, and so on, that from the early days of a human being's life are steeped in social and cultural particularity. How a Japanese actor emits a guttural sound may be imitated by an Italian actor. This sound may then become part of the psychobiological stock of sounds, gestures, and so on, accumulated by theatre anthropology. But the sound produced by the Italian actor may not be emitted in exactly the same way or convey exactly the same nuances - physical, facial, and the like - which accompanied it when the Japanese "model" produced it. As a consequence, this sound cannot evoke the same emotions or communicate the same meanings, whether cognitive, affective, or spiritual. Exact reproduction may not even be possible, not least because one psychobiological factor is not isolated from another. For example, breathing in the emission of the guttural sound is connected with the centring of the body and the carriage of the head. How a performer combines these psychobiological factors when she or he reprocesses the desired sound will depend on how the sociocultural conditions pertinent to the making of this sound made it the sound it is in the first place. These very same sociocultural circumstances contributed to making the performer. Think of the sounds produced by the great Kabuki actor Nakamura Utaemon. Can anyone outside his cultural context actually reproduce them, let alone move spectators in the same way? *This* is the domain of social-cultural signs. No amount of laboratory experimentation in Poland, Italy, Denmark or France can capture cultural uniqueness.

Productions and Cross-Cultural Perception: Some Examples

Details from several productions will now help us to explore a little further the problems that have been raised, as well as introduce a number not yet discussed. Needless to say, this empirical data does not consist of raw facts assembled by a dispassionate observer. It is channelled through the reflections and theoretical categories of the preceding pages, which may allow us to refine the arguments presented and perhaps even consolidate some of them.

The Royal Court, a theatre well known in England for its support of new playwrights, brought to Australia in 1989 a play that had already had considerable success in London. The play, *Our Country's Good*, by British author Timberlake Wertenbaker, is based on *The Playmaker*, a novel by the Australian Thomas Keneally. Keneally had covered all the historical research necessary for the authenticity of his book, and on which the play relied thereafter for its resonance. Thus his research incorporated numerous crucial tasks: identify the convicts who had been sent to establish a penal settlement in Sydney in 1788 and the reasons why they had been so severely punished; bring to light the circumstances in which George Farquhar's *The Recruiting Officer* was the first play to be mounted in the colony; understand the motives of Lieutenant Ralph Clark in staging Farquhar's big hit of 1706 with convicts who were diametrically opposed to the upper-class characters that they were playing; explore the disagreements between the military authorities on how to run the colony, Arthur Phillip, the Governor, supporting Clark's venture while other senior officers were against it.

Wertenbaker pares the mass of historical information available in the novel down to the barest essentials. Her text comprises twenty-one short scenes, all of them made up of sparse, elegantly-proportioned dialogue, verbal ellipses and innuendoes that fill in, so to speak, the silences between words. The scenes have montage-like concision and speed, although the narrative carried by them is linear, respecting sequences of events and the logic of cause and effect. Wertenbaker also uses Keneally's documentation to flesh out protagonists who are faced with the unprecedented situation of a gentleman's play being performed by convicts in anything but a gentleman's setting. These players, needless to say, have virtually no idea of the theatre, let alone of how to perform.

Clark, on the other hand, is knowledgeable about theatre art and is devoted to it. Like Phillip, he has humane sentiments. Phillip argues step by step as the dialogue unfolds that convicts will remain beasts unless they are exposed to the moral, "uplifting" benefits of civilized society. Theatre, to his mind, is a civilizing power. A Scottish officer, who synthesizes the viewpoint of Phillip's opponents, argues that flogging has the best civilizing effect on felons. The debate reverberates with opinions and attitudes to be taken as representative of the colonial policy of the period. In this larger context, Phillip's view increasingly appears to be a personal rather than an official position.

The debate on the side of the convicts revolves around their miserable plight, their disdain for a barren landscape whose strangeness is sharpened by memories of the teeming squalor of London, and their disarray in the face of penal brutality. Pointed reference to their continuing crimes, especially to the theft of food, reminds spectators of the original, frequently petty crimes for which many of the convicts had been transported. The convicts' awareness of how the scales of justice have been, and continue to be, weighted against them is summed up by John Wisehammer, the only convict-actor capable of intellectual rather than visceral criticism, when he composes a poem intended to replace Farquhar's epilogue. Wisehammer's composition, which sounds like a pastiche of Farquhar, concludes with lines on how convicts were transported for their country's "good".

The fact that Wisehammer comes from London's impoverished Jewish population and is described by fellow convicts as non-British provides additional ironic commentary on the ruthless, and in several respects arbitrary, legal system that had rationalized the establishment of a colony in Australia. The actor playing Wisehammer delivers the poem naively, as if it had come to the character spontaneously. Its satirical thrust is intensified because Wisehammer is portrayed throughout as something of a Shakespearian fool. His insight into the grimy realities of colonialism is endorsed by Clark's embarrassed reactions. Clark mutters incomplete phrases until he finally states that the poem might be thought by the authorities to be "political". Wisehammer's epilogue is predictably revised for the performance which is about to begin when the production of *Our Country's Good* ends.

The structure is that of a play-within-a-play since most of *Our Country's Good* is taken up with preparations for, and rehearsals of, *The Recruiting Officer*. It is interspersed with miniatures of the physical, psychological and cultural deprivation endured by the convicts, on the one hand, and with those highlighting patrician confidence, on the other. The whole, while consistently sharp-witted and humorous, never loses sight of a Britain divided into two nations, the privileged and the poor, who, for the purposes of historical accuracy for the production, are the London Cockneys and Irish forming the workforce of the colony. Wertenbaker and director Max Stafford-Clark thus foreground Britain's imperial role, as well as the contrast between her high culture and the low "criminal" culture she exported to Australia. The actors' accents, speech rhythms and pace bear out the social contradictions on which the colony was founded, as do their mannerisms, facial expressions, posture and gait.

The production casts a harsh light on Britain's self-interested pragmatism to which the civilizing force of playmaking is fundamentally subordinated. Nevertheless, it takes an optimistic view of how theatre culture might be mobilized for the purpose of humanizing social groups that operated and survived on inhuman premises. One of these premises, the genocide of the indigenous people, is not approached directly. Allusion to the fact that *Terra Australis* had been populated for centuries by aborigines is made musically. The pulsating sounds of a didgeridoo, the sign of aboriginal culture par excellence, introduces the second Act. The music closing the production is a triumphant symphony. In terms of narrative, it refers to the imminent success of the play. However, since it is so obviously part of the hegemonic culture transferred to hegemonized soil, it can be interpreted in broader social terms. The music's precise significance for spectators largely depends on their own sociopolitical and cultural horizons. Black Australians, for example, could well perceive this music as a statement of British-European domination over them. Given the politicization in recent years of black Australians, their demands for land confiscated from them and their renewed pride in their own culture, a perception of this kind would not only be probable but also pertinent.

Here we are led straight into the difficulty of assessing which audiences are addressed, potentially or actually, by *Our Country's Good*. The production was performed in a Sydney theatre (Sydney Theatre Company) whose spectators are principally drawn from the managerial groups and liberal professions. Among them are spectators from the artistic professions. Few regularly attending this theatre belong to the numerous non-Anglo/Celtic ethnic groups constituting a good third of Australia's "multicultural" society. (The term is in quotes because multiculturalism has been an official policy since the Whitlam Labor period, 1972-75.) When these groups are represented in the audience, they appear through their adult children. The children, unlike their parents, were born and educated in Australia and frequently become detached from their sociocultural and linguistic backgrounds.

These first-generation Australians are upwardly mobile. Those who have not progressed socioeconomically beyond their parents rarely attend professional theatre. But the parents of both groups are even less likely to set foot in theatre houses they consider alien to their culture. Linguistic and class barriers have been too strong for too long. Add to this the geographic location of theatres in the business districts of the inner city where a certain veneer of sophistication creates sociocultural distance. Add again the lack of theatres and even of makeshift performance spaces in the neighbourhoods densely populated by non-Anglo/Celtic communities. And add, among many more social factors, the ongoing discrimination experienced during the past forty years by non-Anglo/Celts. Racial discrimination has bred cultural shame among them. It has also fostered in the Anglo/Celtic majority a hostility towards cultural manifestations that cannot be translated easily into folklore (usually culinary folklore or representations of folkloric characters such as Con-the-Greek-fruiterer who gabbles advertisements on television).

The panorama is not altogether negative insofar as community theatres of a predominantly amateur kind have flourished over the past ten years. Bilingual performances (Italian/English, Greek/English, and so on) have begun to break up the pattern of ghettoization and isolation. And, although institutions and executives are Anglo/Celtic, thereby showing that multiculturalism operates within permissible boundaries, these performances at least give the doctrine of multiculturalism some credibility. The parents of the children attending *Our Country's Good* will not have seen this production. They will have attended, instead, the bilingual performances on immigrant life as they know it. Since these performances take place in "ethnic" zones, that is, working- and lower-middle-class suburbs inhabited also by Anglo/Celts, they will not have crossed the class threshold separating them from mainstream theatre and establishment theatres.[14]

All in all, then, the actual spectators of *Our Country's Good* are primarily of British, if not necessarily English, stock. Much the same could be said of the production's implied spectators, though not only because it was made in England. Its subject matter and performative style anticipate spectators who know the difference between, for instance, an upper-class English accent and a working-class Irish one. These spectators would be just as aware of the myriad of sociological meanings sparked off by each accent. The production works for recognition of this kind and, in this way, indicates whom it is seeking to address in the first instance.

Implied spectators may thus be identified in a reasonably sure manner. Anglo/Celtic Australians would have no trouble whatsoever in making the distinctions requested of them. This is so because the distinction between "high" and "low" accents is reproduced in their own society according to the British model. The model is close at hand insofar as what is called "educated Australian" is an attempted reduplication of its upper-class English counterpart. Meanwhile, the vernacular is aligned to Cockney English and all it implies socially, convict heritage included. Similar comments could be made about the mannerisms, grimaces and other sign processes mentioned earlier. The ins and outs of these details, while communicating maximum meaning to Anglo/Celts, would communicate less to second-generation non-Anglo/Celts and would probably escape their parents altogether. Not only would the sociocultural gap be too great for those parents, but the returns on the time, energy, effort and psychological stress invested in bridging it would be minimal.

What if we were to turn the tables and take the production back to London? London audiences similar in composition, level of education, job-and-culture aspirations, and so on, to audiences in Sydney would also have immediate access to the sign processes interconnecting with each other on stage. Nevertheless, these processes would set limits to the interaction between performers and spectators in London precisely because the latter would respond most to what makes most sense to them, leaving in an incomplete state what they would not have managed to grasp firmly.

There is, to start with, the whole Australian side of the story. What emerges as a potent critique of British dominion from Stafford-Clark's production, however finely overlaid with humour, is mediated from the perspective of the convicts. Secondly, from the standpoint of Australia today, especially since the 1988 bicentenary celebrations, this critique is potentially explosive. Remnants of colonial behaviour survive beneath the skin, ready to leap out at the smallest scratch. Australia is still constitutionally tied to Britain. Prime Minister Whitlam was sacked in 1975 by the Governor-General who, although an Australian, represents the British Crown. Spectators in Sydney in 1989 grasped meanings that spilled over into areas of contemporary importance, the call to Republicanism not least among them.

It is doubtful whether English spectators would be as alert, as sensitive to the implications for Australia's present of a play set in her past. Unless, of course, they were as historically informed and historically astute as Wertenbaker and Stafford-Clark themselves. As for the production's perspective from the vantage point of convicts, spectators would have to accept it in order to benefit maximally from what this perspective was showing. Modern British patricians might well not share its unsentimental sympathy for the damned, nor concur with the interpretation of history filtered through it.

These remarks indicate that the sociocultural meanings permeating a production neither can be nor are perceived uniformly across the different social groups who may be interpreting them. This lack of uniformity becomes a more complex matter still when cross-cultural perception is involved, namely, when Australians view a British production, or the English view it, as occurred in the case of *Our Country's Good*. Imagine Northern Irelanders viewing it today. Or spectators in India who have fought, and whose parents fought, for independence. Or spectators in France, for whom Britain's colonial history may as well have taken place on the moon, so foreign does it appear, despite France's own colonial history.

We have noted how sociocultural meanings are grasped according to varying degrees of understanding within one society. They may undergo profound transformation when they go across from one culture to another. The higher end of the scale of understanding, where sign processes are interpreted on many possible levels of meaning simultaneously, could be called refined perception. But this type of perception depends on the knowledge and heart of spectators or, when a vital component is missing, on their openness, willingness and ability to leap over the chasms separating them from a production. Even so, openness, willingness, and so on, are not acts of magic. They must start from something concrete, from some entrance point that is culturally and historically capable of being an entrance point for them. And even when the conditions of understanding are optimal, each order on the scale of understanding, whether closer to the higher or lower end, is only partial, only part of the global whole that a series of performances of the same production will yield as its "true" meaning.

The difficulties associated with cross-cultural interaction suggest how the assumptions of transculturalism as conceived by Grotowski and Barba founder when they are assessed not from the standpoint of performers but from that of *spectators*. In other words, when performance processes are felt and seen (and thus interpreted) by this or that group of spectators, they are not abstracted from a context that makes them feelable and seeable in the first place. Without concrete points of reference, spectators would be in a state of complete incomprehension. This is called mystification; and mystification is not to be confused with transcendental states of consciousness and related mystical experiences.

Our Country's Good, when performed in Australia, depends on cross-cultural processes of communication insofar as broadly English and broadly Australian sociocultural resonances are not exactly the same, whatever similarities may exist between them. It will be useful, in the framework of this discussion, to look briefly at a production where the distance between two cultures is far greater. The production is *Greek Tragedy* (also performed in 1989) by the English writer, director and film-maker Mike Leigh. Leigh is well known for his unorthodox working methods. He usually develops a script from the social experiences of ordinary people in a circumscribed community or from those of the actors with whom he is working. He then selects ideas, fragments of dialogue and conversation and whatever else may have arisen from the working process and puts them together to form a coherent text. In other words, the text and the preparations for production are closely interconnected, making for an organic performance whole. Leigh was invited to undertake a project of this kind by a Sydney theatre (Belvoir Street Theatre) which, although in the mainstream, welcomes experimentation and hosts a variety of new, marginal or even one-off theatrical ventures.

The script for *Greek Tragedy* was not completed until the opening night. Its subject was ostensibly a day in the life of the Australian-Greek community. Leigh's observing, note-taking, documentary - in short, somewhat positivistic - approach resulted in a naturalistic production. Each and every detail of the decor, lights, corporeal expression and music (Greek bazooka) tells spectators that they are in a working-class environment which, in addition, is meant to be Greek. Just how Greek it is becomes a central question as the performance progresses, and for several reasons, including the fact that the working-class rather than ethnic category emerges as the production's main point of reference.

A small-time Greek-Australian businessman and a female piece-worker who sews clothes at home are the focus of attention. The man is the former employer of an intermediary for another small business whom he encounters in the woman's house on one of his rounds for collecting finished articles. The woman is submissive to her husband and deferential to their successful compatriot. Her sister, who arrives towards the end of the performance, is an air stewardess. She is confident, articulate. Her clothes, make-up, words and movements indicate that, unlike her seamstress sister, she has adopted "Anglo" customs and habits. She is also emancipated, this intentionally suggesting, as does everything else about her, that she has been assimilated into the majority culture. She emulates, in other words, the presumed liberation of Anglo/Celtic women, which the production takes not to be the case for Greek-Australian women in general. *Greek Tragedy* homes in on the oppressive, obtuse vulgarities of the male characters, but is essentially the tragicomedy of a woman imprisoned by her gender, class and ethnicity.

The young Greek-Australians in the audience whom I spot-interviewed after the show felt that the production had exploited national stereotypes. They believed that its negative image of their community was doing a disservice to Greek-Australians (who, in any case, had been fairly systematically represented in a stereotypical fashion in society at large). As another spectator, with another cultural frame of reference, I nevertheless shared the general feeling of these spectators. However, my own criticism went in another direction. It seemed imperative to note how the production had reduced burning social issues to a matter of interpersonal behaviour pure and simple, as if Leigh and his actors believed that only individuals counted, the "social" side of their existence being somehow outside the personal (and domestic) sphere. In the light of the then considerable backlash in Australia against multiculturalism, both institutionally and at the grass-roots level (this regression also expressed in debates on Australia's immigration policy), the production's narrow focus seemed all the more disturbing. Equally disturbing, to my mind, was the way the young Greek-Australians, who were uneasy about the production, had reduced the complicated issues concerning non-Anglo/Celtic immigrants past and present to a question of ethnicity per se, which we could write as Ethnicity in the abstract. It was as if they had formulated their whole notion of ethnicity in a vacuum, well and truly out of the sociological contingencies which were integral to their family experiences. Or was this a case of unconscious amnesia, Ethnicity becoming a scapegoat or at least the instrument for blotting out the memory of painful economic struggles which all the characters on stage had signposted deliberately but had dropped relatively quickly?

A similar bias towards ethnicity as such is to be seen in the production, in that "Greek-Australianness" becomes the centre of the debate between the successful sister and the unsuccessful one and the upwardly mobile male. The actors are all Greek-Australians and are closer in outlook by virtue of age, education and social mobility to Greek-Australian spectators in the auditorium than to their parents. The "assimilated" sister on stage appears to be their image of themselves - a desirable "other" or alter ego who represses the sister who has not "made it". The actress plays the role of the unassimilated sister with finesse, and the way she appears to have been directed by Leigh suggests that he feels deep sympathy for the character. However, in the final analysis, the performance highlights this piece-worker's behaviour without, at the same time, foregrounding the social pressures that help to explain it. This rather descriptive approach is certainly linked to Leigh's working methods, which I have termed "naturalistic". It is also surely linked to how essentialist notions of ethnicity end up dominating the production. And it raises an important question regarding the - to my mind - unresolved tension between what seems to be the director's focus of sympathy and what turns out to be the actors' focus which, as the performance unfolds, gains the upper hand. Does the production express a cultural contradiction between two different views of one subject, Leigh's view (Englishman, "outsider") and that of the performers (Greek-Australians, "insiders")? And is this cultural contradiction exacerbated by the social positions taken, Leigh viewing them from the standpoint of a *working-class* character who is also a Greek-Australian and the performers viewing them from the standpoint of a Greek-Australian character who also happens to be a working-class woman? Since Leigh's method is to go with the material his performers present, the predominance of the second viewpoint in the contradiction noted is not surprising; and is a tribute to Leigh's generous, self-effacing approach.

The processes of abstraction that result from essentialist ideas about ethnicity have other consequences for the production in that, when push comes to shove, *Greek Tragedy* could be about any victimized woman and any sexist men: despite its culturally specific signs, and even its ethnocentricity, it ends up making gender statements which, in turn, are based on an all-embracing abstract notion of the "human condition". Thus the "human condition", gender absolutes and national stereotypes converge. From here to universalism is an easy step, all the more so because any declaration concerning the "human condition" is itself, by definition, universal. However, the universals at the core of the production are situational, namely, in respect of Greek-Australian characters in a Greek-Australian setting. And what emerges from the defined situation seems to be an Anglo/Celtic view of Greeks in Australia. The issue of cross-cultural perception and interaction of concern to us opens onto several hypotheses: director Leigh, although viewing things from the standpoint of the working class, tends to see the situation from the vantage point of the English working class; the performers, although Greek-Australians, have no intention of taking up their parents' mantle and asserting Greek identity; although of dual culture, they opt for a single culture, as expressed by the assimilated sister. The two hypotheses concerning the performers suggest that, in either case, they do not perceive the situation from the standpoint of Greek-Australian immigrants.

The question of point-of-view, which has received enormous attention in literary studies and almost none in studies of the theatre, is crucial for understanding how productions are produced and performances performed. It is also crucial for the sociology of the theatre to which the numerous questions raised in the course of this discussion must belong. It must, therefore, be raised in issues to do with culture, whether culture is situated sociohistorically and its particularity affirmed, or whether it is abstracted out of context in the name of a transcendent sign (which amounts to a negation of culture). There is a great difference between the universalism projected by this or that work and the generalizing power emanating from a work that does not deny its sociohistorical and cultural space. Cultural constraints of some sort might well be necessary, not only for anchoring a production as a work of art, which involves aesthetic evaluation from performers and spectators, but also for communicating emotion and meaning, which involves social evaluation and some sense of cultural appropriateness.

NOTES

1. The philosophical expression of these methodological procedures, which presuppose the virtual non-existence of an author, may be found in Michel Foucault, "Qu'est-ce qu'un auteur?" *Bulletin de la Société française de philosophie* 63 (1969) and Roland Barthes, "The Death of the Author" in *Image, Music, Text*, trans. Stephen Heath, London: Fontana, 1977, pp. 142-8. Both writers develop a discourse theory congruent with the conceptual principles of structuralism and semiotics and which as good as eliminates any notion of the "subject", that is, of a speaking, inventive and doing/acting being. This elimination of the subject who is the architect of her/his own discourse is antithetical to the principle of social agency which is fundamental to sociology.

   It should be noted that, although I refer here to stage productions in order not to create a confusion with "production" in its general sense, I by no means confine my discussion to productions performed on a proscenium stage. My discussion includes productions that may well be performed in all kinds of non-traditional performance spaces. What matters is the fact that these performances are put together by design and are not random occurrences or happenings (although "happenings" can also happen by design, as John Cage, The Living Theatre and others have shown).

2. "The Sociology of the Theatre, Part Three: Performance". *New Theatre Quarterly* V, 19 (August 1989), pp. 282-300.

3. For the requisite documentation concerning these points see Maria Shevtsova, "The Sociology of the Theatre, Part One: Problems and Perspectives". *New Theatre Quarterly* V, 17 (February 1989), pp. 23-35. See also my *Theatre and the New Cultural Policy of France's Socialist Government. Theatre Papers.* Fourth Series. No. 7. Devon: Dartington College of the Arts, 1981. This monograph is not cited in the article above. On questions concerning cultural policy vis-à-vis the theatre, see also *Per una politica del teatro. Atti del convegno sul teatro del partito comunista italiano* (Prato 24-26 September 1976). Rome: Bulzoni, 1977 and Bruno Sanguanini, *Il pubblico all'Italiana.* Milan: Franco Angeli, 1989. For policy in respect of an overview of the arts in general see John Pick, *The Arts in a State.* Bristol: Bristol Classical Press, 1988. For an excellent regional study concerning policy and the arts see Bruno Sanguanini, *Fare cultura: attori e processi della modernizzazione culturale; il Trentino.* Milan: Franco Angeli, 1992. To be noted is the fact that Pierre Bourdieu, in his study of the social distribution of the arts, cultural values, "cultural capital" and related issues characteristic of the author's research, sorely neglects the theatre (though no one, not even Bourdieu, can cover everything!). See *La Distinction: critique sociale du jugement.* Paris: Les Editions de Minuit, 1977. See also Pierre Bourdieu, *Les Règles de l'art: genèse et structure du champ littéraire.* Paris: Le Seuil, 1992 which, as its title suggests, focuses on literature (and especially Flaubert).

4. Paris: Editions Gonthier, 1966. Goldmann argues appropriately that the question of science in the social sciences cannot be broached via the idea of value-free, detached observation which is modelled on the methods of the physical and natural sciences. The researcher, an active subject who undertakes a sociological study of a given object, is always in some relation to the latter by virtue of being *in* society and not outside it. Objectivity in the social sciences, Goldmann argues, is only possible when the ensemble of social relations in a delimited society is taken fully into account. Consideration of this ensemble or "social totality", as Goldmann calls it, protects against partiality of judgement and mere opinion, on which subjective assessments are founded. A clear view of the social totality requires placing it in a historical framework, this procedure giving the "historical sociology" which Goldmann distinguishes from positivism (and thus positivistic sociology), empiricism and other methodologies that Goldmann deems to be parcellized and, therefore, inadequate.

5. The theoretical underpinnings of the concept of social sign used here are to be found in the works of Mikhaïl Bakhtin (and notably in *Marxism and the Philosophy of Language*, trans. Ladislav Matejka and I. R. Titunik. Cambridge, Massachusetts, London: Harvard University Press, 1986; original Russian 1929). I discuss the implications of this concept at some length in "The Sociology of the Theatre, Part Three: Performance" as noted above.

6. As occurs, for example, in Brook's *Mahabharata* where martial art exercises, particularly those requiring sticks, practised during the "training" periods of the actors, are left behind almost intact in the production.

7. See, in particular, *Les Ombres collectives: sociologie du théâtre*. Paris: Presses Universitaires de France, 1965 and *L'Acteur: esquisse d'une sociologie du comédien*. Paris: Gallimard, 1965.

8. *The Empty Space*. London: Harmondsworth, Penguin, 1968. It is also useful to consult *The Shifting Point*. New York: Harper & Row, 1987. For an excellent "summary" of Brook's achievement up to *The Mahabharata* see David Williams, ed. *Peter Brook: A Theatrical Casebook*. London: Methuen, 1988.

9. For material relevant to some of these issues see Patrice Pavis, *Theatre at the Crossroads of Culture*, pp. 160-216, trans. Loren Kruger. London and New York: Routledge, 1992 and the essays in Patrice Pavis, ed. *Confluences. Le Dialogue des cultures dans les spectacles contemporains: essais en l'honneur d'Anne Ubersfeld*. Saint-Cyr L'Ecole: Prépublications, 1992, as well as his "Une Rencontre interculturelle: Wilson, Brook, Zadek". *Théâtre/Public* 105 (May-June 1992), pp. 36-45. See also David Williams, "Remembering the Others that are Us: Transculturalism and Myth in the Theatre of Peter Brook". Forthcoming. It should be noted that there are slight, though not insignificant discrepancies of meaning between Pavis' "*interculturel*" and Williams' "transcultural" and, it seems, between the latter and my own use of the term.

10. "Theatre Anthropology". *The Drama Review* 94. 2 (Spring 1982), p. 5.

11. Barba's search for resemblances, for variations on a given, stable theme is, in my view, comparable to Foucault's quest, notably in *L'Archéologie du savoir*. Paris: Gallimard, 1969. See also, in the framework of the present argument, Foucault's *L'Histoire de la folie à l'âge classique*. Paris: Gallimard, 1961; *Surveiller et punir*. Paris: Gallimard, 1975; and *L'Ordre du discours*. Paris: Gallimard, 1971.

12. "The Fiction of Duality". *New Theatre Quarterly* V, 20 (November 1989), p. 312.

13. ibid.

14. These observations are largely, though not exclusively, based on my research by questionnaire on audiences attending Italo-Australian productions in Sydney. For some general reflections relevant to the present discussion, see my "Théâtre multiculturel, nouveauté et perspective ethnique". *Sociologie de l'art* 5 (1992), pp. 69-79.

PART II

PRODUCTIONS

3

PEER GYNT IN FRANCE DIRECTED BY PATRICE CHEREAU

In 1896, Lugné-Poe staged *Peer Gynt* in Paris, the very first production of the play in France. From then on until May 1981, when Patrice Chéreau presented his interpretation of Ibsen's masterpiece at the Théâtre National Populaire in Villeurbanne, Lyon, *Peer Gynt* had enjoyed a mere thirteen French productions. This figure can hardly compare with the number of times other European plays have been mounted in France since the turn of the century. After Villeurbanne, Chéreau's production went to the Théâtre de la Ville in Paris for the 1981 winter season.

It is true that *Peer Gynt* seems to pose special difficulties because of its length, apparently rambling structure and call upon stark, striking images of mountains, deserts and mythical, magical or nightmarish landscapes, all of which give it the distant, other-worldly and epic quality that held delights for a visionary symbolist like Lugné-Poe but was daunting for lesser mortals nourished on theatrical realism or even on formally experimental theatre. Chéreau, then, rose to the challenge by mounting a mega-production equal in daring to the fantasies of the Norwegian author. His *Peer Gynt* defied decorum in that it was divided into two parts which were performed in a consecutive sequence over two days. The spectator, in other words, had to come to the theatre twice running to fit the pieces of Chéreau's creation together. The different parts were called Day One and Day Two, each playing for three and a half hours. This marathon, which refused to make any concessions to the rules of entertainment defined by the *théâtre bourgeois* of the nineteenth century, is nevertheless the apotheosis of nineteenth-century theatre - particularly as it had come to be at the end of the century - at this, *our* twentieth-century *fin de siècle*.

Chéreau, though, is not inspired by the symbolism that enraptured Lugné-Poe. He responds to the terrestrial desires which, in art and in the culture generally, were known by the name of naturalism; and thus his spirit moves with Antoine and Zola, both of them great champions of Ibsen. Antoine's production of *Ghosts* in 1890, which he describes as having "the sombre grandeur of Greek tragedy", introduced Ibsen to France. No one was a more tireless campaigner and noisy publicist for naturalism in the theatre than Zola. Antoine and Zola's aim of bringing about a theatre capable not only of portraying real life but also of outdoing it, that is, of being *larger* than life, is magnified - perhaps to an unprecedented degree in the theatre - by Chéreau. Chéreau also surpasses their commitment to truthful representation through ordinary, unadorned "natural" detail. Chéreau, as if thumbing his nose with a grin at Antoine and Zola, puts a real pig and a real horse on the stage. The pig and the horse, albeit natural animals ridden by an actor playing a fictional character, do not simply represent themselves. They are the signs of tragic destiny in that they help carry Peer inexorably into his grave.

Such tricks and effects as the pig and the horse, although fulfilling specific directorial intentions, are flirtations, even whimsical references to nineteenth-century naturalism. They are, at the same time, humorous quotations of the artifices used by the *théâtre de boulevard* - the worst kind of *théâtre bourgeois* according to Antoine and Zola, and whose social and cultural values these naturalist purists abhorred. Yet naturalism always *was* paradoxical. It imitated nature through icons which, instead of looking natural, only stressed their own artificiality. It demanded high seriousness through representations which, by their very exaggeration for the purposes of mimesis, could not help but be comical. Today's audiences laughed at a real pig and a real horse on the stage of the Théâtre de la Ville, just as loudly, and with the same sort of complicity, as audiences did at a puffing engine on the stage of the Châtelet, a non-serious, *boulevard*-style theatre. The puffing engine had appeared several months earlier in a production of Offenbach's *La Vie parisienne* (first performed in 1866, and so well before the refinements of Lugné-Poe's *Peer Gynt*). The Châtelet is directly opposite the Théâtre de la Ville. It became famous for its productions of music hall and musical comedy, giving rise to the widely-used, familiar expression *"du Châtelet"*, which means corn and kitsch. Chéreau's knowing exploitation of gestural and vocal gags, particularly through Gérard Desarthe who plays Peer, is both a return to, and a wink at, the Châtelet tradition. So, too, is Chéreau's use of painted backdrops, which he combines with a device that became the hallmark of naturalism in the theatre, namely, the extension of the decor beyond the visual field. The purpose of this illusionism was to suggest continuity of space, as in real life.

Yet Chéreau's amalgamation of modes does not altogether explain why the term "apotheosis" used above is appropriate for his work. The most important factor is the tight collaboration between Chéreau, Richard Peduzzi, his scenographer, François Regnault, who translated the Norwegian for this production, and every other participant, not least the actors. Although Antoine and Lugné-Poe executed works differently, they both conceived of the *mise en scène* as an orchestrated ensemble of specialists, the director at their head. Their expectations now meet in a *mise en scène* which is given maximum possibilities for collaboration. However, collaboration is no longer understood to be one between craftsmen, as was the case at the turn of the century, but between technologists. Peduzzi, scenographer-engineer, manipulates equipment worthy of Zola's conviction that science stretches theatrical semantics; and that science for society is progress.

While it is banal to say that a performance cannot exist without space, this banality cannot be repeated enough regarding any performance, let alone one thoroughly determined by Peduzzi's massive architecture. For this reason, my analysis starts with, and concentrates on, space. Secondly, Regnault's translation into colloquial French, and into prose and verse metres as close as possible to Ibsen's, divides Acts into Scenes (not in Ibsen) which are Chéreau and Peduzzi's guide for the division of space.

There is no need, here, to enter into theoretical problems on the relationship between a written text and the "text" which is the performance. *Peer Gynt*'s collaborators have simplified the difficulty. My enumeration of Acts and Scenes therefore follows their spatial and narrative organization. In other words, when I speak of Scene y, I mean the scene structured by the performance. If my reader wishes to check the narrative moments being discussed, her/his task will be facilitated: Peter Watt's translation of the Norwegian (Penguin) marks the transitions where Regnault-Peduzzi-Chéreau have marked them. My own translations are from the French script.

This is not the place for a critique of semiotic theory as it has been used in recent years for performance analysis. It is nevertheless useful to note the four principles of a critical nature as regards semiotics that underpin my analysis of *Peer Gynt*.

Firstly, a catalogue of semiotic categories, to which performance signs are made to correspond, produces a dictionary, at best a model, but eschews the whole which is the performance. My aim is the whole, that interaction of semiotic processes where one process is mediated by the next and, simultaneously, is transformed by all the others operating at the same time. While, for the purpose of clarity in writing my analysis, I will give special attention to one sign-process - space, for example - it should be understood that reference to other processes such as movement, voice, light, and so on, keep the whole performance in mind.

Secondly, the notion of signs in theatre theory requires revision. The interaction of play-elements in a given performance produces meaning. But when meaning is defined as the relationship between signifier and signified in a hermetic system, the analyst is confined to this formal construction and to the purely descriptive method it entails. More attention should be paid to how semiotic processes or semioses function in terms of sociocultural meaning, which is absorbed ("encoded" in semiotic terminology) and, of greater importance still, changed by the performance-whole. By looking at a performance as a recipient of signs and, hence, as a passive, "flat" phenomenon where signs appear as so many pre-set pieces, semioticians have neglected the fact that the performance-whole is a dynamic which generates and *re-creates* signs.

Thirdly, a performance *interprets* signs, as does a spectator. Interpretation and, therefore, selection (interpretation is not to be equated here with hermeneutics) play a far more important role on both sides of the stage or playing space - the performance side(s) and the side(s) reserved for the audience - than semiotic theory has admitted to date. Moreover, there is a back and forth movement between performers and spectators. How one reacts affects what the other does, and vice versa. A complex process of interpretation occurs in the interaction between the two. It is to be noted, furthermore, that the audience "side" or space(s) holding the audience may become the arena of performance, thereby merging playing and audience space for whatever duration is required. This mingling of spaces and between performers and spectators strongly affects the back and forth interpretative movement between them. We shall see how important the use of audience space by performers is to the meaning of Chéreau's *Peer Gynt.*

Fourthly - and this is connected to the third point - spectators have a sociocultural existence and a sociocultural memory (witness the laughter at the *Châtelet* pig in Chéreau's production), which are active in how spectators respond to any production and in how every production is made, for whom it is made (which audiences? where?) and what orientation it chooses. The performance's orientation is a crucial component of the meaning that emerges from it, though always with respect to the spectator.

We can take the example of the pig to illustrate these points on memory and meaning. Peer Gynt, having fled his village, meets the Woman in

Green deep in the mountains. Her snout, when she first appears in II v, anticipates the image of the real pig that appears at the end of the same scene. This strong visual image of Pig is repeated and reinforced by the shape of the Troll King's head. The Troll King makes his entry immediately after the pig's exit. The pig-image is strengthened, once again, by the Woman in Green's reappearance in III ii. Its impact on perception and, by now, also on meaning, is extended through an aural image: the Woman in Green tells Peer that the misshapen creature he despises is his son, for "a pig can be recognized by its skin". Peer is the object of her indictment. The recurrence of pig images in one form or another jolts the spectator's memory back to her/his first incredulous view of the real pig. And this corny pig no longer seems to have been there just for fun, or merely to remind the spectators of entertainment conventions past and present. The spectator has begun to realize that the pig images accumulated during performance open a critical perspective on Peer, and not only on him. Since, besides being part of an aesthetic construction, they also operate in a cultural context which does not prize piggery, the spectator cannot avoid recognizing their socially negative associations. The memory required of any spectator for the duration of one performance is constantly doubled by a collective, social memory.

It should also be noted that I am by no means confusing or fusing actors and characters. My attention to acting detail points out the actors' *transmission* of meaning. However, I use characters' rather than actors' names to help the reader find her/his bearings. After all, the analysis below is verbal metalanguage, whereas Chéreau's production, like all productions, is built out of a plurality of "languages" in which words are not necessarily of uppermost importance. Furthermore, by referring to the characters in their fictional universe, I hope to avoid the cumbersome linking that occurs when the separation between actor and character is stressed (for example, Desarthe/Peer).

* * * *

Space in *Peer Gynt* is multiple: vertical, horizontal, diagonal, audience-space and wing-space. To these five spaces that are appropriated by the actors should be added a sixth - the paralinguistic space in which the cries of birds, the barking of dogs and the howl of wolves, wind or sea create volume, distance, or crushing proximity. The position and intensity of non-verbal sounds are regulated according to play. Bird cries, for instance, seem to soar high above the spectators just as the decor outlining mountains and which gives the depth of perspective to the stage zig-zags and bangs into place. The imposing scenographic ensemble announces Peer's monologue in II iv. Towards the scene's conclusion a bird calls from the wings. By this time Peer is sitting on a horizontal plank the length of the stage and which is suspended half-way between the floor and ceiling. Peer turns towards the direction of sound saying "Mother, be quiet". Later, at the end of V vi, Ase's voice is heard off-stage from the same location where the bird called. Thus, not only does Peer associate that particular bird call with his mother, but the very source of sound allows the audience to coordinate bird and mother, whose voice, now that Peer's life is coming to an end, will not be still. Wing-space, at this very moment in the performance in Act V, is the actor's rather than paralinguistic space. However, since Ase is now dead, her voice now belongs to the non-human sphere of animals, trolls and supernatural emanations permeating a forbidding nature. Consequently, it now belongs to the fantastic, phantasmagoric universe that has pursued Peer from beginning to end.

Further examples of how and why non-verbal sound is emitted from either acting or paralinguistic space will be given with respect to other scenes. It is important to state, right here, that my classification of space into six types is for expository concision. These spaces merge in the dynamic of the performance. They criss-cross as the decor changes, which it does especially rapidly in Day One. Similarly, they criss-cross as the actors change position, or according to when and how the actors use the architecture (for example, when Peer is sitting on the plank). The actors' bodies also mould space. (Take, again, Peer sitting on the plank: his vertical body is etched out against the horizontal empty space behind him, making it look quite cavernous.) The production as a whole is built by this complex intersection of spaces and of movements in space.

The preceding paragraphs should have shown how one space connects with or becomes another. Further reference to II iv should also indicate how the simultaneity of different spaces mediates the criss-crossing of signs. Let us take Peer's plank again. It gives the horizontal, which contrasts sharply with the vertical of the walls surrounding him. His seated body accentuates the verticality of the framing sets. (Seconds earlier he was standing, an imaginary perilous drop beneath him. His standing body also accentuated the vertical lines of the set.) His words interweave with paralinguistic sounds such as the bird cry off-stage, or - minutes before - the shrill cry of eagles above Peer's head. Since Peer is standing when the sound of eagles is heard, these sounds seem higher still. Hence three types of space - horizontal, vertical, wing-space - interchange and exchange meaning with gestures, mimicry and speech; with the oblique, low light from stage-right; with the cold, granite-grey of Peduzzi's constructions. And these monoliths connote the cliffs and chasms of a dangerous mountain-scape that dwarfs, crushes and kills.

Colour semiosis contributes, as we shall see, to the interpretation provided by all collaborators of this *Peer Gynt*. Sound semiosis, for its part, incorporates the crash of sets, the marked stamping or running of feet, the music made by instrumentalists on stage and/or in the wings, as well as the electro-acoustic throbs and pulsations produced by sophisticated technology and which appear to come from above the amphitheatre holding the audience. The fluctuations and tonalities of the production's sound scape move in and out of the various phonemes, intonations and cadences produced through both speech and song, the whole creating an extraordinary texture of tempi, beats and rhythms that deserves special study.

Given the above remarks on the numerous and swiftly changing spaces of *Peer Gynt*, it seems almost impossible to claim that the vertical and horizontal axes emerge as the dominant space-shapers of the production. Yet they do, precisely because, with them, Chéreau and Peduzzi can extend or narrow space overall. The interplay between extending and narrowing spaces generates the conditions for all the relations established on stage, for instance, the relation between the architecture, props and light. It concerns, above all, the relations between the actors. The counterpoint established between the extension and reduction of the space in which the actors must play also guides the production's philosophical argument which, of course, is not straight discourse: it is mediated by all the stage processes.

The production's argument, as expressed through language, has a triadic form. The first two elements of the triad are Peer's recurrent "Be yourself" or, paradigmatically, "Be true to yourself" and the Troll King's "Suffice unto yourself" or - also paradigmatically - "To yourself be - enough". These axioms create a prolonged dialogue that lasts for the duration of the Two Days. The dialogue is carried not only by explicit statements like these, but also through a progressively stronger undercurrent of lexical and situational irony. The third element in the triad which, on the one hand, links up with Peer's life principle and, on the other, with that of the Troll King, is Begriffenfeldt's axiom according to which "Being yourself" is the same as "Being beside yourself" (IV xiii). The lunatic asylum run by

Begriffenfeldt is both the realization of, and a metaphor for, his axiom: being yourself *egotistically*, as Peer and the Troll King understand living, leads to being beside yourself, that is, to madness and/or death.

When, at the end of Day Two, Peer, whose shoulders are stooped and whose body is shrunken (Desarthe's illusionistic acting is most compelling), looks up into the Button Moulder's face to ask querulously what "Being yourself" actually means, the Button Moulder's cryptic reply is: "Being yourself means slaying yourself" (V ix). Peer is on the brink of death. The synthesis of the argument set out in words spells death. How the production focuses on physical, moral and social devastation in Act V will be discussed at the conclusion of this essay. The last Act of *Peer Gynt* gazes upon these devastations which, irrespective of the metaphysical sheen that covers them, are shown to be concrete, palpable catastrophes. And this multiple destruction is shown to be the point of departure, the destination and the cohesive principle of the entire performance.

Now that the production's main philosophical content is clear, we can note that spatial shifts transform the appearance of what I described as "framing sets" above. These frames are held in place throughout the Two Days. Wide, flat pillars along stage-left are shortened by a long, low platform which is like a stage within a stage, and ends in steps. Behind the platform is a passage, which is walled in by a vast, grid-like backdrop. The grid is either partially blocked from view by mobile pieces, or disappears behind various backcloths. It is more exposed when it provides a wall for the lunatic asylum. When it becomes a wall, the grid is hemmed in by an equally vast cage-gate from which the lunatics, who are trapped in narrow space, gradually move outwards, some towards the audience. The same grid is the frontier of perspective from V ii till the end of the performance.

Pillars along stage-right, which are narrower than those opposite them and closer to the audience, are mostly used by Peer, notably at the beginning of III i, when he actually chops into the pillar nearest the audience with a gigantic axe. Peer uses the pillars in IV v, when, betrayed and abandoned by fellow merchants, he searches for roots to eat in the desert and finds them among the small plants tucked into the side of the second pillar. He uses them again in IV v, when he spits the roots out and sprawls against the second pillar, a knotted handkerchief around his head, lassitude in his arms, nonchalant wit in his voice. The pillars serve Peer in V vii, when he attempts to seduce Anitra, who is on her back in the shadows. They are particularly important for play from V ii, where they become Peer's hiding place, his space of fear. These pillars, then, are not "dead" decor.

At stage-left - near the audience, though flat against the wings - stands a ruined tower borrowed from nineteenth-century iconography of the romantic or 1890s "decadent" kind. A heap of rubble at its base touches a plank coming down in a low diagonal almost to centre-stage. This diagonal line is echoed by a white curtain hanging further back. The curtain is like a collapsed sail. Above it is a horizontal plank. All these main frames are the basis for the ceaseless transformations of space, colour, sound and play that have a mesmeric quality, irrespective of the sharp jolts to the spectators' perception brought about by the transformations at issue.

* * * *

Day One starts with the diagonal as Peer pushes Ase, who is on her backside, down to the floor-boards. The descending plank carves out a restricted area for their play. Dialogue continues beside it (Peer mostly on his knees, Ase sitting with her legs crossed), on it (when Peer, still on his knees, narrates his tale of the mountain goat), or under it. Peer curls into a foetal position under it when Ase scolds him. He then hooks his legs over the plank as - a truant child - he fiddles with bits of rubble and giggles or mutters to himself in mockery of her admonishments. Action on it occurs again as mother and son exchange affections, one curled into the other and vice versa (here images of maternity glide into those of sexuality), until Ase, who refuses to let go of Peer, is whisked up onto his shoulders, run in a semi-circle towards the horizontal plank, and hoisted up and dumped on it, her legs still kicking, her hands, which had been beating Peer, now gripping its sides.

As Ase heaves herself onto the plank to face Peer and also the audience, the white curtain swings backwards and up, showing rolling clouds of grey with burned orange tips. Shortly afterwards, the curtain is pulleyed forward towards the audience as Peer runs off. After shouting for help - Maria Casarès as Ase makes the situation very comic - Ase sits alone, tiny and still in this enormous concave shape, while two peasant women with bundles of straw on their backs appear and exclaim at how Ase is sitting on a roof. The curtain then sweeps higher, hiding Ase as the two women exit behind it. Thus the curtain breaks the production's opening scene into three sequences and then marks the transition into the next scene where Peer makes it the focal point of his monologues. The clouds drifting across it symbolize his desire to escape from uncomfortable reality. In the meantime, the diagonal plank does not become an irrelevant piece of furniture. Peer scuttles underneath it when he hears voices at the beginning of I ii, and hears, from there, the villagers' disparaging remarks about him. Here again, as often happens in the production, Peer defines his space of frightened solitude.

A sharp click releases the curtain which swirls down onto the stage, indicating that the scene is finished. Peer drags it out as the music and laughter of wedding festivities are heard in the wings. At the same time, a farm landscape slides across the back wall of the stage. Light, which until now appeared dimly and obliquely, irradiates the landscape from behind, giving the actors in this extended space the quality of sculptured figures. The bridegroom enters first, as if in shock, holding space alone as he blindly moves towards the spectators. A violinist, whose notes are discordant though sweet, comes into view at the very back. The guests follow, in twos and threes, attenuating space rather than filling it. A similar impression of emptiness is created by the sporadic noises of clinking and spilling beer mugs. Costumes in beige, black or faded colours harmonize with the soft, autumnal landscape open to view. Meanwhile, the wedding proper continues, not visually but aurally, off-stage, in wing-space.

The composition recalls northern painters of the classical period, its rustic elegance evoking a de Hooch. But its emotional atmosphere is disorder. The invisible musicians, stamping feet and voices filling wing-space produce sonorities which are half-way between folk music and its caricature. These off-stage sound patterns extend the configuration on stage of increasingly drunk young men, simpering young women, and reserved, puritanical elders. Violence increases when Peer, who enters from front left, is progressively driven back towards the diagonal plank, bullied, harassed, derided. The long distances held between the actors emphasize that the social structure is not a community, but a place of alienation.

The same perspective on Peer's society is to be seen when Solveig and her family enter by the diagonal plank. Veritable strangers to the village, they are treated indifferently. A similar indifference characterizes their attitude to each other. (Helga, who clutches Solveig, is an exception to the lack of contact between the people.) The psychological separation between the local inhabitants, which is suggested in how they are placed in twos and threes, only ceases when Peer becomes the subject of collective humiliation. [Plate 1] It is operative when Peer - again on his knees, again on the horizontal line which signifies oppression - bounds up to Solveig,

Act I Scene iii
Photo by Birgit, Paris

veers away from her (gestures she repeats in counterpoint) and finally falls at her feet. Solveig is about to brush past the sloping hills and barns facing her. Peer turns furious circles on his knees, shouting he will go mad if she does not dance with him, obstructing her path, as he will her life, in the mystic union she eventually effects with him.

Desarthe's obsessive head-shaking, his agitated hands, his pigeon-toed feet and averted gaze - and these are constants in his rendition throughout Day One - give a Peer, semi-village idiot and semi-neurotic, who is branded by rejection. Rejection takes multiple forms. It is presented, in social terms, through the image of a brutish, God-fearing, troll-and-devil-fearing peasantry whose protestant individualism Peer adopts as his life principle; and which Day Two austerely exhibits step by step. For instance, the parable of the positive-negative in V x is carefully articulated, vocally and visually, in the open vistas of the last Act. It shows how Peer has inverted the God-law of his ancestors into troll-law. At the same time, it stresses the ambiguities between religion and superstition, individualism and self-reliance and egotism, all of which are integral to Peer's social origins. Chéreau's *Peer Gynt* bids farewell to charming folk-tales.

Rejection is expressed metaphysically by the fixed sets, a metaphor for an estranging - and estranged - cosmos: the domestic landscape on the horizon is also dominated by it. Peer experiences moral and psychological rejection. The villagers treat him as a misfit. But Peer turns himself into a misfit and then an outcast by fabricating myths and fantasies that clash with his small world. These imaginings feed his dreams of becoming an emperor. The small world of his village restricts him. But neither the great plains of America nor the deserts of Morocco and Egypt (Act IV) can fulfil his yearnings and dreams. Furthermore, Peer - a peasant turned capitalist turned pauper - does not know how to fulfil his dreams. Multiple rejection, which is the flip side of multiple alienation, is concentrated in Peer, though is everywhere in the production.

The wedding scene thus prefigures all of Day Two. And it has a specific counterpart in V iv, where the fixed architecture, an orange pillow, bits of bric-à-brac and a battered pram wheeled slowly by a bent, black figure at the back, depict the desolation of old age as Peer and the villagers know it. The physical distances which were observed during the wedding are greater still in this scene, where former noise is replaced by silence and former agility by decrepit movements. Almost all the figures reassemble in shadows that hide faces, light now a long tunnel through the centre of the stage tapering in at the back.

The occasion on Day Two is an auction of Peer's belongings which, as

Peer discovers on his return home, are like relics of the legend that he had become. As Peer stumbles onto the stage, barely perceptible in the gloom, his tired gestures show the futility of his and his compatriots' respective histories. They have emptied these histories of all reality, turning them into mythology. Peer tells the villagers the tale of his odyssey through the world. And, although emblematic, he tells it as if it were just another one of his many fanciful tales. This one time, however, the tale Peer tells is true. It falls on deaf ears. Peer tells his story from the stage within the stage, where he is reduced to a bystander of his own life. His body leans against the huge wall in black - vertical on vertical - while the villagers, who are just as blind to his presence as he is to theirs, drift past just below him and disappear. Peer's personal failure is a social failure which is not his alone. The auction, like the wedding, assembles men and women for acts of callousness, self-centredness and destruction.

The wedding scene, then, is a pivotal scene for the entire production, and in more ways than one. It ends when Peer suddenly bursts from the back of the stage with Ingrid on his back. As he gallops up the steep steps of the auditorium, still carrying Ingrid, the men rush for cudgels (off-stage) and chase Peer through the aisles. Audience space becomes the mountain that the women scrutinize, clustered together on the edge of the stage. During this event - the one act of solidarity that the spectators witness or hear - Ase's voice rises above the din, the only voice besides Solveig's (to be heard in support of Peer later on in the production) that does not clamour for revenge, or retribution, or barter, which are the hallmarks of the social relations others enter into with Peer wherever he goes. Ase's refusal, here, to share her countrymen's harsh outlook confirms her generous words earlier in Act I about her son and about human kind in general. The audience discovers later on that Solveig's refusal to conform to the villagers' views is more radical still. After marching down the amphitheatre through the audience with skis on her shoulder and stocks in her hand (III iii), Solveig arrives on stage to tell Peer boldly and crisply that she has abandoned the village's "airless, hemmed-in domain". We shall return to the question of how the two women's opposition to the norms of their society is situated by the production as a whole.

Act I establishes the domestic, social, cultural and geographic contexts in which Peer's biography is to be situated. Acts II and III concentrate on how he begins to forge his Self. Act II is announced from behind the audience, that is, from the top rows of seats occupied by spectators. Ingrid and Peer are on opposite sides of the auditorium. Audience space now divides them, as do their antagonistic words. Their first seven exchanges are made in the dark, as they go down the amphitheatre steps towards the stage. The darkness in which they make their entry is in sharp contrast with the spotlight that had lit their exit from the wedding. Peer's appearance on stage is synchronized with his violent outburst to Ingrid that he has faith in no one "except for one". This "one" is the unutterable Solveig, who secretly isolates Ingrid from Peer. (A key phrase underlying a sequence's thrust, and which coincides with a given actor's frontal position to the spectators, is a systematic procedure of the production.) The human alienation that spectators cannot help but notice is intensified by the alienation brought about by Nature and which Nature seems to personify. A curled mountain, rock formations etched on its base, clicks into place across middle-stage, its impressive power a warning to all who may dare to transgress its authority.

Alienation is aggravated, yet again, as the curled mountain moves out while three higher, jagged mountains, with gaps and fogs between them, crash deeper into the stage. The scene (II ii) is Ase and Solveig's search for Peer. Solveig's parents take the role of dispassionate spectators. Ase's calls are timed into four movements, the last occurring at the top of the stairs, her voice carrying into the wings. Solveig's are mute as she stares far into the heights formed by the audience. While proxemic relations between the actors repeat the patterns of distance established in previous scenes, they are established here along diagonal lines. Two miniature figures on top of the high central mountain - a man, followed some length away by a woman - provide a mirror image, an allegory and even a parody of the image projected at floor level below the mountain. At the same time, these tiny figures give a sense of the enormous distance crossed by Ase and Solveig and which the spectators have had to cross to keep up with them. [Plate 2]

A similar optical illusion and juxtaposition of images recurs in IV xii, when a figurine of a nineteenth-century bourgeois stands on the Sphinx's enormous head. Visual incongruity, in this case, does not function in terms of spatial depth. It elongates the vertical axis, and points allegorically to the discrepancy between Peer's grandiose ambitions and his reality. Moreover - additional incongruity - Peer, who wants to be an emperor, is about to meet Begriffenfeldt, who will offer him an empire. That empire is a madhouse.

No sooner have eye and mind seized II ii, than II iii is introduced by snow-capped peaks, their base shrouded in white smoke (representing fog). Loud moans in the wings herald the arrival of the three writhing, sliding herd-women whom Peer will as good as rape. Sexuality is in profile and predominantly on the horizontal, as it is when the Woman in Green or

Act II Scene ii
Photo by Birgit, Paris

Anitra is involved. Throughout the production, sexuality is shown to be another form of alienation. Where Peer is specifically concerned, physical desire is just one more of his many spontaneous desires that end in sadness and emptiness, the very words that Peer uses after he has had his pleasure with the three women. The arbitrary nature of Peer's actions and his adventurer's attitude to all things including sex are clear again in II v, which is announced by glaciers and the Woman in Green. Peer sniffs her while crawling on hands and knees, as she does, and imitates her grunts, squeals, wiggling backside and related movements that designate a pig and a troll in one. These comic-grotesque procedures lead to brutal and brutish fornication in front of the glaciers. The glaciers are not simply a setting for action. They express visually the precarious, ice-burning quality of Peer's sexual and other urges. When a real pig abruptly materializes, these urges take Peer, on its back, into the kingdom of the trolls. The glaciers also comment symbolically on Peer's uncoordinated, egotistical desires which come to fruition in trolldom, that is, in the living out of the motto "To yourself be - enough".

Where Scenes iii and v of Act II show how Peer behaves in relation to his desires, Scene iv synoptically catches their dimensions: Peer's aspirations are as big as mountains. The three women drag themselves along the floor and vanish, moaning-sobbing, into the wings to stage-left. Peer is suddenly seen to the right, wedged between the low, snow peaks of II iii and the towering cliffs previously used in II ii. The plank used horizontally in Act I thunders down, barely missing Peer's head. It dives, this time into a diagonal, nose to stage-right. It is almost immediately dipped down in the direction of stage-left, Peer's arm seemingly heaving it across. Peer pushes aside the cliffs, leaving them at a point where they look like massive doors opening from the grid behind. He then bounds onto the plank, first walking on its edge, then sitting on it (the plank now straightened), his body front-on to the audience in both cases. Each phase of Peer's physical exertion structures his long speech into sections. The ebb and flow of his speech goes into the score created by the avalanche-like rumble of the sets. How Peer moves mountains is convenient for changing decor. But the forceful heavy images quickly following each other denote Peer's "You come from greatness/Peer Gynt, one day you will be great". At the same time, they undercut Peer's pretensions. His rhetoric in this sequence terminates in a gag: Peer hits his head on the side walls and falls flat on his face. Desarthe and Chéreau follow Ibsen's stage direction, exploiting it thoroughly so as to ridicule Peer beyond any hope of reprieve.

The fluctuations of depth in the four consecutive scenes just cited give the illusion of an ever-opening perspective. The major contrast, in spatial terms, is the inward-closing area of the Troll King's court in Scene vi. Here, density is created through crowded figures emerging from the dark at the back and, simultaneously, from the abruptly opened trapdoor, which is in shadow. Numerous pig and monster masks, heavy costumes in shades of grey, an iron cage (from which Peer will be released), a piano (wheeled in, its base notes rumbled out by the Woman in Green), pots, pans, steaming buckets, thick books for consultation on how to deform Peer, scissors and other surgical instruments - this multi-layered configuration is thickened further still by the gloom. Dully-lit bulbs, encased in what to all intents and purposes are mini-cages, hang low over the rites of perversion and sadism into which Peer is initiated. The four bulbs, the only sources of light in this scene, whizzed down at the beginning of the scene.

Peer is invaded from all sides at every move he makes. He is interrogated by the King, who flashes a torch that is around his neck into Peer's face. The philosophical dialogue where the King distinguishes man from troll is carried on in a similar, interrogatory manner. Peer is hit, pushed down, then pushed perilously close to the trap's void. He is thumped into it. He tries to clamber out along the diagonal plank that had been lowered down in Act I. The diagonal plank now snaps and rolls into the hole, with Peer still trying to escape on it. Whereupon the trolls draw the trapdoor up against his neck, pinning him down for their operation. (These movie-like stunts communicate danger and indeed *are* dangerous for the actors.) Peer eventually extricates himself as the trap springs open. He runs towards the ladder in the corner of the fixed sets and climbs it, one group at his heels, the other clamouring on the floor-boards. Once again, Peer's attempts to find freedom through his own efforts are a chimera. The ringing of bells, which are pulled by Ase and Solveig, as the audience discovers in Scene viii, disperses trolls, gnomes and goblins. But Peer's failure to be (to exist and survive), let alone be "himself" (forge his own identity), foreshadows Day Two.

If space is narrowed down considerably in the kingdom of the trolls, it is reduced further still in the two subsequent moments that decide Peer's future. The first is his meeting with the Great Curve or Voice (II vii), after which he goes deeper into the mountains to build a hut. This hut is wheeled onto the stage with Peer banging on its roof. The second decisive moment is Ase's death (III iv), after which Peer leaves Norway. Peer's encounter with the Great Curve, the ghost and Peer's double who tells him to detour, occurs in an enclosure blocked by the vast curtain used in Act

I. This time, the curtain billows outwards, recedes and falls, while a new element, a white moon on its clouds, adds to the sensation of mystery. No one is present until Peer's head protrudes from under the heavy fabric. Spectators then see his arm, clutching a forked stick, then his torso. Finally, his whole body slides through. As soon as Peer is out, the curtain becomes the Voice to which Peer's every action is a response. He swings his fork, throws it to the floor, swivels his body and punches the air in his battle with the Voice-curtain, which lunges forward intermittently and finishes by swallowing him up. Henceforth, Peer continues to detour, which by the end of the production means that Peer's deviations result in his finding neither himself nor others.

Ase's death breaks the last of Peer's ties. Narrow acting space, which once again suggests Peer's folding into his own ego, is now locked in by a fire curtain. Ase's bed comes up from the trapdoor, and Peer from the first rows in the audience. Substantially static, III iv shows Peer to the side, behind, in front of his mother's bed-coffin, that is, anywhere but with her, physically and emotionally.

Momentary gestures of tenderness underline the prevailing sense of bleakness. So, too, do Peer's attempts to alleviate his mother's fear of dying when he plays at spurring on a horse by standing on the end of Ase's bed slapping his thighs and whipping a rope, or when he plays at being a horse by pretending to drag the bed along the boards. All these actions concentrate space into an even smaller area. When the fire curtain goes up as the bed-coffin goes down, bleakness is not dispelled. It is, on the contrary, reinforced by the indigo backdrop dotted with stars that stares at the audience and concludes Day One. But then bleakness in Day One is continually present in the actors' eyes, which rarely meet, or cannot be seen to meet in the gloom. Peer, particularly, gazes obliquely; or simply talks with his eyes closed.

* * * *

The exclamatory though cold register of Day One continues in Day Two. My observations will be confined to the principal structural aspects of Day Two, which also lasts three and a half hours.

The varieties of space, and hence the complexities of spatial interaction, diminish in Acts IV and V. Audience space serves the actors four times: the Moroccan thieves run through it (IV iii); Peer arrives at the auction from it (V iv); the Thin Man tries to exit from it, but is stopped, at the tenth row, by Peer's "Wait, wait!" several feet below (V x); the churchgoers walk up, singing, through it (V x). The churchgoers filed past Peer on stage, and on either side of him, without, however, seeing him.

By the same token, the use of machinery to form height is less frequent and, generally, less rapid. What it creates are a stone fortress (IV ix); three sets, which flash by - like slides on a screen - showing the silhouettes of pyramids, palm trees, men on horses and thus denote Egypt (a prelude to IV xi); a construction with two hieratic figures on it in profile, their faces destroyed, designates the colossus of Memnon (IV xi); the Sphinx, also in profile, and with a pyramid smaller than it standing behind and to the side (IV xii). Subdued lighting etiolates the desert tones of these constructions. Where scenography in Day One explored depth, these pieces are flat - photographs or cinema "stills". Once again, a naturalistic principle is observed: the view is blocked, while selected parts of the decor give the eye an escape route. (Antoine, following Zola, called these *échappées.*) Low-lying sand dunes (to be found in IV v, the scene of the horse mentioned above, and in IV viii) have a similar function. All these constructions which appear at the very back of the stage frame "open" space.

On the other hand, space is contracted only once, by a semi-transparent veil with gnarled trees painted on it, providing an unexpected touch of northern landscape (IV vii). A scene showing Peer and Anitra exploiting each other sexually is played out in front of it. Anitra's seated handmaidens can be discerned behind it (another kind of *échappée*). Or their standing bodies are half visible outside it, when they voyeuristically observe the couple's antics. These tricks for the eyes are complicated by carpets, cushions and other insignia of Arabic culture. The view is too much, to this spectator's mind, like an early colonialist's idea of exotica, which is not critically placed by the actors' performance. For instance, Peer's parody of Anitra's dance in Scene vi is cheap, although it is executed according to the principles of vaudeville humour chosen by Desarthe/Chéreau for Peer throughout Act IV. The attempted gaiety of these scenes does not diminish their brittle, even complacent, quality.

Otherwise, space in Act IV is figuratively obliterated when a miniature ship gliding against the whitish backdrop (Scene ii) explodes into fire and smoke. This *coup de théâtre* (and piece of kitsch, too), which is also an ironic quotation of such "stagy" effects, is followed by another: monkey-actors bounce up and down in nets placed high up towards the front of the stage. Peer is levered up on a swing, kicks, fights, is inundated with pellets of excrement, grunts and groans, and swings down and out to stage-left. It is impossible, in our mass-media world, not to think of Tarzan.

Chéreau and Peduzzi's propensity for theatrical-cinematographic effects reaches its climax in V i. An exact replica of a ship-deck, mast and all, seems to heave upon heavy seas as raincoated figures dash out of the trapdoor and from the wings. Meanwhile, Peer sits impassively on a suitcase, in profile to the audience. Apart from the acoustics, which create a tempest, the tempest is fabricated through the actors, who teeter and swing as one, with or without ropes, and in whichever direction the imaginary sea rolls them about. Only the unknown Passenger's feet are steady, indicating, by this, that he is a supernatural being. Like all the other figures, he also appeared from the open trapdoor, where he - joke - lit a cigarette.

As the mast cracks, the sea, thus far rendered through bodies, voices and mimetic sound, "materializes" in a voluminous black curtain that spills out along the floor, sending the sailors flying into the trap. Stupendous waves later - and a tiny, tossing ship on the horizon as well - Peer's diminished torso is suddenly seen clinging to an overturned boat (Scene ii). Up pops the Cook, whom Peer drowns without fuss. Immediately afterwards, the Passenger's head appears from the other side of the boat. The laconic dialogue between him and Peer is accompanied by burlesque actions: Peer, for example, paddles with his hands, while his strange companion swims backstroke. This short sequence makes Peer and his circumstances look ludicrous, but it humanizes the feat of technology (and, in retrospect, a whole array of engineering skills) witnessed by the audience. The Passenger and Peer are then swallowed up by the waves which keep rolling and rolling for one full minute, as if signs and portents of annihilation and doom.

From here on till the end of Act V and thus of the performance, the fixed sets stand in place, untrammelled by the workings of sophisticated machinery. The open trapdoor, though, becomes a centralizing element. The funeral occurs around it (Scene iii), during which time Peer sits, hands limp, on the edge of the platform within the fixed sets and merges into obscurity. (The opening of this scene is skilfully ambiguous: Whose funeral is it? Did Peer drown?) Peer peels the onion - a metonymy of his Self - kneeling in front of it (Scene v). And when he finishes stripping away its layers of skin he discovers that nothing at all is contained in them. The trap also stands for a waste-bin when Peer throws the pieces of the onion into it. These are fragments of his non-being, remnants of the unachieved dictum: "Be yourself". Since the trap served as a grave in Scene iii, it now represents Peer's imminent extinction. He will soon discover "non-being" in the ultimate sense of the term.

The trap is also a metonymic representation of memory, the past and the unconscious in that, from it, emerge - in the form of voices - the words Peer should have spoken, the deeds he should have done and the fears and songs he should have expressed and sung (Scene vi). The women incarnating these voices recall the composition of II iii. Their words remind spectators of IV i, among other scenes, where a wine-laden table on which Peer, first brandishing a bottle, and then a glass, proclaimed that he would be emperor (though of what would he be emperor?), appeared and disappeared through the trap. [Plate 3] By the end of the performance, then, the trapdoor draws together - through its associative, coagulative and even symbiotic functions - the crucial stages in which Peer forged his self-destruction.

The trap shuts, once and for all. From V vii till the conclusion, space is moulded by the tunnel of light mentioned previously. This tunnel appears to be narrower and longer still because of Peer's walking up and down within its confines with his successive partners, who are, at the same time, his secret doubles or alter egos. These partners are the Button Moulder (who comes twice), the Thin Man and the Troll King. The process of doubling, which conveys either a metaphysical or psychosocial meaning, is brought out by how the actors perform their parts. Doubling with metaphysical meaning predominates. The second kind, which emphasizes psychosocial meaning, is expressed through the Troll King. In each case - and for the first time of considerable duration - Peer and his given partner show camaraderie or complicity. For the first time, moreover, Peer actually looks his companions straight in the face.

Played in a dry style which is tempered by whimsy, pathos and buffoonery - this in a current of intermingled nuances - these scenes evoke tragedy without, however, becoming tragic. Their potentially tragic force is checked by the irregular flow of gags. The Thin Man, for example, is something of a high-camp caricature with his prim movements, long nails (which he clips, at one point, under Peer's nose) and weary feet. One of them is a club-foot which he ostentatiously unties while sitting on his suitcase. This is the foot he rubs vigorously. Another example gives us Peer and the Troll King putting their own hats on the other's head, noticing the error, and hastily correcting it.

Gentlemen's costumes on the supernatural creatures emphasize the sober and the comic aspects in one stroke. A pig's head on a tramp's outfit is downright funny. Humour is transformed into uneasiness when Peer and the Troll King, who stand side by side, look and sound like derelicts. The emptied space with its tunnel, where lighting makes the whole decor look

Act IV Scene i
Photo by Birgit, Paris

unreal, constantly generates tension. Distress, however suppressed or distanced, is inscribed in Desarthe's body, particularly in his shoulders and insecure legs. It is embedded, too, in his weakened voice, which musters strength to shout "No! No!" in the face of invading nothingness.

Peer's near-last moments are moving, despite the lofty derision - let us call it - which gnaws into the fifth Act. The final sequence, which sees the reappearance of the hut that Peer was building earlier on, has a similar emotional undertone. Solveig walks in a straight line out of this hut, a Bible in one hand, a blind woman's stick in the other. Once again, her meeting with Peer is presented in an aggressive-defensive, backwards-forwards motion. The ambiguity of these movements is resolved when Peer falls to his knees and curls, foetus-like, against Solveig's legs. Solveig, at this point, is crouching on the floor, her back and arms curved, and her knees bent and open, as if giving birth. In this flashback to Act I, Solveig and Ase fuse into the one image. Solveig sings her lullaby and then lifts Peer to his feet in order to direct him back to the hut. Behind its open door, a sombre, narrow space awaits them (a visual counterpart of the gaping trapdoor) as Peer, eyes still closed, is supported by Solveig and leans against her stick. Blind Oedipus: Chéreau's quotation of a great tragedy closes his drama of a little man. A woman's opposition - the opposition referred to previously - retreats into silence and becomes endurance. But a woman's opposition to her society and its values seems to have no other alternative than to be expressed in the form of motherly love.

Chéreau gives us a maternal *Liebestod.* Wagner's Ring cycle, which Chéreau directed at Bayreuth (1976-1980), leaves many traces in his *Peer Gynt.* So too - and via Ibsen's pessimism - do Kierkegaard and Schopenhauer, those other Nordic philosophers of decadence who, like Wagner, enjoyed a *succès de scandale* at the turn of the century. Yet in this spectacular - and specular - tussle between the tribulations of the ego (Kierkegaard) and the machinations of the cosmos (Schopenhauer), the latter's World as Will and Idea pre-empts everything, and dominates all. Chéreau takes Peer at his word: "I'll watch the battles of heroes for greatness, for good/but I'll remain unmoved (*au sec*) like a pure spectator" (IV ix).

Heroes, however, do not exist in Chéreau's construction. In their place gesticulate creatures who are belittled in more ways than one, starting with the stage architecture. The cosmos of pure spectatorship that Chéreau erects on the stage demystifies the myth of pure individualism, among other myths denounced somewhat sardonically by the production. But it is replaced by a grey nuclear zone of untouched monuments from which the very presence of people has disappeared. Peer jokes about existence preceding essence (IV v). Chéreau, like Peer, forgoes materialist thinkers on existence to joke and play with essences, and with one great essence in particular - Death - on which his production is a long meditation, *au sec*. Ibsen, Antoine and Zola were, in their own ways, materialist thinkers. And they were plagued by the crisis of individualism, which was manifest in social decay. Antoine and Zola, in particular, found a solution in what they thought was science: in the principles of observation, documentation and detachment. Chéreau adopts their conceptual/theatrical principles, supersedes them by far and modifies them through Ibsen. Ibsen's ironic smile at science understood as pure observation is given theatrical expression when Peer jots down notes - "pure" facts - in the desert.

The vision of an implacable destiny, which Ibsen and Zola shared but articulated differently, finds its apotheosis in Chéreau's apocalypse. It is everywhere in the production and perhaps, paradoxically, most explicit in the lighting, which effaces the human visage. Spectators beyond the tenth row simply cannot distinguish faces; and, for the most part, they must strain to distinguish between characters. Human effacement has rarely had such eloquence in the theatre.

Chéreau's great monument of, and to, the twentieth century - the last of its theatrical kind, perhaps? - belongs to Chéreau's directorial vocabulary, as he has used it until now. But it is not just Chéreau's individual idiom, not just his personal *Weltanschauung*. This great monument captures a mood prevalent in our own *fin de siècle*. The organization of any artistic work implies the existence of a particular public or publics. That is to say, a work, both in its preparation and its "finished" state, contains some idea of which expectations it can meet, and from whom they come. Leaving aside aesthetes who valorize form by devaluing content, it is probable that Chéreau most speaks to and for audiences who - at a conceptual level, at least - accept doom as an unalterable truth, as a fact, pure and simple. Desarthe's urgent "No! No!" rings out in protest. Perhaps the actor is also protesting against his director: against a totalizing viewpoint on a devastation so horrendous that only monuments can withstand it and stand unscathed.

PEER GYNT in Two Days by Henrik Ibsen

Translator: François Regnault
Director: Patrice Chéreau
Decor: Richard Peduzzi
Costumes: Jacques Schmidt
Music: Fiorenzo Carpi
Lighting: André Diot
Sound: André Serre
General Direction: Yves Bernard
Props and Special Effects: Danka Semenowicz
Make-up and Masks: Reiko Kruk and Dominique Colladant

Cast

Peer Gynt: Gérard Desarthe
Ase, his mother: Maria Casarès
Solveig: Catherine Rétoré
The Bridegroom: Miloud Khetib
Ingrid: Chantal Bronner
The Woman in Green: Nada Strancar
Solveig's mother: Madeleine Marie
Solveig's father: Jean-Claude Jay
Helga: Sabine Thomas
The Three Herd-Women: Paule Annen/Dominique Blanc/Micheline Kahn
The Voice: Gérard Desarthe
The Troll King: Henri Virlogeux
Dr Begriffenfeldt
The Passenger } Roland Bertin
The Button Moulder
The Thin Man: Didier Sandre
Kari: Paule Annen

And (in order of appearance in various roles)

Claudine Mavros; Roland Amstutz; Andrzej Seweryn; Gilles Gérardin; Benoît Régent; Patrice Finet; Pierre Baillot; Muni; Bruno Cardoni.

Musicians

Roger Germser; Christophe Guiot; Antoine Ladrette; Gérard Vidal; Bruno Sansalone; Christian Boissel.

4

JEAN-PIERRE MIGNON AND *PEER GYNT*: A FRENCH DIRECTOR IN AUSTRALIA

Nothing could be more different from Patrice Chéreau's *Peer Gynt* than *Peer Gynt* staged by Jean-Pierre Mignon in Melbourne in 1990. This French director arrived in Australia in 1978. In 1980 he founded Australian Nouveau Theatre (ANT) which, until very recently, was based at the Anthill Theatre in South Melbourne. ANT has mounted more than fifty productions to date. Among them are Chekhov's great plays, Molière's *Tartuffe*, *Don Juan*, *The Misanthrope* and *The Imaginary Invalid*, Beckett's *Happy Days* and *Waiting for Godot*, Lawler's *Summer of the Seventeenth Doll* and, for the 1992 Melbourne Festival, *La Vida es un Sueño* (*Life is a Dream*) by Calderon. Mignon has not worked exclusively with his own company. He has mounted productions for the Victorian Opera, for example, and the Sydney Theatre Company, including a highly acclaimed *Marriage of Figaro* by Beaumarchais, and in 1992 Strindberg's *Miss Julie*.

Mignon's artistic register thus encompasses European and Australian plays, classic and contemporary pieces and some of the major landmarks of the French cultural tradition, this component perhaps being the most important of them all for an understanding of his work as a whole. Of course, there is no such thing as a uniform *French* tradition. It is multi-layered and multi-directional. Like any national tradition, it embraces many cultures - popular and learned culture, artisanal crafts and fine arts, and marginal aesthetic movements as well as an aesthetic canon. The list would have to continue in order to indicate fully the complexities involved in the terms "national", "cultural" and "tradition". Even so, what Mignon takes from his culture of origin, not necessarily consciously (or what sustains him from it, unintentionally, like rain sustains the earth), is its comic tradition, which arguably realizes its fullest potential in Molière. Molière synthesizes, like no other French playwright, the refinements of artistic elitism, as nurtured by the powerful state of Louis XIV, and the unadulterated "raw" intelligence of a people's culture as expressed, during Molière's time, through theatre *à l'italienne*, whether of the itinerant, rural kind or in its more domesticated guise inside urban theatre houses.

This successful hybridization of opposing social and artistic genres surely goes a long way towards explaining the unique quality of Molière's comedy, its extraordinarily rich tonalities, ebullient confidence and steady aim, which hits its target at every shot. Its distinctive, robust character resurfaces in Mignon's productions and ipso facto in his staging of *Peer Gynt*. Chéreau, as we have seen, embarks on a dark journey where destructive forces predominate. Mignon's *Peer Gynt* makes fun of the lunacies and failings of human beings; and shows that those who over-estimate their own capacities and, consequently, overstep the limits imposed by reason, convention and sense are not cause for despair. They are, on the contrary, cause for laughter which, if not always good-natured, always sings on an affirmative note.

Chéreau, particularly towards the end of his production, appears to interpret Ibsen through Beckett as Beckett was understood during the 1950s and even the 1960s (the "human condition", "existential crisis", "theatre of the absurd", and related notions). The homology of interpretations is perfectly feasible, given the anxieties and austerities felt in France in the late 1970s and early 1980s, which was also a time of renewed fear on a European scale of nuclear war. Mignon, on the other hand, playfully views the insanities of the world. This is why his productions bring out and accentuate the humour to be found in Beckett's texts. We could say that the world view constructed through Mignon's buoyant approach to Beckett has far less to do with the morose misanthropy often attributed to the latter and far more to do with the Molière whose *Misanthrope* sparkles with critical wit.

I asked Mignon to comment on what I perceived to be his special affinity with Molière. Here I referred to the way he had interpreted *Peer Gynt* (content, themes, issues) as well as to qualities of the staging or *mise en scène* (pronounced gestures and vivid mimicry and movement of the actors, who took the performance at a very quick pace from beginning to end).

Mignon replied that his work in the theatre did not depend on intellectual decisions but operated on an organic, instinctive level. Its dynamic and impulses came out of the working process, in the scenes prepared with actors. I had made some remarks earlier on about the energy and, to my mind, the unexpected humour of his production, likening these particular aspects of *Peer Gynt* to his productions of Molière. Mignon noted that Molière was not the only one to have developed these features. He also pointed out that Ibsen had changed style completely in the last scenes of his play. The scenes involving the Button Moulder, the devil-figure, and so on, were written, according to Mignon, in a different kind of verse. With this verse, Ibsen brought vaudeville to his play; and vaudeville was a new element, a new theatrical genre working in the play. The issue led Mignon to compare *Peer Gynt* to Beckett, especially the last Act, whose vaudeville humour illuminates the tragic situation at its core, exactly as occurs in Beckett and had occurred, before him, in Molière. In Mignon's view, what links Molière to Ibsen and Ibsen to Beckett is the counterpoint between comedy and tragedy, which counterpoint is the hallmark of all great theatre irrespective of cultural differences.

The linkages established by Mignon - Chekhov was also cited - prompted me to ask whether Molière was nevertheless an important touchstone for him because he was integral to his cultural "stock". I elaborated by saying that I thought the cultural sources and resources of directors were intrinsic to how they directed; further, that their cultural roots allowed them to develop a theatre practice with a specific character of its own. Mignon tended to agree with this broad principle, saying that Molière as well as the commedia dell'arte tradition in general were to be found in Beaumarchais' *Marriage of Figaro* and Feydeau's *A Flea in Her Ear*, among many possible examples. Here Mignon alluded in particular to how the plots of both plays unfolded from a similar situation (in *Figaro*, Suzanne's writing a letter of assignation to the Count, her would-be seducer, at the request of the Countess).

However, Mignon did not believe that what he called "a snowball effect" was confined to one particular cultural context. This snowballing occurred generally and assured continuity in the *theatre*, which is why Molière is part of Ibsen and Ibsen part of Beckett. It would probably be true to say that, for Mignon, whatever rolls out of one cultural tradition rolls over into another, creating a tradition of the theatre as such.

How, given Mignon's idea of theatrical interaction, does he stage *Peer Gynt*? And does he have an open view, cultural barriers having disappeared from sight, because of his experience of cultural duality which, in his case, has generated freedom instead of conflict? "In his case" because duality or biculturalism can be experienced as tension and closure, as happens with non-professional immigrant groups and sometimes among artists - and certainly among those for whom immigration has meant an end, or virtual end, to their career. These questions, although not broached directly in the material below, are nevertheless pertinent to it. Since, unlike Chéreau's *Peer Gynt*, I was unable to see Mignon's production repeatedly, what follows is not a detailed analysis but a very brief account whose main purpose is to continue the dialogue with Mignon that was begun in my opening pages. My interventions will sometimes distance his voice. But the words running between us will hopefully stimulate reflection on *Peer Gynt* played in quite different cultural spaces and separated by time as well as by the trajectory and goals of two directors whose initial links by birth have been severed by societies.

* * * *

The fundamental and most important element of Mignon's production is space which, as in Chéreau, is adjusted architecturally for the needs of performance. However, unlike Chéreau, Mignon does not rely on an elaborate scenography. Nor does he play off stage-space against audience-space. He resolves the problems of space posed when there is a proscenium arch by doing away with the latter altogether. Consequently, the theatre reserved for *Peer Gynt* was gutted. Its seats were pulled out and its stage reorganized. Long ramps resembling the hanamichi in Kabuki extended from the stage and ran right around the theatre. Platforms joined these ramps, creating focal points for action. There were, in other words, several "stages" and not one, central stage.

In addition, the entire theatre was covered in off-white calico (or similar cloth) which abolished distinctions between stage-space and audience-space. The whole space was playing space, the difference between players and spectators marked by the fact that spectators sat or reclined on large cushions or on the covered floor. The floor was graded, as is usual when rows of seats are built in a theatre. Yet - clever optical illusion - this refurbished place gave the impression that actors and spectators were more or less on the same plane and, therefore, more or less at eye level with each other.

Mignon explained that the idea came to designer Mary Moore in a flash, during rehearsals:

> Her idea immediately seemed right because a painter begins with a white canvas on which you can then put colours; and you can always come back to neutral, to the white canvas. It allows your imagination to float. You can see waterfalls. You can see a desert. You can see snow. You can see

Photo by Jeff Busby, Melbourne

> anything, and also the actors in the empty space. . . . The theatre, before, was horrible, with those horrible theatre seats, some blue, others red. . . . However, we were massacred for what we did. One of the theatre critics gave us a positive review. But you really do destroy the audience when you say "three and a half uncomfortable hours". We lost thousands of people because of that, which is really completely stupid. Firstly, I don't think it was very uncomfortable, and even if it was uncomfortable, people can cope with a little discomfort for three hours!

I remarked that I thought people looked comfortable enough, lounging around and looking around them to follow the performance; also that the white, snow-like space had a fairy-tale atmosphere which prepared spectators for the tale that would be told them. They could sit, stretch, relax and listen.

A number of important points came out of this exchange, not least of which is the negative impact a theatre critic can have on both company and audience (in this case, by driving audiences away!). It is also clear that a director's artistic intentions will not necessarily be perceived by her or his public from exactly the same angle, nor even be evaluated appropriately. In addition, the perception of spectators depends on whether they are looking from the "inside" and, therefore, in terms of the parameters defined by the work, or from the "outside", that is, in respect of other conditions impinging on the work, for instance, the issue of creature comforts raised by our theatre critic.

Let us, however, focus on the "inside", endogenous considerations foregrounded by Mignon and which constitute the aesthetics of his production, "empty space" being its essential component. Needless to say, this space is never empty. It is filled by the actors' ceaseless motion which, as the performance progresses, shifts from sheer physical vitality (some of it, as in the opening scenes between Peer and his mother, expressing the joy of being alive) to a feeling of restlessness, as if the production as a whole was externalizing Peer's psychological fragility. This transition from one kind of physicality to another is to be seen most clearly when the wedding scene is compared with the scenes in the troll kingdom.

The wedding scene takes place right across the whole theatre, all ramps and platforms being used to create the sensation of changing events or environment, and the hustle and bustle and noise of communal activity. These changing, different spaces have a narrative purpose in that they map out the sequence of events until Peer finally runs off with Ingrid. The continuity between spaces is just as important for building up a sense of urgency in which Peer's passion for Solveig beats like a drum. Peer's

Photo by Jeff Busby, Melbourne

erotic desire is articulated through the way he moves in on her; and is then "stated" bluntly when he bites her behind. This "kiss" is given in a knowing and provocative manner, the actor communicating his pleasure through mimicry and gestures that solicit the audience's complicity in his action. The incident is calculated to be as funny as possible so as to show that it, too, is part of the celebration of life and love in which the spectators, by their close proximity to everything happening around them, are totally enveloped.

The verve, excitement and laughter generated until this scene and sustained right through it have an anxious edge in the sequences between Peer and the Troll King's daughter and between him and the Troll King. For instance, the slight waltz Peer dances with the King's daughter when he meets her is mocking, but also suggests awkwardness and even fear. His body, when he meets the King, is menacing. Peer's vulnerability, which his aggressive attitudes can scarcely hide, is accentuated by the shadows falling over him. A small light bulb set at Peer's feet is the only light shed upon him. However, although the visual effect is one of sobriety, the dialogue between Peer and the Troll King on the difference between man and troll is full of punch. A troll dance, where all concerned, including Peer, wiggle their bottoms as if dancing the twist, is caricatural, and anticipates the vaudeville humour that Mignon discerned in Ibsen's text and which he plays to the full at the end of the production.

Of course, the twist-like movements belong to the second half of the twentieth century and not to that of the nineteenth. This semiotic process, then, situates *Peer Gynt* socioculturally, placing it in our time and roughly sketching an image of man or troll today. The fact that the King and his entourage are dressed in ordinary shirts and trousers rather than in specially designed "troll" costumes shows how they double - or are the double of - "normal" human beings. The dialogue on man and troll, which virtually concludes that there is no difference between them, is thus sustained visually.

From here on, a series of visual and gestural jokes keep play big. At the same time, they contribute to the restlessness I referred to earlier. Among these jokes are the chattering white monkeys Peer encounters during his travels, and who throw white fluffy balls (supposedly coconuts) at him from the tops of cartoon-like palm trees; the mock-Hollywood harem Peer acquires in the desert (the women's gestures parody the worst features of neo-colonial films on such "exotic" subjects); the imaginary horse Peer rides, like a child on a hobby-horse; Begriffenfeldt's saying "Here's a knife" to Peer while making the sound of a knife flying through the air; Peer's coronation with straw towards the end of Act IV, which ends with small lights flashing on and off as they do on a Christmas tree.

When the production is looked at retrospectively, Act IV appears to be a prelude to Act V. A violin whistles as if it were the wind. Peer weathers a storm made with lights. The segment where Peer drowns the Cook in the sea exploits burlesque comedy: thus Peer holds the Cook by the hair while the Cook holds his nose to the sound of "glug, glug, glug" as he is meant to go under. The devil-figure who haunts Peer in Act V is austerely dressed as a parson and greets Peer with his arms outstretched in benediction. The devil-parson's eyes do most of the acting for him, their rolling upwards, squinting, and so on, creating a farcical situation in which Peer is the prime dupe. The Button Moulder is very slick in a dark business suit. In his case, hands and feet rather than eyes are of principal importance. Gestures made with them are clear and smooth. His face is impassive. The whole image recalls Molière's famous hypocrites and, as in Molière, unmasks worldly aplomb, showing the fraud beneath it. It would be true to say that all the vignettes combined carefully by Mignon for the last Act and presented by the actors with impeccable timing are examples of exposed deceit of one kind or another. In fact, Molière's presence is so strong in the concluding Act that when the production is taken from the end back to the beginning, Molière seems to loom larger than before. As we have seen, Mignon's conscious, intentional point of reference was not Molière but Beckett, through whom, in any case, in Mignon's notion of cross-influence, Molière passes.

The production closes with Solveig cradling Peer's head in her lap, this gentle, maternal gesture mirroring the opening movement between Peer and his mother. Peer has come full circle. Solveig and Ase are one. Suddenly, at the end of the production, spectators realize fully the significance of Peer's running round and round the white space, cutting off the corners made by ramps and platforms and moving in closer and closer on them. These circles are the production's principal metaphor for its content, which has to do not only with Peer's fate but also with that of the people close to him. Yet this comic tale does not end with a sad moral, nor even - in this spectator's view - with a moral of any kind. It simply states the last event of its narrative, the echoes of the laughter it stimulated still too potent to allow a shift of mood.

Mignon had this to say on the coupling of Ase and Solveig:

> Yes, it's true. It's there in the text, mother/wife. Ase is much more interesting. She is richer, less caricaturized . . . Solveig is very discreet, even retiring, as are most of the characters in the play; and there is something caricatural about her, as happens with the others. The people at the beginning

Photo by Jeff Busby, Melbourne

of Act IV - the American, the Frenchman - are caricatures. They are cardboard characters, which is important because this is an epic play. But everything revolves around Peer.

The issue of how it might be best to understand Solveig was treated by Mignon with reference to his interpretation of the play as a whole:

> In mounting *Peer Gynt*, I wanted to talk about Ibsen's intentions, which are rather difficult to get across today. My impression was that the play was written as a satire of the Romantics. It was also an attack on the people who extrapolated from the Norwegian Romantic movement and made a nationalistic movement out of it. So it's a satire that has lost its flavour today. Our task was to speak to an Australian audience in 1990, which is why we sometimes had to deviate from Ibsen's original intentions but in such a way as to say some new things *with* his text. My feeling is that Ibsen's contemporaries must have laughed at moments where it would be impossible to laugh now. The Romantic aspects satirized have to do with flight into dreams and flight away from reality, as well as with withdrawal into yourself. This is, for example, what the people who wanted to reconstruct the Norwegian language from ancient dialects were doing. We don't grasp these points today. Take, for example, the character in the asylum, Huhu, who is invited to go as far back as the ape. This kind of satire [on the search for origins to justify a nationalistic cause] escapes us today; and so we really had to move away from what Ibsen meant by it.

More questions on what he wanted to say to a contemporary Australian audience led to Solveig;

> We nevertheless kept the major Romantic technique, which was to focus on the principal character - on Peer Gynt. What was pertinent for today was the relationship between egocentrism and individualism. It's what gives us today's yuppies. It's very important at the present time to create a feeling of sympathy for a character for whom, I believe, Ibsen's contemporaries had no sympathy; to keep an audience's interest till the end by developing traits that attach the audience to the character and, at the same time, allow it to be objective about him. I found this to be the most difficult thing to do.
>
> There was another problem, and that was Solveig. I could swear that, when the play was created in 1867, people must have burst out laughing when Solveig reappeared in Act IV and sang about how she was still waiting for Peer. You can't do that today. It's not right, otherwise the character becomes a symbol. And what about the woman? . . . I think that, where sexism is concerned, Ibsen was progressive in relation to his time. Moreover, his works after *Peer Gynt* show it. Even so, he dragged a rather enormous sexist tradition behind him compared with what we would like to achieve today. Although [this tradition is] there, making Solveig ridiculous was out of the question. Peer lives withdrawn into himself right through the play. He refuses to face reality. It takes him ninety years to try and understand that there is something else besides himself. . . . It was very difficult to find the balance between this egocentrism and Solveig.

I asked Mignon whether he thought that it was necessary to distinguish between egocentrism and individualism; also whether he thought that Ibsen had called into question the notion of individualism which had been of such importance to the Romantics. Mignon replied that he thought Ibsen had a positive as well as a negative view of individualism. The positive version of it in *Peer Gynt* was projected through the tale of the young man in Act III who cuts off his finger in order to avoid being sent to war. This brief episode in Act III is picked up in Act V. Peer returns home to a funeral - the funeral of the man who had cut off his finger. We learn that he had led a life of great hardship but great generosity, especially towards his children. Mignon explained that he had deleted this episode from Act V (and, therefore, the reference to the man earlier on) because he thought that the audience would have difficulty in sustaining interest throughout the Act which, to his mind, was problematical enough with fewer details. However, Mignon stressed that the man's story, while paralleling Peer's, was also in opposition to it. In Mignon's words, "The man lived for himself as an individual, but lived with love and faith and passion for others". Peer had not done this.

It is clear from Mignon's account of the parallel stories how he distinguishes between egocentrism and individualism as these categories concern *Peer Gynt.* And what his account raises in a very precise and important way is the issue of how absences and silences in a production can be as relevant to its sociocultural meaning as its representations. Mignon's decision, after spending time on the funeral scene, to eliminate it for the sake of tightness and, therefore, greater communicability with the audience, cost him - and the audience - as he acknowledged with some anguish, depth of exposition of what he perceived to be the major themes of the play. An unrealized potential left the field open for the comedy that held sway and, in my view, undercut the tragedy which Mignon saw working in counterpoint in Ibsen.

Yet the decision was made with a contemporary audience in Australia in mind. Does this suggest that the cultural climate in Australia in 1990 was conducive to comic genres, and particularly to burlesque, vaudeville and farce? And does it show a concordance between the sociocultural values embodied in the stage work and its imputed or expected audiences? One of the main values upheld by the production might be called realistic, individual - but neither individualistic nor egotistical - apprehension of the world, which is anything but Peer's approach.

Mignon had no doubts as to Peer's exploitative, unscrupulous self-centredness, to which the Troll King draws attention early and again late in the play. As he sees it, Peer confuses self-sufficiency with rapaciousness and in this is like a modern capitalist or modern yuppie whose motto could well be "Live for yourself and crush others". How do audiences receive this message as Peer incarnates it? Is their laughter critical as well as the laughter of complicity? Mignon's vibrant production opens up, all over again, the problematical issue of laughter and its shading - when it is merely "fun" or satirical, high-spirited as well as serious, high-spirited but vacuous, and so on - all shadings not only being a matter of theatrical genres but of how they are determined culturally.

It was important, in the context of the discussion on *Peer Gynt* for contemporary audiences, to ask why Mignon had chosen to stage it, a rare choice, especially given that *Hedda Gabler*, *A Doll's House* and *Ghosts* are taken to represent Ibsen, and not only in Australia. Mignon replied:

> The play is rarely performed because it represents enormous risks, starting with those concerning Peer, Solveig and the caricatural figures when viewed from a present-day perspective. Still, it's very important to be able to deal with an unfamiliar Ibsen, an Ibsen who precedes *A Doll's House* and *Hedda Gabler* and who is really in the middle of the nineteenth century and shows himself to be a precursor of modern theatre. You can find Strindberg, Bulgakov and Beckett in him. He brought a goldmine to the middle of the nineteenth century, going against the current of romanticism. It is important to know about this in Australia today. It is not a great play, dramatically and theatrically speaking. There are strong moments; but we have lost a lot of its original intentions and meanings. It is also over-written. It contains too many words. Even so, it's a work worth communicating to others.

PEER GYNT **by Henrik Ibsen**

Australian Nouveau Theatre

Translator: May-Brit Akerholt

Director: Jean-Pierre Mignon

Designer: Mary Moore

Lighting: Nigel Levings

Music: Sam Mallet

Cast (in order of appearance)

Robert Menzies (Peer Gynt); Julie Forsyth (Ase); Louise Newey;

Jennie Robinson; John Howard (Troll King); Jo Kennedy (Solveig);

John F. Howard; John Penman; Sergio Tell; Jacek Koman; Ian Scott;

Jane Conroy; Hope Csutoros.

NOTE

Paraphrased passages and transcribed extracts are from my interview in French with Jean-Pierre Mignon in Melbourne, in December 1990. The use of French was determined by factors of no relevance to the present text, Mignon being perfectly fluent in English.

5

THE THREE SISTERS IN FRENCH AND RUSSIAN (Théâtre de l'Enfumeraie and Teatr Tembr)

The stage is small, its floor and walls covered in white cloth. To the right, close to the edge of the stage, stands a half-size grand piano and a chair. Behind the piano, ten white columns in the style of classical Greek architecture are spaced out evenly in a semi-circle, leaving room between them and the back wall for movement. As the spectators settle in for the performance, a man dressed in early twentieth-century costume comes in and plays the piano, his sounds - many of them discords - becoming increasingly urgent. His tones echo Scriabin, Rachmaninov, Debussy, Satie and Ravel, but are not the music of any of them.

This is the setting of the first two Acts of *The Three Sisters* directed by Nika Kossenkova and Pascal Larue in May 1993. In the last two Acts, there are twelve columns grouped diagonally to the audience in rows of two and three. The piano now stands at the back of the stage, but does not close up the space leading to the back wall that had been left open at the beginning. The music played and sung throughout the performance was composed by Svetlana Golybina, a concert pianist, who plays the piano in the scene changes between Acts II and III and contributes by her special skills to the profoundly musical quality of the production as a whole.

The production was performed by Teatr Tembr, founded by Kossenkova in Moscow in 1987, and the Théâtre de l'Enfumeraie, which is based in Allonnes, near Le Mans. Kossenkova started out as an actress, playing in Tashkent and Magadan, the Siberian town where Stalin had built a number of particularly infamous concentration camps. In Moscow, she was a driving force of the experimental "studio theatre" movement, including in her repertoire Ludmila Petrushevskaya's *A Suitcase Full of Trivia* and her "monoperformance" rendition of Marina Tsvetayeva's play, *Phoenix*. Both plays by these controversial women, each one haunted, in her own way, by the history of her period and generation, were staged by Kossenkova for the very first time. For twenty-five years and more, Kossenkova has created, developed and taught her own voice-training method.

The Théâtre de l'Enfumeraie has been working as a closely-knit group for the past ten years. It essentially grew out of performances mounted by Larue as part of a campaign organized by Arianne Mnouchkine and supported by theatre workers across the board to free Vaclav Havel from prison. The group has been particularly interested in contemporary pieces, notably by Brecht, Le Clezio and Genet. Larue was a pupil of Jacques Lecoq whose principles regarding expression through the human body have deeply influenced his approach to the theatre. This explains why Kossenkova sees her collaboration with Larue as the meeting (in her words, "marriage") of movement and voice.[1] *The Three Sisters* is their first production together.

Moreover, the production is their first attempt at combining two languages. Thus Olga, Natasha, Andrei, Vershinin, Soliony, Chebutikin and Ferapont, who doubles as Fedotik, speak French. Irina, Masha, Anfisa, Kuligin and Tusenbach, who doubles as Rodé, speak Russian. The actors never switch languages, although key sentences delivered in Russian are occasionally repeated in French for reasons that will be discussed shortly.

The few phrases that appear in Chekhov in French to mark not only the social status of the characters but also their genuine accomplishments are delivered in the production in English. Apart from eliminating the difficulty posed by using French for special resonance and meaning, as Chekhov intended, in a production *played* in French, the phrases delivered in English illustrate Andrei's contention that, between them, his sisters speak English, French, German and Italian, as well as their native Russian.

Andrei's gentle, wistful remark on the "useless knowledge" their General father had given them is framed by the production so as to indicate that their being cultivated neither can nor should be dismissed. The three sisters, Andrei and the officers who come to their home certainly belong to a privileged caste. But together they represent the Enlightenment values of critical reason, productive knowledge, social justice and personal ethics, as well as the Renaissance ones of individual liberty, honour and dignity. Soliony continually quotes Lermontov in whom, arguably, all the European currents relative to early nineteenth-century Russia meet. And references to Voltaire and Shakespeare, which are enunciated very clearly by the actors as if to draw attention to their significance, show that the production positively evaluates the knowledge and culture, whether of languages, literature, philosophy or music, of its protagonists.

Language, then, for the production, is not merely a matter of grammatical and syntactic combinations. Nor is voice, for Kossenkova, a matter of diction pure and simple. Let us put it this way: what Kossenkova highlights throughout the production is the idea to be found off stage, in the works of Mikhaïl Bakhtin, that language is, above all, a matter of utterances uttered by speakers whose particular "accents" (values, emotions, world view, position in society and vantage point from which action springs) are invested in their utterances.[2] Speakers and speech, in other words, are inseparable; and they are inseparable from the situation which defines what kind of speech is uttered.

This axiom allows Kossenkova to develop her work on voice for the production. When the actors speak, sing, or hum, or produce whatever sound is necessary for an action, they do not simply produce sounds with their mouth (diction). They draw on the resources stored in their entire being. The being summoned up in the sound emitted by a performer has a whole cultural history that is embedded in her or his individual make-up or psyche. Consequently, voice, as Kossenkova understands it, coordinates actor, character, the context of the play, and the social contexts of the play and the performers (besides demonstrating certain technical and aesthetic achievements without which the coordination at issue would not be possible). This, at least, is how I interpret Kossenkova's work.

The way that voice *is* utterance and everything - socially, culturally and psychologically speaking - that an utterance conveys, helps explain why an utterance pronounced in a foreign tongue (foreign, that is, to the character who is speaking) does not appear artificial. Thus Masha, for example, when she speaks in English, "inhabits", as Bakhtin would say, her utterances. Yet her capacity for inhabiting language which, Bakhtin argues, is the very condition of language itself (because language is always the utterance of someone and, therefore, of *their* voice), is predicated, in Chekhov, on the learning and culture of Masha's milieu. Masha inhabits her milieu. This means that when she speaks in a foreign language (at other points she speaks in French), she conjures up all the ambiguities, tensions and social contradictions - elegance and cultivation in some quarters, vulgarity, ignorance and opportunism in others, poverty and other forms of disadvantage elsewhere - that exist in the Russia of her time and penetrate the sisters' household.

The character who crystallizes this situation is Natasha who, in Act II, is already the mistress of the house and about to evict the sisters from it by sheer power of coercion. She is also about to become Protopopov's mistress. When, in Act III, Masha turns in fury on her heel towards the audience and, referring to Natasha, spits out "sale petite bourgeoise", the clash between two types of society and culture could not be more obvious.

Masha's sudden switch from Russian into French shows in a flash the great pain she had accumulated, and had been hiding, on her brother's and sisters' behalf, as well as her own. Masha, Olga and Irina stand for civilization which, although peopled by the Voltaires of history, is incomplete unless it encompasses kindness and consideration towards others, whatever their social rank.

This notion of civilization seems to underpin the scenes between the sisters and Anfisa, for example, which, if a little awkwardly played, are clearly meant to be portraits of mutual respect and warmth. Where the sisters envelop Anfisa in their solicitude, Natasha stumbles over her (Anfisa sits on the floor instead of on a chair) without bothering to see who or what obstructed her path. Along with Protopopov, she stands for a new order run by self-interested pragmatists. Natasha, after all, is an efficient manager of people and property. Protopopov is a successful small-time bureaucrat.

The sociopolitical implications of the Natasha-Protopopov couple are suggested by the production rather than projected explicitly, Kossenkova and Larue preferring, it seems, an ambivalent view of what this duo might be carrying into the future. However, the directors openly highlight the humanistic perspective that guides, like a compass, the three sisters' deeds and words. The directors also bring into full view the humanism embodied, albeit differently in each case, by Andrei, Vershinin, Soliony, Tusenbach and Chebutikin. The humanistic world view, which filters through these characters and, through them, fills the production drop by drop, modifies Andrei's "useless knowledge". Instead of being merely a humorous or flippant epithet, Andrei's phrase underscores the burning desire and struggle of all the characters cited above - the three sisters being in the vanguard of this struggle - to make their knowledge *useful*.

The links made by the production between civilization, humanism and productive work (connections not altogether unlike those of the "narodnik" - populist - ideology that motivated sectors of the progressive intelligentsia during Chekhov's lifetime) explain why talk of work, which rings right through Chekhov's text, resounds in the actors' voices, their words on work bouncing back and forth between them like notes caught up and sung in different timbres in a choir. Here, too, Kossenkova's attention to the quality of sound is crucial to the kind of meaning that sound is supposed to communicate.

Precision as to the meaning they were looking for prompted Kossenkova and Larue to reject translations that gave "superfluous" rather than "useless", both of them arguing, correctly, that the latter term captured more accurately what Chekhov's Russian wished to say. They finally settled for Elsa Triolet's translation of 1954 on the grounds that it was the closest one to Chekhov and the one that best suited their own purposes. Adjustments to Triolet's translation were made here and there according to the demands of performance.

These remarks indicate how foreign speech accentuates the importance of voice-utterance to the production. However, its voice-utterances are principally in mother tongues: French for one group of performers, and Russian for the other. Which raises the question of how such problems as gimmickry, artificiality, clumsiness, and many more that are incipient in a bilingual enterprise of this kind, are overcome in performance.

Needless to say, work like this requires a long preparatory process. It also has to rely on what might be called "reciprocal tuning-in" - linguistically, emotionally, psychologically and in terms of life-style, habits, cultural baggage, and so on. Communication between performers in a common language and, through it, to an audience can be difficult enough at the best of times. Doing it through two languages, where neither party is fully conversant with the language of the other, might well seem too difficult by far.

The co-directors began to tackle this potential nightmare by having the actors learn from each other's working principles. Larue invited Kossenkova to give a series of workshops to the Théâtre de l'Enfumeraie on how to produce and sustain sound from multiple sources (for instance, from the toes, the top of the head, an elbow). Her method may be described, perhaps not altogether adequately, as the production of infinite variations on tone, nuance and timbre (hence her company's name), which are produced through the vibration of any given part of the human body. This means that the body resonates exactly like a stringed instrument. Kossenkova's method, apart from nurturing powers of vocal expression, as well as releasing a wide range of expressive capabilities through the body into the voice, aims to give performers the ability to create and project sound without strain.

Larue, for his part, taught the Russian actors the rhythm and fluency of movement; also the lightness and humour to be captured from movement. His work with the neutral mask which, as is well known, is a hallmark of Lecoq's teaching, allowed them to explore communication through motion, gesture, and the smallest details of physical activity. As these observations hopefully suggest, the physicality of Larue's approach complemented Kossenkova's focus on vocality which, after all, depends upon physical transmission.

The coordination sought between companies through these kinds of sessions was extended to - let us expediently call it - "cultural immersion".

The Russian actors (as well as the composer and costume designer) were steeped in their hosts' cultural environment during their visits to France. Their French counterparts went through a similar process during their month's stay in Moscow. While in Moscow, they not only experienced the vagaries of daily life, but also climbed the higher planes of inspiration by rehearsing *The Three Sisters* in Chekhov's house, which is now a museum. Art and life, in other words, blended together for concentrated spurts of time over several years.

This immersion, through a common project requiring continual energy and effort, in each other's aesthetic, cultural and daily world - not to mention their respective world's economics and politics - brought about something of a symbiosis between the two groups. It is general knowledge, at least among linguists, that immersion in a targeted environment stimulates and consolidates language acquisition skills. Kossenkova pointed out that the members of the two companies who had had little or no knowledge of the partner language now either understand or speak it with varying degrees of competence by sheer dint of their constant interaction in two languages in work situations, as well as out of them.

Kossenkova's reflections on this spin-off from their project led me to observe that what I have called "symbiosis" had an impact on the performance. That is to say, instead of severing the production in two, a possible outcome of a bilingual and bicultural venture, the two parts crossed over each other. They did not merge. But nor did the seams holding the two together stick out. Obtrusiveness did not happen because the symbiotic relationship between the performers allowed them to listen to each other so sensitively that the criss-cross of languages simply flowed on, as if they were listening and replying in one language.

Bakhtin's term "polyphony" is by far the most appropriate one for the construction, and effect on the listener, of this production. The polyphony at issue not only concerns the two languages as distinct entities we call "Russian" and "French". It involves the process of interweaving, by multiple speakers, of voice-utterances. And it involves the dialogic relationship (Bakhtin, again) between sound (Kossenkova's forte) and movement (Larue's). The symbiosis between the *performers* at a professional/personal level facilitated at the *artistic* level, during performance, the co-existence of multiple elements characteristic of polyphony. Kossenkova and Larue surely did not set out to "materialize" or even "illustrate" Bakhtin's theses. Nevertheless, the result of their interchange is remarkably Bakhtinian.[3]

The decision to work together came from the shock of recognition, from the realization that the "Other" could provide what "I" lacked. Larue describes his initial encounter with Teatr Tembr as a *coup de foudre* - love at first sight. It was his idea to stage Chekhov. The choice of play was made together. If the preparatory work took some two years, the production lasts, Kossenkova notes, one hour and fifty-two minutes. She stresses that all pauses in Chekhov were scrupulously observed, and not one line of his text cut. The brevity of the performance alone suggests that the dreadful inertia so often attributed to Chekhov is out of sight and sound in this production.

Although the idea of playing Chekhov came from Larue, I was interested in knowing what the stakes were for Kossenkova, what her aims were in combining two national languages and two types of play. I asked this question, remarking that I presumed she did not do experimental theatre solely for the sake of testing an idea, or "laboratory theatre" (here taking up Kossenkova's terminology) for the sake of pure research.

Kossenkova replied that she wished, first of all, to show the beauty, poetry and musicality of Chekhov's language, his Russian having great richness of intonation which, she believed, Russian had in general, and far more than French. (She hastened to add that the French people with whom she had discussed the second point agreed with her.) Chekhov's tonal richness was such that it gave layers and layers of meaning to words, which explained why his plays could be translated adequately into a wide range of languages and be understood. Hence his "universal" quality. Even bad translations could not cover over his particular intonation, his unique poetry. This, she felt, was true of all great poets, Shakespeare among them. What Kossenkova most wanted to do was to bring Chekhov close to the hearts of French spectators by having them hear him properly.

Kossenkova develops her point:

> There are directors who see, and Pascal Larue is one of them. I *hear* things. I hear everything in a voice. A voice is like an extract from a whole person. I look for the voice a playwright is speaking in. When I find the intonation, I find the [speech] genre someone is using. I find the right rhythm, the right vocabulary. I can change speech, but I always keep the author's rhythm . . . I try to find the inner voice of a play. Chekhov's voice is inscribed in *The Three Sisters*, as are the voices of Euripides, Pushkin, Shakespeare. When a character says "Shakespeare" or "Voltaire", I have to find them, hear them in the text. . . . Chekhov belongs to a whole group of our early twentieth-century poets - Kruchenykh, Khlebnikov, Andrei Bely, Mayakovsky, Pasternak, Akhmatova - all of whom were great masters of voice. They read their own poetry out aloud. They heard their own voice. Well, Chekhov also heard his own voice out aloud when he was writing.

These and related observations on intonation led Kossenkova to stress that, to her mind, the problem did not lie in the translation of words, but in how they were articulated, enunciated or pronounced. And this fed into my questions concerning the difficulty of working in two languages on stage and off, given especially that all issues of musicality aside (intonation, rhythm, and so on, included), language carries semantic content, as well as a whole host of cultural assumptions which musicality alone cannot communicate.[4] Did she, therefore, encounter any particular difficulties with actors who, having a Lecoq training, could be said to have come out of a theatrical context that was *culturally* constructed? Did they, in other words, have suppositions about how to perform that did not necessarily coincide with how her own actors conceived of performing?

The replies from Kossenkova concerned both groups. The French actors had difficulty, for instance, in understanding what it might mean to play a Russian officer. First of all, they were anti-militarist and found Kossenkova's military exercises, in preparation for the roles, personally distasteful. Secondly, they appeared to reject the sign systems that went with officers (signs to do with social class, heroism, honour, chivalry - the latter involving some resistance as to how Irina, an upper-class young lady, might react to Soliony's tempestuous advances). Thirdly, they did not always see the point of working on detail, whether of physical or vocal presentation. In addition, not all of Kossenkova's explanatory references met with the same flash of comprehension. References to Dostoevsky, for example, triggered off an immediate response. References to Pushkin, who is one of Kossenkova's main interpretative touchstones for *The Three Sisters* - if not the principal one - fell flat, without echo.

The Russian actors, for their part, were not easily able to abstract from a situation. Nor, consequently, could they give an action the lightness or deftness sought for it. Kossenkova explained how difficult it was for them to play a clown "in general". They had to have concrete indications as to what sort of clown they were, where they were, why they were there, how they were dressed and who they were with. Kossenkova's affectionate, almost parodic account of her actors was followed by an affirmative answer to my question on whether their predilection for such precise contextualization had something to do with the Russian theatrical culture, perhaps even with Stanislavsky's influence on it. She observed, however, that notwithstanding their "Russian" preoccupation - and certainly Chekhovian preoccupation - with shading and detail, the Russian actors were less disciplined than the French ones. This, she believed, was bound up with how much psycho-emotional energy they invested in their work, leaving them quite tired after a few hours of exertion.

If the actors of Teatr Tembr were uncomfortable with the hours and pace of preparation set by their French partners, they were not thrown off course by most of the theatrical, literary and philosophical references made by them with respect to France. And they were least likely to be puzzled by Kossenkova's discovery of a key to the production in Pushkin. Pushkin is a strong enough cultural icon to spark off a certain degree of consensus among artists as to what he might signify for the show. One of the most important connecting links for the production is that between Pushkin and Lermontov. They stand for similar values, for similar heroism and grandeur, and for a similar inner, moral nobility which, for this spectator at least, distinguishes all the male characters of the production. Whether we take Soliony, who is physically modelled on Pushkin and Lermontov's heroes, or Vershinin, who is portrayed as a man of moral integrity and refinement, or again Andrei, who is shown to be nobody's fool, but suffers from an over-developed sense of decorum - each male character may be said to be a variation upon the themes of dignity, courage and the desire to do something meaningful for self and others.

What is, in fact, striking about the production's male figures is how their image recalls the intelligentsia of the *beginning* of the nineteenth century, as if the ideals of that particular intelligentsia illuminate Chekhov's world and serve as a model for the present. Kossenkova's allusions to the finer details of these cross-references are of a more personal nature. Thus she explained that Pushkin's death in a duel, at the hands of a Frenchman, inspired her conception of the rivalry between Soliony and Tusenbach which led to the fatal duel where Tusenbach is killed. She also explained that, given the association she made between Soliony and Pushkin's biography, it was imperative that Soliony be played by a French actor. By the same token, Olga, who, Kossenkova argues, announces the play's themes, also had to be performed by a member of the Théâtre de l'Enfumeraie. If we follow Kossenkova's reasoning, it seems that the characters who provide the exposition and the action are played by the French performers.

The issue of casting brings us back, of course, to the use of two languages in the production. It was planned that *The Three Sisters* would travel to Russia after performances in France. What this may well suggest are changes in how much Russian is inserted in dialogue delivered in French, since the aim will be to communicate as much as possible, with language and irrespective of language, to Russian-speaking audiences, as was anticipated for French-speaking audiences. It is likely that more spectators in Russia will understand French - or, at least, enough of it to get the gist of interchanges in this language - than was the case of Russian for spectators in France. Assumptions as to anticipated audiences may well determine not only the quantity of French used, but the very purpose and function of speech units in French and of the bilingual aspect of the production as such.

These reflections remain in the realm of hypothesis. What is sure is that the version intended for audiences in France used Russian phrases, or simply isolated words, in French speech in order to echo the most important thoughts and emotions of a particular character. This procedure of picking out refrains that highlight the motifs weaving in and out of scenes and binding the whole is continued through the production - from the very beginning right to the end. In other words, selected phrases echo the themes to be found in the whole, exactly as occurs in music; and, as in music, they give the major or minor key, and the modulation or transposition of a specific theme.

The production's musical structure is especially evident in how French phrases come in and out of speech in Russian. The fact that there is marginally more French intercepting Russian dialogue than there is Russian in French is hardly surprising, because the audiences watching the performances are taken to be French-speaking before all else. What *is* surprising is how *little* French is used. And this indicates that French, when used in Russian, has minimal expository, explanatory and narrative purposes. Its main purpose is to gather together the leitmotifs that are repeated throughout the performance, and not only through words. One of Irina's leitmotifs, for instance, is "We must work". When she utters this sentence in Russian, she repeats it in French. Thus, it becomes her sign without being exclusive to her. It distinguishes her, but also links her to others, since almost everyone at some point in the performance talks about the necessity of work. The work leitmotif, in other words, can be heard strongly enough in the speeches of those performing in French (for example, Vershinin and Tusenbach) for its brief appearance, in French, in Irina's usual Russian, to have a special impact.

Let us look at a few more examples. Masha takes up the theme of living. She utters "We must live" momentarily in French as if to bring into focus the central importance of this line of thought for the whole production. The theme of love, which Masha carries through with Vershinin, is brought out in a similar manner. The fact that she speaks in Russian to him, and he in French to her, emphasizes the way the motif-fragment "I love" is borrowed from one language (Masha's borrowing from French, for example) and echoed or re-echoed in the other. (Thus Vershinin says "I love" in Russian immediately after having pronounced it in French.) Olga, who also carries several themes at once, states in French (since this is the language of the actress) a number of times throughout the production that she is tired. Irina, when she goes to work at the telegraph office, repeats the theme of fatigue in Russian. One or two words here and there uttered by her in French are variations upon the same theme. But the same theme recurs through most of the other characters, whatever language they speak, precisely because it underpins Kossenkova and Larue's interpretation of Chekhov.

What the production is careful to show through *all* semiotic processes - and not only the verbal ones highlighted by bilingual means - is that the fatigue cited by the characters is neither metaphysical nor psychological (or, for that matter, imaginary or neurotic), but is closely bound up with how much they work and how much more they want to do so. They may say they are tired, but the stage shows them to be seemingly inexhaustible. The striving for life, love, achievement and purposefulness (the opposite of what is "useless") is marked out so clearly by the performers for their characters that the last scene, where the sisters are grouped together and return - as if in an opera trio - to their main motifs (working, living, learning) has nothing mawkish, defeatist or pessimistic about it. The production closes with the sisters looking straight at the audience and speaking to it in intimate tones, communicating what amounts to a message of hope.

The musical effects brought out verbally through two languages and, above all, through the voices in which utterances are uttered, are sustained by music right through the production. All the characters, at some point, play the piano. Piano playing continues the flow between Acts, scene changes thus not interrupting the rhythm and beat established. It anticipates or introduces dialogue, signals a change of direction in dialogue or accompanies dialogue. Masha, for example, in her conversation with Vershinin in Act II, covers a good deal of what she has to say while she is playing. This lieder-like component is foregrounded through the numerous songs that are sung on stage and off. Most of these songs are folk songs. Others are lullabies. Still others are cries of pain. Take, for example, Masha's singing fragments of her love for Vershinin when he leaves forever. Kuligin, Masha's husband, cradles her in his arms like a child and half-sings words of comfort to her. His half-lullaby, half children's rhyme, fades into a hum.

Humming, like singing, has enormous emotional force in the production.

At the beginning of Act II, humming in the wings merges with the music of the piano on stage. It then takes off on its own, its power and rhythm - all notes in harmony recalling orthodox liturgy and folksong in one - creating a snowstorm. The landscape created through sound gives the winter scene of Act II, which ends with Natasha going off for a ride in a troika with Protopopov. By the same token, the sound gives the characters' inner landscape, which is exteriorized by them through action. Their turbulence, motion and passion - including Masha and Vershinin's passion, which becomes the dominant voice in Act II - is captured in the choral humming whose acoustic images are all the more compelling because those producing them are out of view.

Voices also fade into the distance, as does the humming, like the motion of a troika. So do the voices calling in the forest, echo upon echo upon echo, when Soliony kills Tusenbach. Trailing off into silence, before words and movements take up the rhythm of life again, is used with great economy in the production. It is used poignantly, lyrically, at the beginning of Act II where the flicker of candlelight, traced out by the movements of the characters bringing the candles in, composes a choreography almost without sound. It is used at the end to accentuate Tusenbach's tragic fate.

A similar process of the trailing-off of sound occurs at the beginning of Act III. This time, movement in almost total silence comes from Natasha, who paces around the Greek columns in authoritative and authoritarian mode, and fades into them, as if a spy closely watching what has now become *her* household. The choreographic impulse of movements like these materializes elsewhere in dance, especially in the waltzes and folk dances which are performed and which unite the different social worlds that Olga and Anfisa (Olga perhaps being the closest to Anfisa) represent. Perhaps this is the production's ideal for the future. The Greek columns, meanwhile, stand still and, whether taken as the columns of a noble family's house or the columns of ancient tragedy, remind spectators of the past. The tragic undercurrent of this production, which surges through the actors' play, is caught, as if quintessentially, in the sign of the columns.

***THE THREE SISTERS* by Anton Chekhov**

Théâtre de l'Enfumeraie and Teatr Tembr

Translator: Elsa Triolet

Directors: Nika Kossenkova and Pascal Larue

Scenographer-Consultant: Yuri Kononenko

Decor and Lighting: Cyrille Guillochon, Benoît Sari and Rodrigue Montebran

Costumes: Irina Titorenko

Music: Svetlana Golybina

Cast

Natasha: Annick Augis

Masha: Irina Borisienko

Kuligin: Vladimir Douchine

Vershinin: Jacques Gouin

Tusenbach, Rodé: Sergei Grousdev and Franck Trillot

Soliony: Pascal Hatton

Irina: Nathalia Orekhova

Olga: Valérie Pourroy

Andrei: Pierre Sarzacq

Anfisa: Maylis Verseils

Ferapont, Fedotik: Christophe Virlogeux

Chebutikin: Jean-Paul Dubois

NOTES

1. Direct quotations and my occasional paraphrasing of Nika Kossenkova's words come from conversations with the Russian director in Paris in May 1993. However, since most of my commentary on the production is my own particular interpretation of Kossenkova's work, her and my voices should not be confused; nor, in consequence, should my views be attributed to her. The director, it may transpire, may not agree with them!

2. Bakhtin's theory of language, in antithesis to theories derived from or related to Ferdinand de Saussure, stresses that language is primarily a matter of speech. Saussurean and almost all other linguistic theories, by contrast, give priority to the notion of language as writing, which has a system of grammatical and other rules that are integral to the structure of language. Bakhtin consistently argues against the notion that language has a structure as such in abstract and which precedes, and even transcends, the speakers who use it (in writing, as well). Since, for Bakhtin, language comes into being between speakers, it is always alive to their shared needs and intentions in a given social time and place.

   This not being the appropriate context for a detailed discussion of Bakhtin's theory of language, attention must be drawn to *Marxism and the Philosophy of Language* (which was published originally under the name of V. N. Voloshinov), trans. Ladislav Matejka and I. R. Titunik. Cambridge, Massachusetts, London: Harvard University Press, 1986 and *Speech Genres and Other Late Essays*. Caryl Emerson and Michael Holquist, eds., trans. Vern W. McGee. Austin: University of Texas Press, 1986. For a useful exposition of points relevant to my remarks above on notions developed by Bakhtin around the concepts of speech, utterance, discourse, and so on, see James V. Wertsch, *Voices of the Mind: A Sociocultural Approach to Mediated Action*. Cambridge, Massachusetts: Harvard University Press, 1991. For further details of my own exposition/interpretation of Bakhtin's theory of language, see my review of Wertsch's book in *Science and Society* 57. 1 (Spring 1993), pp. 98-101 and my "Dialogism in the Novel and Bakhtin's Theory of Culture". *New Literary History* 23. 3 (Summer 1992), pp. 747-63.

3. Bakhtin develops his concept of polyphony in *Problems of Dostoevsky's Poetics*, trans. Caryl Emerson. Minneapolis: University of Minnesota Press, 1987.

   Since I had been so deeply struck by the Bakhtinian quality of the production, I could not resist asking Kossenkova about it. It turns out that Kossenkova considers Bakhtin to be one of her "great masters", stating that he is indeed one of the main touchstones of her work for the stage. She gave, as an example, her attempt to create a dialogic relationship between actors and spectators by having the former speak to the latter as if they were the interlocutor to whom a given character was speaking or had just spoken (for example, Soliony's addressing Tusenbach and then looking at, and speaking to, the audience as if the audience were Tusenbach). This form of direct address to the audience, which is not a break between stage action and audience (as occurs, say, in Brecht) but a *continuation* of the dialogue on stage, is a way of including spectators in the action and placing them in the role of participants (even if they do not actually *do* actions), as was the intention of participatory theatre to which belong, among the most famous productions, Arianne Mnouchkine's *1789*, *1793* and *L'Age d'or*. "Participation", in the case of these particular productions by Mnouchkine, means that spectators were able to move from tableau to tableau and thus walk around the different podia designated for performance instead of being glued to their seats.

4. The question of semantics brings up, of course, the issue of how spectators react to and understand a bilingual production when they do not have a grasp of both languages used. This issue will continue to be relevant as long as words are intrinsic to performances and not merely decorative or aleatory. It does not arise in dance performances, for example, which do not incorporate verbal means of sense-making and communication in movement (as do, on the other hand, such genres as the dance theatre of Pina Bausch or Karole Armitage's mixed media compositions).

A study of audiences for this *Three Sisters* was not on my agenda. Nor can my informal, conversational mode of eliciting commentary from spectators here and there claim to have any scientific value. Nevertheless, a spot-check of a few spectators suggested that those who claimed to know the play well or who were theatre practitioners were not concerned by the semantic loss. Those who did not know the play well and felt that understanding the meaning of words was crucial to a complete understanding of a performance felt that they had lost too much from not understanding Russian. It would have been illuminating to converse with spectators who were not theatre practitioners and who did not place great importance on the meaning of words, letting the remaining semiotic processes do the work of communicating meaning to them. The question, then, would be to see just how much they understood from and of the performance, and in what sense of the word "understand"! Understanding, after all, is not purely a matter of cognition.

PART III

SPECTATORS

6

SOCIAL AND CULTURAL ELITES: AUDIENCES FOR *THREE SISTERS* DIRECTED BY RICHARD WHERRETT

Introduction

The material presented here with regard to *Three Sisters* is part of my research on theatre audiences, where empirical data and methodological and theoretical considerations are closely connected. In other words, my research is not being carried out in a positivistic manner. It does not, therefore, assume that facts can be organized without the intervention of interpretative principles.

Those who are familiar with the work of Pierre Bourdieu will have understood from the title of this essay that I am referring to some of Bourdieu's major conceptual categories. However, it will become clear that, although these categories help shape my interpretation - at least for my present purposes - I by no means follow Bourdieu step by step. This has nothing to do with the fact that Bourdieu does not study the theatre. It has everything to do with my premise that theories neither can nor should be "applied" mechanistically.

As for matters of method, questionnaires devised by me have been my source of information on audiences. Numerous methodological issues are involved in constructing and distributing questionnaires and then in assembling replies from respondents. Let me cut through a long argument by saying that questionnaires are adequate for gathering sociodemographic data, that is, quantitative data, but are notoriously difficult when it comes to evaluative, *qualitative* information. I have attempted, in my audience research as a whole, to highlight spectators' interaction with whatever production is at hand, as well as to highlight other qualitative responses from them. I link these evaluative areas of inquiry (and they are far from straightforward) to quantitative material which, if less troublesome than the former, is certainly not trouble-free. The linkage between the two allows what would otherwise be purely statistical data to take a human form. This human form is theatre played by and to living beings in society.

My last general introductory point concerns spectators' awareness of the formal-stylistic qualities of *Three Sisters* and their sensitivity and receptivity to these aesthetic qualities. The kind of awareness spectators may have can only be gleaned from their observations on the production. Thus, by the phrase "aesthetic education" I am referring to the awareness, receptivity and sensitivity as articulated by, or deducible from, their remarks. I am not referring to the teaching programs of schools, universities, specialized arts institutions, and the like, where spectators may have learned about the theatre or developed their capacity to talk about it.

Some Explanatory Remarks About Qualitative Questions

It was not possible, for many reasons, to have the questionnaire focus on the stage processes - use of space, gestures and movements, music, lights, and so on - which together, in play, constitute a production's formal-stylistic qualities as well as give it sense and meaning. Spectators were asked to rank their enjoyment of *Three Sisters* on a scale of 1 to 5. They were then asked to explain their ranking. This open question assumed that unprompted and, as it were, "spontaneous" replies would mark out the spectators' immediate frame of reference, whether to do with stage processes or, say, thematic structure or didactic "message".

The next question "What do you think *Three Sisters*, a Russian classic, has to say to theatre audiences in Australia today?" principally sought information on cross-cultural perception and evaluation. It also solicited thoughts on the term "classic". Since the question referred to a specific production of a specific classic, it hoped to stimulate further commentary on the staged version (which, in fact, it did). I worked on the hypothesis that additional commentary on the production would provide clues to spectators' sensitivity to its aesthetic (which happened in a number of cases).

Other evaluative questions targeted their aesthetic education according to the meaning assigned to these two words above. This was also the target of questions probing spectators' overall assessment of, and attitudes towards, the work of the Sydney Theatre Company as a whole. One question asked what interested them about STC productions. Another asked what kinds of plays and productions they would like to see more of by the company. Yet another asked what they thought was the main purpose of theatre. The assumption behind the "purpose" question was that spectators would indicate their perceptions of the social role of the theatre, as well as suggest their expectations of it.

It should be clear from my remarks that my notion of "aesthetic education" cannot easily be separated from what I call "theatre culture". Indeed, the questionnaire was designed in order to keep the two in tandem. Thus questions on the frequency of spectators' attendance at play productions, ballet and contemporary dance performances, and performances of opera aimed to find out something about their theatre culture, now measuring it quantitatively. This statistical data was to provide support for the qualitative material coming from the open questions. Furthermore, it situated playgoing in the broader spectrum of *spectacle*. By doing so, the notion of "theatre culture" was able to appropriately embrace several different performing arts while, at the same time, allowing play production, which is integral to theatre culture, to be singled out for special attention. The second, narrower concept underpins the request to spectators to name the last production they saw, and where, before *Three Sisters*.

Brief Theoretical Remarks

The first point to make is that what Bourdieu defines as a social elite is predominant in the sample audience. By educational qualifications and profession, it belongs to the intellectual strata of the dominant classes, if not necessarily to the intelligentsia as traditionally conceived. Two questions emerge in respect of all the information I have gathered, a selected part of which is included here. Does this social elite have an aesthetic education? Is it also a cultural elite? It must be remembered that the term "cultural" includes, but is not exclusive to, my notion of aesthetic education. When these questions are set in the context of Bourdieu's theory, they may be conflated roughly as follows: Are those who possess social capital also possessors of cultural capital?

We must keep in mind the fact that Bourdieu makes distinctions between social, economic, intellectual, and cultural capital. Nevertheless, he maintains that there is a tight relationship between them, even though they do not always directly correspond with each other. For example, those with economic wealth do not necessarily have intellectual or cultural wealth. Just the same, Bourdieu argues, the relationship between these different forms of capital usually makes them overlap. As a result, a disposition towards culture is acquired by individuals through family environments that look favourably upon culture. This disposition is nurtured through schooling, whether at high school or university, and whose real benefits are contingent upon the family milieu which has already encouraged an interest in, and competence in, cultural activities. In the case of the class fractions at the top of the social hierarchy, a disposition towards culture is fostered by the culture inherited from the same class, both disposition and inheritance usually being linked to economic well-being. From here follow Bourdieu's theses on the reproduction of privileges: the benefits derived from social status ensure greater gain from the educational system; the surplus value culled from education guarantees greater access to the professions (especially to "top" professions), as well as to cultural goods; the cultural capital already accumulated generates more of the same capital; the classes or class fractions who have already accrued multiple riches, cultural wealth included, become entrenched and reproduce themselves; their reproduction (moreover within a structure that, extrapolating from Bourdieu, could accurately be described as oligarchic) occurs alongside the serial self-reproduction of the remaining classes.[1]

Bourdieu's theory, although theory and thus having generalizing power, essentially responds to the socioeconomic, institutional and historical structure of France. My data regarding audiences for *Three Sisters* suggests that the tight relationship between the different forms of capital identified by Bourdieu may not hold for Australia today - or, at least, not for Sydney society.

Results

My data comes from 551 completed questionnaires which represent 25% of the audience for four performances, or 2% of the total number of viewers of the production (24,190 total viewers).

Of the 551 total, 60% belong to the two upper classifications "managers and administrators" and "professionals" defined by the Australian Bureau of Statistics. The largest groups in the 40% left are clerks and students (8% each). Those classified as paraprofessionals (mostly nurses in our sample), and as salespersons and personal service workers account for 4% each. Of particular note, where distribution by social class is concerned, is that two people are drivers, while another two (nurse's aid and concierge) fall into the lowest category of "labourers and related workers". No factory, farm or other "hard" labourer appears in the sample. As for the middle class primarily serviced by the STC, the academics and teachers included in it (24% of the two upper categories combined) cannot be said to comprise the economic elite, even though they are in the country's higher salary brackets. Lawyers and doctors, on the other hand, arguably do constitute an economically superior group. So do, in general, the company directors, bankers and various managers belonging to the first classification. The majority of them are university educated, by which fact they join the professionals to form an intellectual elite. However, since their social status is perceived to be more important than their scholarly achievements, they are not commonly identified with that elite.

Over half (57%) of the elite, whether "intellectual", "social", "economic" or whatever description best suits pockets in it, ranked the production at 4 and 5. Explanations as to ranking may be divided into two large blocs: the first to do with the playtext as such, and the second to do with the stage production.

Answers in the first alluded to the play in general ("good", "marvellous" and similar expressions of appreciation), picked out specific elements of composition - story, characters, dialogue ("as in real life") - or talked about its themes and their relevance (here anticipating the next question). Very few refer to the play's structure, a male lawyer noting, however, that it is "beautifully structured" despite its "typical Russian length".

Those scoring below 4 thought the play was "ponderous", "wordy", "boring", or "depressing", sometimes linking their judgements to what they believe are national-cultural traits (thus, for example, "turgid", "typically Russian", or "another inexplicable Russian dirge of a classic").

Very few, whether making a positive or negative statement about the playtext, attempt to situate it sociohistorically. Those who dislike its characters usually cannot be bothered to explain why. An exception, therefore, is particularly noticeable, as in the case of an accountant for whom the characters are "superficial upper-class snobs". He continues: "They justify Stalin's purges"(!).

Answers in the second bloc are grouped around components of the stage work: acting, sets, costumes, lighting, pace, spatial configuration, choreography, music and atmosphere. I have listed these components in order of importance according to the number of times respondents refer to them.

A good 40% of the respondents were sufficiently struck by the actors' work to comment upon it, usually in enthusiastic terms, while a few found the parts "over-played" or "played too sweet". In addition, respondents refer either to the production or to the direction/director, thereby suggesting they have taken in the ensemble, the director being, of course, its guiding force. Put mathematically, this means that 23% of respondents indicate they are taking into account the whole stage work, albeit without specifying which features in particular have captured their attention.

There are about the same number of references to sets as combined references to production and direction. It must be stressed that respondents who appreciated the scenography usually took note of the actors and/or the production or direction. Just the same, references solely to the sets were recorded, thus swelling the count for this word and its collocations. The sets were central to the production's sense and meaning. Furthermore, even if their interpretative function vis-à-vis everything else on stage escaped notice, they could hardly be missed. They were sumptuous in the first Act where they depicted a dining room-cum-salon, design details such as billowing curtains, piano, candelabra and masses of flowers having considerable visual impact. They were stately, though austere, in the open-air, autumnal scene of the closing Act. In fact, given their importance and visibility, references to them were disappointingly few.

Richard Wherrett, when I interviewed him about his overall conception of the production, spoke movingly of the relevance of scenic detail to it. When queried about the elaborate sets, he replied that they faithfully followed Chekhov's stage directions. When asked whether a less ornate, or even bare, stage would have done just as well, he replied that this would not have been in accord with Chekhov's intentions. Nor, in his view, would have been direction of the actors' voices, gestures, and so on, outside the parameters of realism. Wherrett, in other words, synchronized his stage interpretation with what he believed was true to Chekhov's text.

And here it is worth adding that only one or two isolated remarks from spectators pin-pointed such details of acting as diction, accent (denoting the class difference between servants and gentry) or gesture (putting feet on a table which, one respondent noted, was inappropriate for women at the turn of the century).

By the same token, when we measure statistically, a mere two references to choreography and spatial configuration pale into insignificance. So, too, does one perfunctory mention of music, and, again, of atmosphere. Considering that Richard Wherrett gave a great deal of attention to the use of space, to movement and steps in space (dance steps included), to the narrative and evocative powers of music, and to changing atmospheres - each of the four Acts marked by a distinctive mood - respondents' inattentiveness to these elements is disappointing. Much the same could be said of the insignificantly few remarks on lighting. The second Act, for instance, is an arresting tonal composition of light and shade, which gives subtlety to the dialogue uttered, the events taking place, the interaction between actors and their characters, and the temporal transitions binding the parts to the whole (day turning to night, summer to winter, and years past to years future).

Now, we must remember that the information here presented can only chart trends. It can only give an impression, an overarching view, of respondents' aesthetic awareness and receptivity. The extreme difficulty of tabulating qualitative data is compounded in this case by the fact that most of the respondents who say something about the stage work usually note several points, for example, acting as well as direction and/or sets. What this indicates, however, in terms of an overarching view, is that a relatively small minority are *most aware* of the constituent elements of a production. When these "most aware" respondents are added to respondents who show a little awareness (defined, for my purpose, by referring only to one element or by merely stating "production"), they make up 34% of all respondents belonging to the social elite as demarcated above. Our figure may have been higher if all the people who gave information about their occupation and formal education had answered the question to do with the production.

Whatever the case may have been in ideal circumstances, the results we have are striking in that spectators record, above all else, their awareness of, and response to, acting - this followed some way behind by their allusions to sets. Secondly, all other stage processes, which are inseparable from a production's aesthetic, seem to recede so far from sight as virtually to disappear from the horizon.

If our elite appears to have limited aesthetic vision, it is by no means short on intellectual comprehension, as is clear from answers regarding "a Russian classic". Observations, here, are wide-ranging, though give discernible motifs: times, life, people, problems, dreams, human nature and human emotions have not changed very much since the turn of the century; Chekhov examines interpersonal relationships, marriage and the family, and the social condition of women; the play is about the meaning and purpose of life; act instead of being a "passive bystander" because, now quoting another spectator, "only we can control our destinies"; goals must be striven for and achieved. All these reflect the motifs of the production itself.

When spectators are not explicit but say "themes", they invariably describe them as "eternal", "timeless" or "universal". A few of them point out that this is precisely why classics are "classics" and yet are pertinent today regardless of racial, social and cultural differences. Some insist, on the contrary, that the play is irrelevant to Australia in 1990. Those who are not totally dismissive as to its contemporary significance find it "historically interesting". Not one single spectator, not even the actors in the sample, refers to the challenge of performing as well as viewing classics, the training ground they provide for theatre workers, or any other matter in respect of theatre art.

We cannot draw definite conclusions from our respondents' remarks as to whether they dissociate artistic processes from content-substance - the relationship between form and content being one of the thorniest issues in aesthetics, and not only with regard to classics. Yet the attraction of classics for our managerial and professional group is great, judging by the number of times individuals in it state they would like to see more classics mounted by the Sydney Theatre Company. When a count is made by author, Shakespeare comes out well and truly first. Chekhov is named extremely infrequently by comparison. Tolstoy rates a mention.

A count by national identity shows a very marked preference for more Australian plays. They are followed, although a long way behind, by British, then American, and, further still, by Russian plays. Spectators' predisposition towards Australian works is not altogether well defined in that some speak of "Australian classics" (such as, for example, Ray Lawler's *Summer of the Seventeenth Doll*), while others either state "contemporary Australian plays" or merely "Australian". Furthermore, when spectators' expressed desire to see more classics is compared with their wish to see more contemporary works, the first just about matches the second. This is corroborated by what spectators say about their interest in STC productions, where interest in classical and contemporary plays is virtually equally weighted.

A count by genre puts comedies at the top of the wish-list, followed by drama and musicals, which, if graphed, would show a noticeable distance separating them from comedies. The term "tragedy" does not turn up once. Does this mean that the tragedies of Shakespeare are peripheral to our respondents' idea of Shakespeare, who is at the summit of their hierarchy of desires?

Whatever the answer may be, Shakespeare is clearly part of their theatrical canon. And their canon duplicates *the* canon, as is evident from the playwrights cited, going from Marlowe via Ibsen, Shaw, Wilde, O'Neill, Tennessee Williams to Beckett. These are the dramatists of university courses. They are also integral to the STC repertoire. Thus our elite's theatre culture, whether acquired at the theatre or through schools of one kind or another, or both, is aligned to established culture. Moreover, by expressing the desire to see more of what they already know, members of this elite not only demonstrate their orthodox taste, but also suggest they are happy to reproduce it.

It would, of course, be inappropriate to isolate the theatre culture absorbed by the elite from the culture available to it on the Sydney stage. A glance at the productions viewed by spectators before they saw *Three Sisters* shows a fairly narrow margin. The productions in it belong principally, though not exclusively, to the STC. The concentration can be partly accounted for by the fact that most of our respondents are subscribers to the STC.

Productions named by them were either performed during earlier seasons or ran in the season including *Three Sisters*. The production immediately preceding the latter, *Hot Fudge and Ice Cream* by Caryl Churchill, was cited more than any other. Unprompted, respondents gave a negative assessment of it, their asides suggesting a distaste for what they perceive to be "avant-garde". The next most frequently cited production was *The Tempest*, mounted shortly before at the Belvoir Street Theatre. The fact that the range of productions available in Sydney is greater than appears from the data may suggest that the upper echelons attending performances at the STC are not, on the whole, predisposed to broadening their theatre culture.

Yet the upper echelons are accustomed to the theatre. Half of them see at least five or six productions per year (six being offered by a subscription). Another third see up to twenty productions annually. Their attendance at ballet or contemporary dance performances is lower. Half of them see none, most of the remaining respondents seeing up to three per year. As for opera, slightly more than half never go. Most of the rest go up to three times, as occurs for ballet/dance. Their theatre culture, then, is principally shaped by verbal theatre.

Furthermore, this elite believes in quality. A good quarter of its members, when talking about their interest in STC productions, mention quality or use terms like "standard" and "professionalism" to convey a similar idea. Quite a large number of them were among respondents, for the same question, who specified that acting, casting, or the productions of the STC as integral entities held their interest before all else.

Although the creative side of the STC's work certainly did not pass unnoticed, what scored highest, numerically speaking, was the company's repertoire as such, for which the terms "variety", "diversity" and "range" were used repeatedly. By comparison, only a very small group focuses its attention on scenography, lighting and costumes, these aspects of *mise en scène* being the only ones mentioned. In other words, well below half of the social elite articulates an awareness of stage processes/aesthetics. What occurs at a non-articulated, subliminal level is anybody's guess.

To all appearances, then, the information coming through suggests that our socially privileged spectators place aesthetic concerns low on their list of priorities. The same information also suggests the relative weakness of their aesthetic education. This is confirmed by their opinions on the main purpose of theatre. Time and again they note the words "entertain" or "entertainment", which, when the count is made, gain an overwhelming majority. Other purposes are by no means excluded. Those noted most frequently give the following summary: the main purpose of theatre is to educate (with several variations on the themes of teaching and learning), provoke thought, stimulate intellectually, and deal with ideas, issues or views (notably of the author). However, none of these options can begin to compare with the vote for entertainment. They fall well behind even when they are merged into one. Even such qualifying statements as "educate in an entertaining way" do not significantly affect the results.

As for aesthetics, a mere 16 out of 332 spectators constituting the social elite refer to this area in some way. Thus, for them, theatre is "Art", "artistic creation", "fantasy", a place for "new art forms" or a "vehicle for artistic excellence and originality". Some in this tiny minority believe theatre's main purpose is to allow audiences to enjoy talented performers, performance styles, words, visual images and music. A musicologist believes it must appreciate the "art of the author", who is a "master craftsman of language". He cites wit and elegance as examples of verbal craftsmanship.

Theatre understood as a facet of culture fares worse still. Here and there an isolated spectator suggests that theatre opens a path to foreign cultures or gives people insight into their own culture.

Conclusion

Bourdieu's categories as regards various elites or types of elite have been relevant and useful for organizing the information gathered on spectators attending performances of *Three Sisters*. The elite at issue here, which is a composite elite incorporating variations that stress this rather than that factor (economic rather than cultural, and so on), concerns the 60% majority of the audience who belongs to the managerial and professional groups discussed above. We may conclude that our elite is a social one that has financial access to established culture, its buying power varying according to different pockets or class fractions of it. We may also come to the conclusion, on the basis of the data available to us, that the "establishment" (in some sense of the word) which is formed by this elite and established culture support each other. However, we may also have to conclude that the cultural status of our elite does not match its social status. I am here drawing on, though not relying solely on, an elevated concept of culture-cultivation inherited from the upper-middle class or the *haute bourgeoisie* and which encompasses the idea that proficiency in artistic matters is integral to being cultivated.

Whatever we decide, it appears that the theatre, for our social elite, is firstly a matter of entertainment and, secondly, of education. This data may suggest that the social elite is primarily a pleasure-seeking group. The value it accords to entertainment may well be indicative of how the theatre is evaluated socially in Australia today. The question to ask, then, is whether the elite of a given society fixes or determines value in such a way that the value set by it is - or becomes - the going value across the board.[2]

NOTES

1. See, notably, *Les Héritiers* (with J-C. Passeron). Paris: Les Editions de Minuit, 1964; *L'Amour de l'art* (with Alain Darbel and Dominique Schnapper). Paris: Les Editions de Minuit, 1969; *La Reproduction* (with J-C. Passeron). Paris: Les Editions de Minuit, 1971; *La Distinction: critique sociale du jugement.* Paris: Les Editions de Minuit, 1979; *Homo academicus*. Paris: Les Editions de Minuit, 1984.

2. When raising this question, it is useful to remember Antonio Gramsci's argument on how dominant classes propagate their values through all social institutions, art institutions included, thereby ensuring their hegemony as a class and their values (political, ethical, artistic or whatever values are at issue) as *the* legitimate values to be accepted and emulated by all other classes in society. See *Antonio Gramsci: Selections From Cultural Writings*. David Forgacs and Geoffrey Nowell-Smith, eds. Harvard University Press, 1985.

7

AUSTRALIAN VIEWS OF A FRENCH CLASSIC: AUDIENCES FOR *PHEDRA* DIRECTED BY MICHAEL GOW

Prologue

Several points must be made by way of a prologue to this discussion. It was not possible, in the case of *Phedra*, to give questionnaires to spectators before the show and briefly explain the purposes of my research to them. I had adopted this direct approach in my studies of audiences for the Sydney Theatre Company's *Three Sisters* directed by Richard Wherrett and for *The Tempest* directed by Neil Armfield at the Belvoir Street Theatre. I had previously used a similar method in my research on audiences for Italo-Australian community theatre. Questionnaires for *Phedra* were placed on the seats of the Wharf Studio, which holds 140 people. The lack of contact with potential respondents had a negative effect on returns. Thus compare a 67% return on questionnaires distributed for *Three Sisters* and 62% for *The Tempest* with 19% for *Phedra*.

The low return for *Phedra* may mean that the sample is not altogether representative of the production's audiences as a whole (a total of 4,125 viewers). Nevertheless, I suspect that the demographic profile available would not have been radically altered by an increased number of completed questionnaires. The results suggest that we would have been dealing with a select audience, whatever the size of the sample. The people who took the trouble to reply - a good half of them by mail - are connoisseurs and perhaps even a coterie especially tuned in to "art-theatre". *Phedra* was the first of three productions directed by Michael Gow for "New Stages", an experimental project of the STC. The play had never been staged before in Australia. Gow, who describes the play as "great" and sees it as one of several models for writing in this country, did not underestimate the novelty of the event.

While the size of the sample may not be a troublesome issue from a demographic point of view, it is quite possible that a higher return would have given a more finely contoured picture of spectators' assessment of the production. The data to hand shows spectators who are extremely enthusiastic or extremely critical, the first group well and truly outweighing the second. Another hypothesis cannot be excluded, namely, that a higher return may have expanded the group of critical viewers, although without necessarily changing the polarization evident in the sample. What is clear from the replies is that our spectators, by their literacy, cultural know-how and interpretative skill in respect of stage processes, constitute a sub-group or fraction of the hypothetically select audience to which I referred above. Hence my term "connoisseurs" for these spectators. It must be noted that the most detailed and often most articulate responses came in by mail. Unfavourable commentaries were written especially carefully. Time to think through their ideas and feelings about the production was obviously a contributing factor to the quality of these replies, some of which had a decidedly studious ring. However, those who completed questionnaires straight after performances, although generally using fewer words, were no less competent for want of time for meditation.

The questionnaire, apart from aiming to map out the social composition of audiences along with other quantitative data, focused on specific aspects of the production. This series of questions began with a request for an overall assessment, my assumption being that an overview would include features that had had a particular resonance for respondents (which was indeed the case). It continued with questions on the set and lights. In order to elicit interpretative rather than merely descriptive answers, these were put in the form of "Do you think the set [later "lights"] contributed to the meaning of this version? Please explain". The following question centred on the actors' performances. It was unguided insofar as it did not single out any particular play element for discussion. Spectators were left to pick out whatever had caught their attention. I chose the set and lights for commentary, rather than, say, costumes or sound, because Gow and I had agreed they were salient features of the production - not to the exclusion of the others, but probably more tightly bound to Gow's conception of the work. I assumed, Gow here also agreeing, that other stage processes would be mentioned according to respondents' aesthetic disposition - which proved to be correct. The whole point of my asking precise and what may well have appeared to be pedantic questions about the production's aesthetic was to discover just how alert or sensitive spectators were in respect of the work's stylistic qualities, this perhaps also indicating the degree to which they were responsive to, and/or knowledgeable about, theatre aesthetics in general.

The series of interpretative questions was prefaced by a "Yes/No" question asking whether respondents had read the play. There was a two-fold purpose behind this question: find out whether spectators were familiar with the playtext, their familiarity or lack of it possibly affecting their interaction with the production; relate this data to information coming from answers that sketched out their theatre culture. Two questions regarding their theatre culture asked, firstly, whether they related *Phedra* to other plays they knew and, secondly, whether they related it to other plays besides those by Shakespeare that have been called classics. There is a certain degree of overlap between these two questions, but the point of asking the second was to link it with another in which "classic" is a key word. The third question, then, in this bracket, asked whether they thought *Phedra*, a French classic, was relevant to audiences in Australia today. Here, although searching for additional clues to their theatre culture, I was seeking respondents' ideas about what constituted a classic as well as how they perceived the production in cultural terms. Would they, for example, refer to the French context of *Phedra* and compare and contrast it with Gow's particular vision? Or would they by-pass references to French culture, drawing, instead, on some other cultural framework that, in their eyes, helped explain the tone and temper of the production? I was looking, in other words, for what might be called cultural interaction or cross-cultural apperception.

This discussion will concentrate on respondents' observations on staging, connecting them where possible with the broader cultural issues that I have briefly outlined. My intention is to construct a dialogue between spectators, Michael Gow, and Rose Clemente, who played the role of Phedra, so that we may look more closely at the interrelationship - imputed, perceived and real - between spectators, performers and director. After all, performance is the process constituted by them collectively. I am using material from interviews I conducted with Gow and Clemente independently of each other after the run of performances had ended. The dialogue or dialogic encounter, then, is a reconstruction from multiple voices discussing the production from their respective positions, my own voice included.

Social Composition

The social composition of our spectators - 161 in all - may be summarized as follows. One hundred of them are women. Grouping by age shows 23% between 31 and 40, and 21% each between the ages of 21 and 30, and 41 and 50; 16% are over 61. I am giving a detailed breakdown because the composition by age does not altogether correspond with Gow and Clemente's imagined audience. Both of them thought *Phedra* would attract "younger people", this principally meaning people around twenty-five, if I am interpreting their words correctly. Clemente, whatever her precise definition of youth may be, added that she envisaged spectators "who wanted to be excited, people who wanted to be amazed" and who "were interested in the possibilities of where theatre could go". She contrasted her imaginary spectators with "the usual people who go to the STC". Clemente's remarks are to be understood in terms of her view of *Phedra* which, she believes, transcends the emotional boundaries that usually constrain Australian productions. In Clemente's words: "I think that it is really useful for an Australian audience to be confronted on the emotional level because it confronts something very basic to the Australian psyche, which does not want to deal with emotions at all, which is a complete denial of the emotional side of life, and of spiritual life as well". She goes on to explain that "art creates the soul and the conscience of the nation", which, in her view, is not properly recognized in Australia. Hence the "emotional side of life" continues to be denied, in the world as well as in the theatre.

Gow, for his part, explains that he wanted to start "full on" and not "let up" at any point. However, this intensity was not unique to *Phedra*: it was the goal of all his productions for "New Stages". Gow does not explicitly compare his intentions with those of any other type of theatre, as Clemente does. Nevertheless, he seems to be drawing on an implicit comparison insofar as, to his mind, emotional intensity appears to be part of what is "new" about the project as a whole.

Most of the spectators responded favourably to the high pitch set by Gow and the performers, one describing it as "over the top", which, she believes, "suited the old ale"; another, as if echoing Gow's words, says the production was "full on"; yet another speaks of its "overblown emotionalism", explaining that she especially liked this in Clemente's performance. A particularly blownout spectator exclaims: "Fuck!!! I had to scrape my jaw off the floor!" Another said she was "too moved to complete the survey". We shall return to our spectators' emotions shortly.

Grouping by formal education shows that 74% are university educated. Classification by occupation, here using the categories of the Australian Bureau of Statistics, gives us 54% who are professional people and 4% listed under "managers and administrators". A clear majority, then, belongs to the top two categories, 16% of whom work in the arts. The next largest groupings are students and retired people, neither of whom figure in the ABS categories, but were required for the sample taken. Even so, at 14% and 11% respectively, they fall way behind the occupational elite. In short, our audience of connoisseurs has the educational qualifications and professional status fit for connoisseurs, even if it may not necessarily have the financial and other privileges to which connoisseurs might like to be accustomed.

Finally, my group includes ethnic identity, which is usually missing - and wrongly so - from surveys of any kind, the paltry few on theatre audiences across the world being no exception. The fact that the Australian census is an exception to the general rule only confirms the rule. The great majority (80%) comes from English-speaking backgrounds: 68% of the total number of respondents define themselves as Anglo/Celtic-Australian; 12% are American, English, Irish (born in Australia or the U.K.) and New Zealanders. The remaining 20% accounts for Australians of non-Anglo/Celtic origin as well as those who do not claim to be Australian in any shape or form (6%, who describe themselves, for instance, as "French", "Mediterranean" or "European").

Is it possible to conclude from such a small sample that "wogs" do not perceive "New Stages" to be for them, not least when (and perhaps least of all when) a grand foreign tragedy is on the boards? What must be addressed first and foremost through this question is the different class status of "wogs" in Australia. The non-Anglo/Celts viewing *Phedra* at the STC belong to various fractions of the middle class. This indicates that relatively privileged non-Anglo/Celts go to "established" or "mainstream" theatre even though they are a minority in respect of the total audience, which is dominated by Anglo/Celts. And this suggests that, although ethnic identity is crucial (for a start it delineates the cultural parameters of individuals and groups), it cannot be given mythical proportions. In other words, ethnicity per se cannot be given priority when inclusion in, or exclusion from, the "high" arts is under discussion: ethnicity can neither be separated from social class nor elevated above class.

And this brings me back to my question. I believe that the sample *is* too small to allow us to draw any definitive conclusions in reply. However, when my data for *Phedra* is placed in the context of my research on audiences to date, exactly the same pattern recurs, albeit on a bigger scale: that is to say, middle-class non-Anglo/Celts are always a small minority; their lower-middle-class or working-class counterparts are always virtually invisible; the latter only become visible at community theatre performances. What the overall pattern emerging from my research suggests is that "establishment" or "mainstream" theatre primarily plays to the Anglo/Celtic middle class, however class fractions within it are described. Secondly, it suggests that non-Anglo/Celtic community theatre, by virtue of the kind of spectators to which it performs and which, to a certain extent, it creates, fulfils an important role for so-called "ethnic" communities, the so-called "community at large" and for the theatre as such, precisely because it creates new spectators for the art. This conclusion, even if incomplete, cannot be ignored when the social role of theatre is at issue, as it must be when spectators are at issue.

Let us now look at the subject of "wogs" from the theatre-preparing side of the stage. Gow commented on my questions about casting with some humour: "I wanted to emphasize their foreignness [that is, of Phedra and Oenon] by casting Rose, an Italian, as Phedra, and Arianthe Galani, a Greek, as Oenon, whereas all the others were terribly Aryan; so that it was very much an Anglo-centric court with two wogs in it, causing all this trouble, as wogs do". To my prompt on whether he was making a specific political point through his casting, Gow replied: "That's what part of the problem in the play is. Everyone keeps talking about the "*foreign* woman's son" or "Hippolytus has got a bit of wog blood in him" . . . and everyone keeps saying "the daughter of Minos and Pasiphae". It's like calling her a Balt or a reffo." Rose Clemente, when interviewed, spoke positively about her Italian culture, claiming it gave her the emotional and imaginative resources required for acting per se, let alone for the role of Phedra. Phedra, she believes, is "a monster of passion and emotion" that cannot be held back by the rules of decorum of the kind that reign in inhibited social groups, whether one wishes to describe them in specific cultural terms or not. Her Italian background gave her an understanding of how to "let go", this being essential because, in Clemente's view, "the audience and the performer in *Phedra* should be completely shattered by the end of the performance" and also be as "elevated at the end" as the character is herself.

Text and Production

Now to the spectators' observations. Forty-eight of them had read the play, 14 among them giving a highly critical account of the production. Some of these spectators found the translation "disappointing", "poor" or "bad". Several of those who had not read the play thought the translation became "too colloquial", giving as an example Theseus' "What's going on here?" Most of those who liked the translation ("fantastic", "excellent", "superb") had not read the play, some commenting on its accessible language and general clarity. Accessibility seemed to be a pervasive theme of commentaries, whether they referred to the text/script or to the production in its entirety. Several of those who were familiar with the text noted that what they liked most about the production was that "someone had taken the trouble to produce it". One retired woman over sixty takes up this line of thought saying she liked "the attempt to come to grips with the problems of staging a French classic of a Greek myth in a modern theatre".

We should note that, when *not* prompted to talk about a "French classic" (this question coming later), very few people refer to the play as French. Those who situate it culturally describe it primarily as a "Greek tragedy". This association is very pronounced in subsequent answers to the question asking spectators to what other plays they relate *Phedra*. "Greek tragedy", whether cited generically or named by title or author, comes way out on top, *Oedipus* well and truly the first on the list, *Medea* still prominent though some way behind. A mere six references to French theatre (three of them to Racine) pale into insignificance. However, those who give a negative assessment of the production argue that it pays little or no attention to Racine's *Phèdre* or to anything to do with seventeenth-century French drama. Gow's reflections in my interview with him suggest that Ancient Greece rather than France is his touchstone. Clemente unambiguously refers to the Greeks as the guiding force behind her performance. All of which suggests that, on this issue, the dialogue between the director, actor and spectators is not at cross-purposes, dissenting voices simply underscoring what was intentionally realized on stage.

The spectators who engaged positively with the production responded overwhelmingly to its "power", "passions", "emotions" and "intensity", these key words allowing linkages with such adjectives as "compelling", "riveting", "involving" and "breathtaking". A number stress the "simplicity", "sparseness" or "concentration" of the whole. Admiration is expressed for the performances in general or for Clemente in particular. For the sake of order in my exposition, I shall include this in my summary of answers to the question referring specifically to performances. A small group (considerably smaller than the one focusing on performance) praises Gow's direction, some noting his wise decision to carry through without an interval, which "would have lost the tension". What is also noted specifically (as distinct from generalities like "well-directed") is the "relentless quality [or "relentless pace"] of the direction" which, according to one student, "worked well to oppress the audience into a feeling of helplessness similar to that of the protagonists". About the same number of people like the intimacy of the venue and/or the close contact between audience and stage, this contact, in their view, intensifying the drama played out. A significant number of those reacting enthusiastically to the production/performances/direction also refer to the set which is invariably described as "simple", "sparse", "bare" or "minimal" - all terms concatenations of each other. The set, then, is very much part of the impact made by the production on spectators.

Set, Colour and Sound

The question concerning the set elicited clear responses (including three indignant "What set!"). They may be grouped as follows. The first and largest group concerns explanations as to how the set "did not distract from" or "allowed me [or "the audience"] to concentrate on the "language", "text", "dialogue" or "words", the "action", the "actors" or "performances", the "emotions" or "passions" and the "characters". As one woman puts it: "It's about passions, not furniture". I have listed all quoted words in descending order, that is, by how frequently they are repeated.

The second, smaller group concerns answers that attribute meaning to the set. Put differently, we could say that they attempt to link set, content, context and execution organically. Thus, for example, the set was "stark like the theme"; it "reflected the characters' trappedness and isolation"; it "gave the impression of a closed and oppressive situation"; it was "one contained but undefined space"; or, in the words of another spectator, it "supported the unity of the piece". The person I have just quoted notes "Time, Place and Action" in parentheses by way of commentary on her notion of unity. Her allusion to classical conventions joins up with allusions scattered here and there to the production's classical "elements" or "mood". Others felt the "abstract" set had a "timeless quality" or conveyed a sense of "universality".

Located in the same group of interpretative answers are those focusing on the double doors upstage and three door-like openings at stage-right. The double doors were ensconced in the bluc carpet that covered the floor and swept up the walls in one bloc of colour. The openings at the side were diagonal to the audience. They were orange-red, blue and green and were illuminated by strong shafts of light coming from off-stage. These stark colours and light threw into relief the bodies of the performers entering, standing or moving out of view through them.

Very few discuss these openings and doors, but all agree they suggest a "world outside" or some sort of external force impinging on the characters, whether "the gods" or "fate". One spectator elaborates: "I thought the fourth door representing the tragedy of fate/destiny was quite an effective contrast to the three doors of "freedom" of everyday life". Another writes: "the corridor-like entrances created a sense of confinement, a space at once connected to and cut off from the outside world". Those who single out the double doors, described by one as "opening magically", agree it symbolizes Hell, Hades or Death. One states that "it obviously led to Hades as it was through that door that Theseus returned". This is exactly what Gow had intended to communicate.

However, a relatively large number of spectators were puzzled by the side-openings and doors, asking whether they were meant to symbolize anything in particular or stating flatly that they did not understand their significance or symbolism. One or two explain they have little knowledge of "production techniques". Another one or two say they had tried to follow the actors' entrances and exits to see if these movements traced out a meaningful pattern. Several wonder about the colours of the side entrances, usually expressing their uncertainty by a question mark. A few venture an interpretation. One spectator answers decisively that red is for passion, green for youth, and blue for the state - this being the only reference ever to the high politics of Racine's play. The reference is, to my mind, all the more astute because the politics of state, even if narrowed down to a matter of struggle for political power, is fundamental both to Racine's tragedy and Greek tragedy - which feature, however, is not explored by the production.

As for the blue carpet enclosing the space, only three people attempt to decode it, one saying it has a "timeless sea-bound effect", another referring to Neptune (and presumably here connecting blue to narrative and thematic structure as well as to the denouement in Hippolytus' death). The third says the blue set reminds him of an airport lounge. If colour inspires attention, the sound effects marking a turn of events draw little attention. One or two associate them with the sea. One remarks that "the deafening noise at the end signifies the wrath of the Gods and Phedra's final destruction". Another is reminded of a 747 taking off or landing.

Actors' Performances

The actors' performances sparked off what might be called - when reconstructed after the event - a heated debate between an enthusiastic majority and a critical minority. A relatively small cluster of lukewarm reactions takes the middle ground.

The majority uses words similar to those appearing in accounts of the production ("passions", "emotions", and so on). There is also a new vocabulary. Thus, spectators speak of the faultless, unaffected, bold, brave, consistent, authentic, convincing, straightforward or unashamedly honest work of the actors. Respondents occasionally elaborate, as does, for example, a drama teacher who, having referred to honesty, adds that she finds it "quite refreshing" because "there is so much half-hearted rubbish around". We could say that, in cases like this one, aesthetic evaluations also articulate the cultural values of the speaker. This is probably just as true of commentaries homing in on the terms "passion" and "emotion", that is, these are the very qualities considered worthy of dissemination in and through the theatre. Our spectators seem to be suggesting, particularly through their own insistence on these qualities, that the theatre does not make enough use of them.

Accolades for Clemente virtually double when respondents are asked to concentrate on the actors' performances. And, although there is a good deal of material on her, it is probably best summarized by the following assessments: "Clemente plays through her body"; she "is a portrait of obsession"; the "no frills, uninhibited, unglamorized quality of Clemente's performance was superb". Arianthe Galani is praised consistently. Those who develop their thoughts point out, for instance, her "dignified beauty", "restrained characterization" and "modulated voice". Josephine Byrnes as Aricia is noted for her grace and Don Reid as Theramenes for his maturity. Brian Vriends as Hippolytus and John Walton as Theseus are rarely cited positively. They receive far more attention on the contra side of the debate.

However, from whichever side of the debate we look, we find spectators frankly bemused by Hippolytus' nakedness in the opening scene and by the fact that his torso remains bare some way into the performance. The only person who offers an explanation may be taken as providing a reply to the queries raised. She talks about Hippolytus' "stages of loss of innocence" right up until he is "clothed in a full-length coat". Our spectator hits the mark in that Gow, when discussing Hippolytus, also stresses the latter's innocence; and apart from making statements about Hippolytus, Vriends' states of undress and semi-dress were to be taken as a metaphor for the processes of hiding and disclosure enacted throughout (my paraphrase of Gow's words). Clemente is particularly interesting on Hippolytus, whom she sees as representing the virility, independence and above all freedom that Phedra desires for herself. These motifs run through Clemente's account of Phedra. Her image of Phedra as a wild stallion who, when locked in, *will* kick the walls down, eloquently synthesizes her conception of her role and how she had hoped to execute it.

Spectators in the minority - 17% of the total number of respondents - may not have missed the point, but interpret Phedra's lashing out as hysteria. Several of them feel the role required "greater depth and subtlety" and notably at the end when, in the words of an irritated respondent, "Phedra has just told us that she is dying and Panop confirms it, yet she stands up there like a prize-fighter and doesn't even totter". The same person says of the whole production that she "was longing for a change in tempo, pauses, a silence or two, in those long streams of words". Her sentiments are echoed by others who found no change in pace, tone or pitch, no shades of emotion (or "too much shouting" and variations thereof), the lines "spoken too fast", the "diction muffled" and a "lack of ensemble acting". A few found the production verged on comedy or caricature, one of them pointing out that the audience laughed at inappropriate moments. A retired doctor who liked Galani and Reid's performances exclaims: "Where was the nobility? The main characters were royal, for heaven's sake. Where was the mighty Theseus, slayer of monsters, lover and leaver of women, communicator with gods? We had a weak and vacillating man". This woman also modestly states that, although she noticed the lighting and its changes, she was "not at all knowledgeable about its use".

It is worth noting, albeit briefly, that commentaries on the light design refer to the play of light and shade, generally relating it to the characters' predicament or to the sequence of events. Many of them speak of the bright light on Phedra at the end which, in the words of one representative spectator, "had the effect of clearly exposing Phedra's torment to full view". My questionnaire did not ask about costumes. It was therefore all the more gratifying to find remarks on them, most of them favourable. A number of respondents expressed uncertainty as to why the costumes were inconsistent or so mixed - ball gowns versus Hippolytus' "Alain Delon musketeer shirt", as one spectator put it.

What can be concluded from all this about our select audience, apart from the points regarding the actor-director-spectator nexus emerging from my discussion? There does not appear to be a pronounced tendency, by whichever invariable we break down the data, that is, by age, gender, education, occupation or ethnic grouping. In other words, favourable interaction is spread across the board in proportion to the number of spectators grouped under each invariable. The same holds for those interacting unfavourably, except for one factor: academics who give a negative assessment slightly outnumber those who give a positive account. Still going with critical views by occupation: of the 26 arts workers noted earlier in percentage terms (16%), only two are critical - a male German-Australian sculptor and a female Anglo/Celtic producer. When we distinguish by ethnic grouping in order to see whether differentiation by culture is possible, we find that very few non-Anglo/Celts, even in proportion to their small number, evaluate the production critically.

Thus, in the absence of pronounced differentiation, we may have to conclude that our audience, which is privileged by virtue of its education and occupation, also constitutes a select audience by virtue of its ability to observe and record what occurs on stage, whether favourably or not. In addition, one-third of our audience is composed of STC spectators, some of whom last attended an STC production a year before seeing *Phedra*. Spectators who had been to the Belvoir Street Theatre before coming to *Phedra* follow a good way behind. Other theatres named cannot begin to compete with the number of times respondents refer to the STC as the theatre where they last saw a play production. Does this mean, contrary to Clemente's hopes and perhaps also to Gow and the STC's aspirations, that "New Stages" fundamentally plays to "old hands"?

8

CULTURAL VALUES AND THE PURPOSES OF THE THEATRE: SPECTATORS, BRECHT AND BENJAMIN

Bertolt Brecht, arguably the most important theorist in the twentieth century of the social purposes of the theatre, developed his ideas in a period - from the 1920s to the early 1950s - that had already been converted well and truly to the cinema, but had not yet invented television. Thus Brecht's concept of "epic" theatre, which he distinguishes from "dramatic" or "bourgeois" theatre, draws on the world of films so as to define more sharply those features of stage work that are the most attuned to modern times.

Take, for example, Brecht's use of montage, "splicing" and voice-over techniques for both writing and staging plays. These techniques were commonplace in the cinema, but were extremely rare in the theatre. Or, again, take Brecht's insistence on presenting surface facts and events without recourse to complex explanations as to the "deep" or "inner" psychological motives of characters who bring about events or are caught up in facts. The way films externalize rather than internalize whatever is necessary for narrative is an aspect of film that Brecht admired immensely. He admired this procedure not least because, on the one hand, it corresponded with his own ideas on making theatre and, on the other, allowed him to intensify his criticism of "dramatic" theatre, which theatre, in his view, dwelt on the psychological sub-surfaces or "hidden" motives behind actions, thereby condemning the theatre to an antiquated, regressive form that was neither good for the art nor good for society. "Dramatic" theatre is the "culinary" theatre, alias the theatre of consumerism, that Brecht despised.[1]

Now, Brecht's awareness of the technical and technological advances made by the new medium of film is not to be taken out of context, namely, the context of Brecht's socialist convictions. While Brecht appreciated the innovations of film, he linked innovation with film's capacity to reach mass audiences. We should remember that the term "mass" has a specific colouring for Brecht: it refers to the large bulk of the common people whom the arts under capitalism had ignored and whom the theatre, like film, can serve, educate and inspire - preferably to change the existing social structures. Consequently, the notion of "mass communication", when communication has a didactic-political-social purpose, is by no means a pejorative in Brecht's framework of ideas. This helps explain why, in his twenties and thirties didactic pieces (*Lehrstücke*), Brecht cast hundreds of performers in Greek-style choruses and attempted, as well, to play to hundreds of spectators. These spectators constituted a "mass" audience ("mass" defined in numeral terms) who, like his performers-workers on stage, came from the popular classes (the "masses" in political terms).

What all this suggests is that Brecht's production values were not only aligned with his particular theatrical vision, which was inseparable from his social vision, but were also directly engaged with the great debates in Europe during the inter-war and, then, post-war periods. And, as is clear from the cataclysmic upheavals of the time, the debates at issue, which can be crudely discussed in ideological terms as fascism versus socialism, were not merely a matter of images and words. Just how pertinent this context was to Brecht's definition of his theatre, understood as both social purpose and aesthetic form, is illuminated by his negative experience, as a man *of* the theatre, in America. His texts, whether plays or film scripts, as well as his directing approach, were considered too "experimental", too "European" both for Broadway and Hollywood. They were, in other words, out of step with the sociocultural conditions of America which made x rather than y accessible to American audiences and, therefore, appropriate to them.[2]

The general issue being raised, then, by these preliminary remarks is that the cultural values ascribed to the theatre, and from which can be derived the purposes attributed to it, are bound to time and place, as well as to the social space occupied by those who evaluate the theatre in the way they do. The convergence of time, place and social space occupied by social actors goes a long way towards explaining why Brecht's conception of the theatre is quite different from that of Stanislavsky, his *bête noire*. Stanislavsky did not espouse a revolutionary cause for the theatre. He was content to have it stay in touch with psychological and emotional "depths". The principle of particular convergence referred to here also helps explain why, say, Artaud, who saw the emergence of fascism, turned his back, unlike Brecht, on the potential for social intervention of the theatre; and why, say this time, Vilar, who in the early fifties preached the virtues of a "theatre for all" in France (thus supporting what could be called a democratic "mass" theatre), enveloped his mission in the language of moderation and reform. Such a language, and the political perspective which it articulated, were foreign to Brecht at the Berliner Ensemble in the GDR. Time, place, social space and social agents all pulled together differently, distinguishing the Berliner Ensemble from the Théâtre National Populaire occurring, so to speak, in parallel under Vilar's leadership.

Similar contrasts could be drawn between directors and companies who command attention today. Look, for example, at Jean-Pierre Vincent and the Comédie Française, Peter Brook and the CICT, Georgio Strehler and the Piccolo Teatro di Milano, Tadashi Suzuki and his Company of Toga, and so on. An interactive process, as happens in the cases just cited, can be discerned between the artistic objectives of these ensembles and the cultures, broadly speaking, which generate their work, and the cultures, more narrowly speaking, to which they address this work. It is a truism, for sociologists, that individuals are members of identifiable social groups, castes, strata, class fractions or whole classes - in short, members of a collectivity of some sort. It is equally true that collectivities of the kind referred to here fashion and define their specific character through the activities, values and mores that are integral to them, this being the narrower notion of culture from which broader notions such as "national culture" can be distinguished. In other words, the culture of a specific class, for example, which is only part of a society, cannot be confused or merged with the culture of a whole nation as such. Brecht did nothing less than point out this difference when he argued that dramatic or culinary theatre was *bourgeois* theatre, a theatre created by and for the middle class in accordance with its world view and tastes. Epic theatre, then, was far more than an alternative theatre contesting the dominant artistic procedures from the sidelines of society while nevertheless sharing its space and the values filling it. It was a theatre with a high vocation that attacked from within the very heart of the social bastion in order to accomplish, hand in hand with political action, the revolutionary transformation of society, in which process the bourgeoisie would lose its political and economic power and thus also its cultural hegemony.

Walter Benjamin, one of Brecht's first commentators, was quick to reiterate his friend's theses, not so much on the political goals of epic theatre as on the linkage between its purportedly filmic qualities and its educational function and effects. The 1939 second version of Benjamin's essay "What is Epic Theatre?" shows very clearly how Benjamin opposes the empathetic experience that he and Brecht believed was undergone by audiences for dramatic theatre to the experience of recognition and, consequently, of learning supposedly undergone by spectators at epic performances. Thus audiences for epic theatre respond with what Benjamin calls "astonishment" to the display on stage that they nevertheless fully recognize as being pertinent to them, and do so precisely because performances incarnate their didactic purposes without effort.[3] Performances, Benjamin seems to be saying, communicate their didactic intentions easily when they and the actors performing them are as relaxed as the audiences supposedly anticipated and formed by epic theatre as such. Benjamin sets a good deal of store by Brecht's idea that the attitude of spectators towards what they see should be "a considered and therefore a relaxed one", this considered relaxation being possible - according to Benjamin - because didactic play, which is the very stuff of epic theatre, is predicated on the "interchangeability of actors and audience, audience and actors".[4]

The interchangeability at issue has nothing to do with a symbiosis between actors and audience (which, in Benjamin's terms, would be a matter of empathy between them). It has to do with a capacity they share in common, namely, that of grasping and understanding what they are about and what they are doing in the social world of their making. And if Benjamin links epic theatre too closely to film (arguably more, in fact, than Brecht does), it is because film provides him with the most useful metaphor for explaining why epic theatre does not seek to arouse deep emotions but aims, instead, at the thinking and critical faculties of its viewers. Film, he argues, works in fits and starts and relies on interruptions to the narrative which keep audiences alert as well as make them aware of the fictitious and factitious character of the procedures (that is, "art") before them. Being aware of the technical or of what could be called the "making" processes of a stage production is, in Benjamin's view, essential to the role of spectator or at least to the spectator worthy of this name. It may be possible to extrapolate further from Benjamin's argument - Brecht's own arguments helping us along the way - and suggest that Benjamin implicitly posits a distinction between the spectator as understood above and the audience for dramatic theatre who, by supposedly being unthinking about her/his world (as well as being unaware of the factitious procedures on stage), is merely a consumer.

In fact, the notion of the spectator as a critical observer is probably better explained by Benjamin in his reflections on film than on Brecht. In his defence of film and of the "mechanical equipment" that is integral to this new medium (which, Benjamin argues, provides the perfect occasion for a fusion between art and technology-science), Benjamin notes how incomparably precisely film can represent the environment, analyze human behaviour, reveal aspects of reality that do not appear to the naked eye (or have become invisible for having been seen too often), and, as well, reveal the underlying structure of the subject of presentation, thereby penetrating through to the very reasons for the phenomenon's being what it is. This might well fit what Brecht meant by his (in)famous *Verfremdungseffekte* (translated as "alienating" or "distancing" technique). It is certain that Benjamin's discussion of how a film actor's work is split "into a series of mountable episodes", making his creation a composition of "many separate performances" and obliging her/him to present an acting self to the public rather than getting inside the skin of somebody else, corresponds with Brecht's idea of how the epic actor should work so as to prevent facile identification between the actor and her/his character, and the character and the audience.[5]

Nevertheless, the whole thrust of Benjamin's attention to the mechanics of film-making is to point out the virtues of the "age of mechanical reproduction" of which film appears, in his eyes, to be the paradigm. Film, by the very way it operates (giving the precision, analysis, grasp of reality, and so on, as noted above), puts the public in the position of knowing spectator and therefore of critic. The public is also in this position because mechanical reproduction takes away the cult or ritual value of art, leaving spectators free to stand outside the art process and survey and seize it. These spectators, who supply the "increased mass of participants" created by the mass art of film, necessarily have a collective experience, the "public", as Benjamin understood it, being a positive collective force. Brecht's notion of spectators is similarly oriented to the idea of a collectivity pulling together rather than separating off into isolated individuals. A fairly straight interpretation of Brecht gives us the following axioms. Dramatic theatre isolates people, closing them in on their emotions. Epic theatre, by contrast, is able to create a collectivity because it fosters perceptiveness and comprehension and inspires action for a common cause. By doing so, it also gives theatre spectators a status that they had never enjoyed before but which, in the modern age - or in "mass society" - is commensurate with the task of intelligent restructuring and construction required by the age.

These considerations are among many underpinning my research on theatre audiences, of which a very small part is summarized in this essay. My research was spurred on by the fact that all of the stage directors here cited - Brecht foremost among them - presuppose the existence of an interactive relationship between spectators and the stage. Their presupposition is based on hypotheses as to who their audiences *might* be, or who desirably they *should* be, given the objectives incarnated in the works presented to their audiences' gaze. Thus, what is assumed is an ideal audience, an imaginary group of spectators built out of the information theatre practitioners have about their society in general, and, in particular, about the selected groups or even coteries that go to the theatre - or who are thought by practitioners to be theatregoers.

Yet ideal audiences are not necessarily real ones, as even the artists most confident about the identity of their public are aware. Nor do targeted audiences necessarily agree with theatre artists' view of the purposes of the theatre. It would be instructive to know, for instance, whether Brecht's view of the theatre as an instrument for social change was shared by his spectators. Were they as convinced as he that theatre in the age of mass communication was not merely a transmission channel? Further, that in an age of commodity exchange, theatre was not merely an item for consumption? I embarked on my research with questions like these in mind; and based it on the hypothesis that the social composition of audiences made most sense when it was linked with spectators' evaluations of what they saw, and with what they thought to be the purpose of the theatre as such. My aim, in other words, was to flesh out a demographic profile so as to see what the theatre meant to which people, and why it had a particular value for them.

Of course, the issue of the social composition of spectators calls upon the variables usually used in surveys, that is, gender, age, education and occupation. I have used an additional one, which is the category of ethnic identity. This category generally appears in surveys only when researchers are involved in, or focus on, ethnic studies. I have used it in the area of the arts for three main reasons: firstly, because in a country of immigration like Australia the ethnic composition of the population is far from homogeneous and certainly not exclusively tied to the Anglo/Celtic origins of its colonizers and early settlers; secondly, because one of the crucial questions to ask about the arts in Australia is whether non-Anglo/Celtic minorities, in all their ethnic diversity, both contribute to and benefit from artistic activity; thirdly, whether, as a consequence of their minority status, they are included in a predominantly Anglo/Celtic established culture while, at the same time, attempting to preserve and/or develop their own culture of origin as part of Australian culture as a whole.

These questions are contingent on a number of facts determined by the

1986 Census, namely that (a) 40% of Australian residents have at least one overseas-born parent; (b) residents of non-Anglo/Celtic background who emigrated in the post-war period mainly came from Southern Europe and Eastern Europe: they are now increasingly from the Middle East and Asia; (c) Australia's multi-ethnic population has given rise to an officially endorsed multicultural policy, including a policy for the arts. The term "multicultural arts" thus refers to the arts generated by the non-Anglo/Celtic communities.

The next methodological point to make as regards this essay is that two different types of theatre and also of stage production are involved in my discussion. The first, the Sydney Theatre Company, is a state theatre and enjoys the governmental subsidization, status and prestige of its institutional rank. The second is the Belvoir Street Theatre which, although not altogether out of the mainstream, is considered to be more innovative, more adventurous and politically less conservative than the STC. The productions whose audiences I have surveyed are *Three Sisters* by Anton Chekhov at the STC and *Love and Magic in Mamma's Kitchen* by Lina Wertmuller at Belvoir Street. The first is a frequently performed classic. The second is written by a well-known film director, this being one of only two little-known plays by her, neither of which is performed frequently.

Three Sisters was staged in a traditional, realistic way with relatively detailed sets and costumes that reconstructed the sociohistorical context of Chekhov's protagonists. This gave resonance to the psychological and emotional structures of the characters which the actors developed thoroughly. Whether looked at from a directorial, acting, scenographic or musical point of view, the whole conformed to familiar images of Chekhov. The production deviated from the norm, however, in that it sought a more vigorous and optimistic interpretation, particularly of the end of the play, than is usually visible on a non-Russian stage. Even so, its performance processes were hardly calculated to challenge the Stanislavskian conventions that are integral to the STC's work in general, give or take "Australianized" variants of these conventions.

Love and Magic, by contrast, was designed to question a number of theatre practices, not least that of performing in one language. The English translation of Wertmuller's text was readjusted by director Teresa Crea. Crea translated segments of dialogue back into Italian and put key lines into Neapolitan with suggestions, here and there, of other regional languages from the south of Italy. She also inserted a number of Italian folk songs and political songs which increased the Italian-language component of the production. All told, there would not have been more than 20% of the total dialogue and songs delivered in Italian. However, this was enough to convey the impression that the production intended to be bilingual; and enough to solicit commentary from quite a few spectators who, when noting down their evaluation of the production, either wished they knew some Italian or wished that the lines comprehending spectators were laughing at had been said in English.

It must be added that, for all its openness to new plays and off-beat playing groups, this was the very first time that Belvoir Street had hosted a bilingual production. This was also the first time that Teresa Crea had directed an all-female cast in a mainstream theatre and in rehearsal conditions quite unlike those she enjoys with her bilingual ensemble, Doppio Teatro, in Adelaide. For instance, Doppio Teatro researches and prepares a work collectively. Furthermore, it takes much longer to mount a work than the four weeks of rehearsal assigned to *Love and Magic*. Doppio also devises its own playtexts, which are invariably based on aspects of Italian immigrant life in Australia. Its members are also accustomed to performing bilingually. *Love and Magic* was performed by seven women of whom all but one were of Italian background. Only two of the women had any experience of performing in Italian, one being a permanent member of Doppio, who had come across with Crea for the show. Another woman of Italian background had buried her ethnic roots so deeply that she virtually had to learn Italian to deliver the lines in the language accurately.

Apart from the novelty, for Belvoir Street, of a production in Italian and English, *Love and Magic* relied on a rhetorical, rather declamatory style of presentation which had little in common with the inward-looking refinements of Stanislavskian realism. Play was very physical, demonstrative and extroverted. It used a whole array of cinema effects (montage, zoom shots, flashbacks, break-up of sequences, and so on). None of this is surprising given that Wertmuller's text has the "feel" of a script for the cinema, her principal medium. The production's cinematographic quality, along with its theatricality, bring it into the sphere of Brecht. So too does its bizarre, larger-than-life story which is set in Naples during the fascist period. The story tells of Leonarda who, having buried twelve children, later secretly kills and dismembers three of her friends in order that her thirteenth child may live. The deaths are due, she believes, to a curse placed on her by her mother. The tale of ghosts, magic and superstition is interspersed with brief, sharp scenes that evoke the fascist period and refer, particularly, to fascist support for the war (hence the singing of *Giovinezza*, a rallying fascist march). Wertmuller is said to have based her play on the true story of Leonarda Cianciulli, whose macabre case went to the courts in 1945.

Now, given these different theatre houses and two quite different productions, what kind of audiences did they attract? And how, after having seen such productions, did these spectators formulate their ideas on the purposes of the theatre?

The audience of *Three Sisters* is predominantly composed of the social elite - thus described because of its high level of education and occupation. Of the 551 total who completed questionnaires (distributed over four performances), 60% belong to the upper two occupational classifications, "managers and administrators" and "professionals", defined by the Australian Bureau of Statistics. The largest group in the 40% left are clerks and students (8% each). Of particular note, where distribution by social class is concerned, is that only two people go into the category of "labourers and related workers".

Breakdown by ethnic grouping gives the following: 67% are Anglo/Celts; 14% are residents and/or naturalized citizens from other origins, the largest group among them being Hungarian-Australians; 10% are from English-speaking backgrounds but do not describe themselves as "Australian" (among them are American and Canadian tourists); 5% are from non-English-speaking backgrounds, but do not describe themselves as "X-Australian" (e.g., Hungarian-Australian) and therefore cannot be grouped with the 14% above. In short, Anglo/Celts are very well represented in proportion to their percentage of the total population of Australia. Minority Australians (X-Australians) are proportionally very under-represented. It should also be noted that 51% of X-Australians are university educated while 53% are in the upper two occupational categories. Compare this to 61% and 63% for Anglo/Celts. The majority of non-Anglo/Celtic Australians at *Three Sisters*, then, are similar to Anglo/Celts in that they belong to the same social elite.

Their status rather than ethnicity appears, in fact, to be the determining factor in why they come to the STC. When asked in the questionnaire what interests them about STC productions, members of the two ethnic groups here discussed uniformly refer most to the "variety", "mixture", "selection", "choice", "range" or "diversity" of shows. Similarly, when asked about the purpose of the theatre, they converge most on the term "entertainment". The terms that then appear most frequently, and can be grouped in one bloc, are "education", "instruction", "enlightenment" and "information". It must be noted that, whilst the words "entertain" and "entertainment" appear relatively frequently as single-word answers, they are more frequently linked with something else. More often than not, the linking words are "education" or "thought-provoking". The first tends to be the preferred term of non-Anglo/Celts; the second of Anglo/Celts. Hungarian-Australians almost without exception state "entertain and educate", but add nothing else. Occasionally, a more eloquent spectator elaborates, as does this Austrian-Australian: "to entertain, to educate and stretch the boundaries of our thinking and imagination, i.e. to hold a mirror up to life". Or take this Anglo/Celtic Australian: "entertain, challenge, provoke, inform, provide a social microcosm or surreal view of society".

When we take the 551 total of spectators, we find "entertainment" at the top of the list. It is cited 402 times. "Education" and variations of the same notion form a bloc of 155. That the theatre aims to present or explore values, ideas or issues is recorded 48 times. That it strives to express or touch feelings is recorded 15 times. That it has anything to do with culture also has a low score at 15 times. But lowest of all, at 8 times, is the view that the theatre is a means of communication.

The huge discrepancy between the top and the bottom of the scale suggests that our spectators place the theatre well and truly in the "entertainment industry", which industry today incorporates film, television, video, recordings, rock concerts, and so on - including the Three Tenors! Yet what kind of entertainment is it for those in the sample? The terms "enjoyment" and "pleasure" appear 39 times, which is a paltry figure compared with the score for "entertainment". Does this suggest the idea of entertainment *without* pleasure? Or is the notion of pleasure, for the sample spectators, built into the term "entertainment", therefore not requiring specification for them? It is certain that our spectators believe that the purpose of theatre is *instructive* entertainment.

It is now useful to note that more spectators in the sample see more theatre than films annually. However, when it comes to seeing more than 20 stage productions or films annually, the 20+ filmgoers exceed by far their theatre-going counterparts. Put differently, this means that there are more great enthusiasts for film in the sample than for theatre. When viewed in proportion to their number in the sample, non-Anglo/Celts are foremost among these great enthusiasts.

In order to follow up the data on the theatre in relation to the cinema, I asked other audiences at the STC, this time for Racine's *Phèdre*, to explain why they went more frequently to the cinema. (The play, directed by Australian playwright Michael Gow, had never been performed before in the country.) The spectators, on this occasion, could be described as belonging to the intellectual stratum of the social elite. Two-thirds of this stratum goes more often to the cinema than to the theatre. The overwhelming reason is cost, that is, the cinema is cheaper. Among the secondary reasons, which are all cited roughly the same number of times, is a preference for the cinema because it is "often better than the theatre". However, all told, this kind of evaluative-aesthetic-cultural judgement is outweighed by an ensemble of pragmatic concerns which, apart from the price of tickets, include the convenience of sessions and locations for film, and the fact that seat reservations are not required.

How do spectators at *Love and Magic* compare? We are here dealing with a 353 total, also over four performances. There are, for a start, marginally more non-Anglo/Celtic Australians (18% compared to 14% for *Three Sisters*). These spectators are also concentrated in the younger age bracket (21-30 years old), which was not the case at the STC. This may well suggest that the younger generation of non-Anglo/Celts who, unlike their parents, feel relatively empowered vis-à-vis the dominant culture, are nevertheless more inclined to go to a theatre perceived as "alternative" rather than "establishment". The choice of play is bound to have influenced them, as probably did its bilingual presentation - unheard of in "straight" mainstream theatre. The fact that well over half of the non-Anglo/Celts are Italo-Australian and Italian (36 of them compared to a mere 4 at the STC) supports my contention. It also suggests how, in an era of television where people surmount cultural obstacles by staying in the privacy of their home, ethnic minorities might be drawn out of their houses and into the theatres: namely, by the theatres' appealing to their cultural parameters, no matter how discreetly (or inadequately) these parameters are defined by the theatres themselves.

This, of course, still leaves us with the vexed question of whether, in an age of mass communication and art industries (with art commodified as never before - Brecht turn over in your grave!), the theatre is increasingly condemned to being a luxury item for elites of one kind or another. We have seen how the intellectual elite at Gow's production of *Phedra* nominated cost as the most important reason for going less frequently to the theatre than to the cinema. Now, while it is well known that traditional intellectuals are today pauperized, economic factors go hand in glove in society with cultural ones. And art culture is necessarily linked to education, if only because inculcation and instruction expose people to the arts, develop their capacity to absorb the arts and, occasionally, refine critical apprehension of them. Pierre Bourdieu, needless to say, has hammered home these points long enough. They have stuck and continue to be valid, despite the fact that his critique of "distinction", which is conferred upon individuals by virtue of their "bourgeois" education, undercuts those aspects that he concedes are positive in "bourgeois" education, even if it is profoundly inegalitarian.[6]

In the framework of these issues, it is relevant to note that exactly half of the Italo-Australians and Italians at *Love and Magic* are tertiary-educated, professional people. Moreover, none of them is from the lower occupational categories. Which data suggests once again, as in the case of the STC, that ethnic minorities who either objectively have access to the theatre or subjectively choose to have access to it are predominantly from the middle classes.

Reflections, by this group, on the purpose of the theatre revolve around "cultural development", "to be exposed to a different frame of reference to mine", "to see people's different viewpoints" and "to communicate ideas". Yes, "entertain" appears with these observations. It also appears with "educate" or "enlighten". Italo-Australians and Italians are not particularly distinguished, as a group, by their viewpoint, except for the fact that none of them refers to the theatre as a forum for social commentary or for social change. On the other hand, this type of Brechtian observation distinguishes Anglo/Celts, Secondly, when offering their assessment of *Love and Magic*, Italo-Australians and Italians almost invariably approve the use of two languages in the production. None of them, however, goes so far as to say that one of theatre's goals in a multicultural society could be the dissolution of cultural-ethnic distance and fear. It takes a number of Anglo/Celts to voice strongly their approval of how "our multicultural society" is celebrated by the production. One of them proclaims triumphantly: "all women, all wogs - only at Belvoir!"

When taken as a whole, the audience orders and ranks its terms much like the audience for *Three Sisters*. Thus "entertainment" comes out on top, followed by "education" and its collocations (quoted 204 and 82 times respectively). What distinguishes the perspective of the audience of *Love and Magic* is, firstly, its proposal of a much wider range of purposes, and, secondly, its emphasis on the theatre as a medium for showing social conditions, developing social awareness and working for social change. In these respects, Belvoir Street spectators may be said to have a Brechtian streak. The range of purposes, apart from the socially oriented ones just mentioned, and which are fifth in order after "entertain", "educate", "provoke thought" and "stimulate", are the following (most repeated ones only): "artistic expression", "portrayal of life", "presentation of ideas", "challenge", "communicate" and "express emotions". Emotions are towards the bottom of the list, as for *Three Sisters*.

Is it possible to conclude anything about the cultural horizons, if not expectations, of *Love and Magic* spectators? Is entertainment the prime value of their national culture, as well as of their group/class culture? It is clear that they share this value with spectators at the STC; and, like STC spectators, they place cognitive apperception above creativity and emotions. A few spectators, unsolicited, refer to "old Italian movies", which *Love and Magic* reminds them of, or to Lina Wertmuller's films. Or else, when not directly speaking of Wertmuller, they refer to the cinema, stating, for example, that the theatre is "more spontaneous" and "more in the present . . . of what is happening". One respondent (New Zealander) who cites entertainment last in his commentary explains that the theatre's purpose is to "discuss/reflect on issues in society in a personal/direct way (compared to film/TV, for example)".

It would be hard to resist, in the context of a discussion where Brecht is relevant, the reference to Brecht from a German woman academic when she speaks of the production's *Verfremdung*. As is well known, Brecht invented the concept in order to help define what he meant by "epic" theatre. *Verfremdung*, then, was the principle of non-sentimentality, of direct communication and appeal to reason which allowed spectators to grasp the sense and significance of what they were viewing and encompass in their comprehension of theatrical fiction a critical understanding of social realities. This so-called "distancing" principle or "effect" (*Verfremdungseffekte*) was a prerequisite for the development of the spectators' consciousness of themselves as agents of action belonging to some larger social whole. The spectator here quoted who refers unpretentiously to Brecht's celebrated concept is just as direct in her assessment of the theatre's role in society. For her, the theatre's purpose is to "overcome individual isolation, create group-consciousness". This, too, is suitably Brechtian.

NOTES

1. For a detailed statement by Brecht on the difference, as he understands it, between "dramatic" and "epic" theatre, see "The Modern Theatre is the Epic Theatre". *Brecht on Theatre*, trans. John Willett. London: Methuen, 1964, pp. 33-42, and especially p. 37 for the famous table drawn up by Brecht in which he itemizes the characteristics of each type of theatre, each item defined in terms of its opposite in the opposing category. Needless to say, all of the writings by Brecht which are translated and annotated by Willett in the book cited are relevant to the discussion above, as are Brecht's commentaries and essays on the cinema. For the latter, I especially refer to Bertolt Brecht, *Sur le cinéma*, trans. Jean-Louis Lebrave and Jean-Pierre Lefebvre. Paris: L'Arche, 1970 and *Journal de Travail: 1938-1955*, trans. Philippe Ivernel. Paris: L'Arche, 1976.

2. For an illuminating account of Brecht's differences of opinion with women and men of the theatre, though certainly not only with them, on matters of art, society and politics, see James K. Lyon, *Bertolt Brecht in America*. London: Methuen, 1980.

3. Walter Benjamin, *Understanding Brecht*, trans. Anna Bostock. London: New Left Books, Verso Editions, 1983, pp. 15-22.

4. ibid., p. 15 and p. 20 respectively.

5. Reference here is to Benjamin's celebrated essay "The Work of Art in the Age of Mechanical Reproduction". *Illuminations*, trans. Harry Zohn. London: Collins/Fontana, 1973, pp. 219-53. The phrases cited are on p. 232.

6. The "classic" work by Pierre Bourdieu on the subject is, of course, *La Distinction: critique sociale du jugement*. Paris: Les Editions de Minuit, 1979.

9

SPECTATORS, THEATRE TYPES AND THE SOCIAL PURPOSES OF THE THEATRE

Four Types of Theatre

The material I am presenting here is based on a small portion of my research on audiences for different types of theatre. Although categorizing them is not a straightforward matter, they may be described as establishment-mainstream, radical-mainstream, workplace-community theatre and bilingual-bicultural theatre. The theatre companies/venues and productions which I have taken to represent these four types are as follows: *Three Sisters* directed by Richard Wherrett in 1990 at the Sydney Theatre Company; *The Tempest* directed by Neil Armfield in 1990 at the Belvoir Street Theatre in Sydney, and *Love and Magic in Mamma's Kitchen* directed by Teresa Crea in 1991 at the same theatre; *No Fear* directed by Joan Murray in 1991 for the Melbourne Workers Theatre; *Tinti di rosso/Red Like the Devil* directed by Teresa Crea and performed by Doppio Teatro in 1991 in Canberra as part of the Australian Theatre Festival. The bilingual title of Doppio's production indicates that it was performed in Italian and English, both languages being more or less evenly mixed for the whole show. The company's very name - "doppio" means "dual" or "double" - shows clearly its aim of developing its work from two languages and two cultures.

It must be noted further that, although *Love and Magic* and *Red Like the Devil* were directed by the same person, they were not performed by the same performance group. *Love and Magic*, in other words, was not a Doppio Teatro production. It was staged on the initiative of Belvoir Street as this theatre's contribution to Carnivalé, the annual, so-called "multicultural" festival held in Sydney where non-Anglo/Celtic "ethnics" - generally, though not exclusively, those who live in or near the metropolis - showcase their particular heritage and talents. What is displayed, then -

often with great flair and vitality - ranges from the folk arts of cooking, costumes, dance and music to the more formal arts of play production, poetry reading, concert recitals, and so on. Since Belvoir Street makes a point of welcoming performance groups that have quite different artistic and gender politics and styles, *Love and Magic*, for all its linkage with "multiculturalism", can be considered without any difficulty as a Belvoir Street production. Teresa Crea was sure in her own mind as to how *Love and Magic*, albeit not to be confused with her usual Doppio work, fitted into her artistic biography. She explained in an interview I conducted with her in Canberra that members of Doppio work collaboratively, generally taking three months of preparation for a show. During this time they work hard physically on scenes, moulding them and the text used for them according to their explorations together. A draft text is usually prepared in the months preceding the workshops, as occurred in the case of *Red Like the Devil* whose material Crea had researched and assembled before Doppio colleagues tried it out for elaboration and refinement. This process of collective preparation for a text and a show where the two organically grow out of each other has nothing in common with the rules of play of mainstream theatre. The rules provide, to boot, a statutory four to six weeks of rehearsal, which allows little time for experimentation with physical movement and expression from whose immediacy artistic decisions may be made collectively. *Love and Magic*, while shaped by Crea in the light of her experiences with Doppio, essentially had to stay within the managerial and practical limits set by Belvoir Street Theatre for productions mounted under its auspices.

Nevertheless, although *Love and Magic* is to be put under the heading of radical-mainstream theatre, it must be cross-referenced with *Tinti di rosso/Red Like the Devil* because of its affinity with the bilingual and bicultural world of the latter. *Love and Magic* intermittently uses Italian - sometimes rather extensively, as occurs in the opening scenes - in order to stress the play's cultural context, the production's cultural horizons and the director's and actresses' cultural origins. All but one of the seven actresses who perform in the show are of Italian background, north or south. Teresa Crea's family is from the south. The script is by Lina Wertmuller, who is from the north. It is the second and last that she wrote for the stage. Wertmuller, of course, is highly celebrated internationally for her zany films, most of which show the clash between northern and southern social structures, belief systems, mores and customs - the northern, industrial sphere asserting its hegemony over the rural, economically impoverished south. The motifs, emotional and imaginative excesses, and dark humour of Wertmuller's films mark the script of *Love and Magic* deeply.

A few more points regarding the typology of radical-mainstream theatre should now be included in the discussion. Audience members who completed questionnaires distributed by me in both 1990 for *The Tempest* and 1991 for *Love and Magic* invariably refer to Belvoir Street as "innovative", "experimental", "risk-taking" and "off-beat". These terms are among numerous variations on a theme that draws attention to the specific character of this theatre venue and how it differs from other well-established, well-viewed theatres. Comparison between theatres, which was not solicited by my questionnaires, was volunteered spontaneously by spectators. Thus they tend to cite the Sydney Theatre Company as a point of reference. The STC, in their opinion, is a mainstream theatre from which Belvoir Street must be distinguished. When they use the term "mainstream" for Belvoir Street, which happens frequently in their remarks either on the production being surveyed or on what they like generally about productions at the theatre, they almost invariably qualify the term with some complimentary statement as if to show that "mainstream" is not being used in a pejorative way. Hence phrases like, for instance, "mainstream, but risk-taking" or "mainstream, but original" appear in spectators' remarks. Descriptions by spectators like the ones I have just cited, together with the general reputation enjoyed by Belvoir Street Theatre as well as its management's goal of keeping it in the mainstream without, however, forgoing its "avant-garde" aspirations, help explain why I am using the name "radical-mainstream" for it. Armfield, whose production of *The Tempest* was received enthusiastically - and sometimes rapturously - by most of my respondents, is something of an in-house director of Belvoir Street and may be said to have contributed greatly to its reputation for originality and artistic quality, which these respondents seemed to think of as a feature of "good" mainstream theatre.

There is another important link between the productions chosen for survey, other than the one between *Love and Magic* and *Red Like the Devil*. The link, this time, concerns *The Tempest* and *Three Sisters*. These two productions were performed within a few months of each other, *The Tempest* coming first. Their consecutive appearance on the Sydney stage suited my research purposes in that my project as a whole incorporated a number of questions concerning classics. One of them had to do with how audiences interact with classics mounted at different theatres. My assumption was that different theatres acquire different styles over a given working period; also, that they project the vision of their artistic director or mainstage director, this projection being part and parcel of their "house" style. At the STC, for example, the title of Chekhov's play lost its customary article "the" because director Richard Wherrett wished to extrapolate from Chekhov's Russian world and give its situations universal meaning. In other words, in Wherrett's view, the unfulfilled hopes and dreams of three particular sisters could well reflect the disillusionment of any three sisters anywhere in the world. Richard Wherrett was the founding director (1979) of the Sydney Theatre Company, from which he resigned in 1990 - *Three Sisters* being his last work for the company - to become the director of the Melbourne International Festival (formerly the Spoleto Festival founded by Gian Carlo Menotti, who is the founder of the Italian original). The STC is a state theatre subsidized by both the state and federal governments in accordance with its official status (hence the term "establishment" for it).

It is interesting to note that Wherrett's conception of this particular classic as having general applicability across social time and space is echoed by quite a large number of spectators. One of my questions asks them what they think a Russian classic has to say to audiences in Australia today. Again and again spectators explain that classics are "universal" and "timeless", and deal with the "human condition" which, because it is a condition of being human as such, is eternal and can never change. The spectators in the sample, in other words, interact with the production *within* the parameters set by the director. Or else, putting it differently, they share the director's viewpoint on what defines classics. It could perhaps also be claimed that the concordance between Wherrett and those spectators who are in tune with him is due to the climate of interdependence built up between the STC, Wherrett's productions during the years he spent there, and their audiences over the same period of time. We should also consider the hypothesis that an interactive climate of the kind at play here is fostered by what may be called the dominant culture. The culture holding sway may well be generating and propagating through the institutional channels at its disposal (theatre houses, the media, schools and other educational institutions, and so forth) the idea that theatre classics are unbounded, universal and "timeless" rather than phenomena bounded by, though not necessarily restricted to, the societies and cultures from which they emerge.

The whole issue of how so-called classics are spatially, geographically and culturally specific and yet able to cross cultural borders and communicate sense is indeed very large. It involves, among many aspects, the strictures of time. The passage of time and, with it, the processes of history *do* make plays and productions outdated, outmoded, and even irrelevant in respect of a short time-span. The very same thing occurs across long periods of societal development. Are some of the plays which are deemed to be outmoded "classics"? Why, when and for whom are designated works "classics"? And when, why and for whom do they cease to exist as "classics"? Sociologists of the theatre must take into account, in some way, the complex issues raised by these and similar questions in order to understand the multiple threads that bind theatre works to their audiences and, through their mutual dependence and interaction, to their societies. Theatre works and their audiences share to a lesser or greater extent the society that they are both in and shape and form. The network of actions implied in this schema makes theatre an institution that, for all its durability, cannot escape changing historically. The transformations undergone by the theatre as a social institution provide clues to its purposes, perceived and real, for this or that collectivity at particular points in its history.

Chekhov's *Three Sisters* and Shakespeare's *Tempest* are too well known to require a synopsis. The staging of each play, on the other hand, does require several comments. The *mise en scène* of *Three Sisters* emphasizes the life-like, sociopsychological truthfulness of the characters and their dilemmas. Consequently, the actors pay attention to detail, to what might be called the outward expression of their characters' motives. Attention is paid to the interaction between characters. The performers take care to create what Wherrett, in an interview I conducted with him, calls "the appearance of being real". His intention is repeated in the stage design, costumes and props. All visual effects capture the play's historical period, the seasons marking the passage of time, and the time zones separating morning and evening, and day and night. Time is central to the production for it underpins the transitions undergone by the characters. The lighting design is of special importance in that, translucent or opaque, light accentuates the temporal context of events. This, too, makes concrete Wherrett's intention of conveying clearly and simply the themes of time, displacement and passivity which he discerns in the text and to which he wants to be faithful.

The Tempest, by contrast, is a symbolic and suggestive production. The actors are barefooted and sit, slide, crawl or glide on the floor, their positions and movements generating considerable visual impact. Moods, whether mysterious, magical, foreboding or humorous, blend into each other. Sensory perception is heightened through such arresting images as the earth-covered stage, the metal and stick bric-à-brac lining one of the stage walls, and floor lights that flash on or off, sometimes in unison with sound effects that conjure up a storm, or Prospero's incantations, Caliban's entrances and Ariel's exits. In the opening scene, a toy ship tossed upon black oilskins figuratively represents the storm and shipwreck that bring Prospero and Miranda to Caliban's island. The lights, earth and bric-à-brac are concrete images for place and narrative sequence, Prospero's discourses on nature and art, Prospero's construction of Caliban as a "natural" savage to be tamed though not civilized, and so on. Ariel weaves in and out of various spaces, from spaces she commands on the stage to several spots she makes her own in the audience. The fact that the part is played by a woman accentuates the master-slave relationship between Prospero and Ariel, and, in another vein again, between Prospero and Caliban. Caliban's enforced obedience to his master is symbolized by the long rope which is tied around his neck and drags along the earthen floor. For people who are familiar with the work of Peter Brook and Patrice Chéreau, the production is like a compilation of citations from these masters, or a homage by citation to them. For instance, no one who has seen Chéreau's *Peer Gynt* can fail to recall that production's extraordinary storm scenes in which a miniature ship is thrown up by a huge black cloth stretched across the entire stage and simulating waves that rock, toss and roll a real ship trying to battle against them. The rather unconstrained and unconventional - for Australia - presentation of *The Tempest* both from a performance and design point of view stimulated a number of spectators to comment on the "exciting", "unusual", "daring", "alternative" style of production that they associated with Belvoir Street Theatre.

Now for a few words on the subject matter of *Love and Magic in Mamma's Kitchen*, which does require a brief introduction. The play is the story of women during the fascist and war period, and particularly of Leonarda who, from southern Italy, is moulded by her region's religiosity and superstition. Leonarda's thirteenth and only surviving child is at the war. In order to save him, she placates the evil spirits that she believes have cursed her by killing three close friends, dismembering their bodies and turning them into soap. Wertmuller bases this bizarre fiction on equally bizarre fact. The real Leonarda went on trial in Italy where she shocked the national consciousness and died in 1945. The production, for its part, foregrounds Leonarda's cultural icons - a mixture of phantoms, witches and madonnas, and spells and prayers. These icons authenticate Leonarda and her friends' cultural world and, at the same time, make it alien, distant, "other", much as Wertmuller does in her films on southern immigrants going to the north of Italy. The production works in with the filmic quality of the script and, as occurs in Wertmuller, highlights what can be rendered in a comic-grotesque fashion. Crea's principles of short, sharp narration and splicing and montage, besides recalling Wertmuller herself, conjure up the memory of Brecht.

The third type of theatre of interest here is the Melbourne Workers Theatre. This theatre is probably a unique genre, at least in Australia, in that it was formed in 1987 "in response to the growing attacks on trade unions and their members". These words come from the company's policy documents. The MWT is a professional theatre ensemble in residence at the Jolimont Train Maintenance Depot which is in the centre of the city. It is not only workplace-based but is also worker-controlled insofar as the union support group, which advises the company's management committee, consists of union organizers, shop stewards and rank and file union members. The union support group, the management committee and the artistic advisory group, which develops theatrical projects, cooperate and work together. Their principal aim, as formulated in their 1991 statement, is "to make theatre for, with and about working-class people in a way that reveals the complexities and contradictions of current working-class struggles to improve living conditions". There can be no doubt, following this formulation, about the MWT's interventionist purposes on the social, pedagogical and political planes.

Every production mounted by the company is usually first performed during the lunch break at the Jolimont canteen. It is then toured to other workplaces, generally, though not exclusively, for lunchtime performances which last for 25 minutes during the 30 minutes assigned for lunch. Sometimes the break is extended through agreements with employers and unions, allowing 50 minutes of performance time. What all this means is that there are essentially two versions of the same production, the longer version adapted to fit the predicted constraints. Evening performances take place in community halls and, when possible, in prisons. They usually give the long version. Community-hall performances are the company's public performances, that is, they are not confined to people actually working on the job, whether in railway yards, factories, building sites, and so on. The fact that productions, besides being oriented to workers in general, address workers of selected immigrant communities indicates how the MWT strives to reach the non-Anglo/Celtic groups that are integral to the Australian working class in toto. By doing so, the company shows that it properly includes in its horizons members of diverse ethnic communities: it is not, in other words, ethnocentric, which in Australia's history has entailed Anglo-centricity to the exclusion of all "wogs", alias non-Anglo/Celts. The MWT's principle of inclusion by ethnicity means that members of a given ethnic community, who are not always necessarily railway, industrial or white-collar workers, are not necessarily doomed to the status of outsiders because they are linguistically and culturally disadvantaged. Disadvantage through language and culture is determined by their being non-Anglo/Celtic immigrants per se.

This state of marginalization in respect of the dominant culture, which is mediated through English, especially affects relatively recent immigrants such as the Turks, the Vietnamese, the Chinese and various Arabic-speaking groups. Most of them are politically and/or religiously vulnerable, as is the case of the Turks, among whom - to complicate matters from an ethnic-political point of view - are a significant number of Kurds. If the so-called Turkish community in its entirety is somewhat alienated vis-à-vis the majority culture, the Kurds are doubly alienated. They are an ethnic minority in respect of Turks (this situation originating in Turkey) and are a minority in respect of Anglo/Celts in the host country. What is, then, a source problem for Kurds is compounded by the conditions of the target society to which they emigrate.

These are among the considerations that prompted the MWT to turn its attention in 1991 to the Turkish community. And, in order to understand the community better as well as communicate more effectively with it, the company hired a Turkish liaison officer to be part of its artistic advisory group. The result of the MWT's collective work was *No Fear*, a production whose protagonists are Turkish workers. The script devised for the performance was inspired by events that began to occur in the Ford car plant in Melbourne shortly before the company started its research. Ford's management was attempting to bring in a trade-off for wage rises by introducing a process called "rebalancing". This "rebalancing" essentially amounted to demanding that workers speed up production, thus changing their current ways of working and giving them a greater workload than before. A Turkish shop steward who claimed that he had tried out the new production method and had concluded it was impossible to use was sacked, according to the company for refusing to work. After the shop steward was sacked, some 200 workers on his shift stopped work. The shop steward went on a hunger strike to protest against the company's treatment of him. The Vehicle Builders' Union, in the meantime, had accepted the decision of management and expected the rank and file to rally round. Most of the 200 workers who had originally gone out in support of their shop steward went back to work, leaving about 20 who refused to resume work in the current circumstances. They were subsequently sacked. The shop steward continued his hunger strike for a month. He was joined towards the end of his campaign by two or three more hunger strikers. None of them was reinstated. The real-life events provoked enormous debate on whether individuals, especially those who were also union members, were empowered to act against union resolutions. The debate was all the more inflammatory because the workers who had gone on the hunger strike had opened up the issue of what a unionist's position should be with regard to individual extreme actions.

The incident takes on a new dimension in *No Fear*. Instead of going on a hunger strike, two Turkish workers, a man and a woman, occupy the factory manager's office. Their action is not premeditated. It happens spontaneously after they are sacked for refusing to trial a new speed line. The turn of events sparks off a heated discussion between them as to the significance of what they have done. The argument is subsequently developed from a different angle by the union organizer, a woman, with whom they had been debating while she was locked outside the office and whom, after much persuasion, they let in. The performance concludes with their capitulation to the union's demands without, however, leaving the impression that their show of force was totally useless. The fact that their fellow workers go out on strike against the new speed line, thereby showing their solidarity with them, suggests that collective action negotiated through unions (and with their backing) in the interests of workers is possible, and desirable.

The production goes at a quick pace. Turkish actors play the workers. An Anglo/Celtic woman plays the union representative. Gestures and movements are open, lively. Props are at a minimum. Black, metal, wire-mesh boxes serve as tables, chairs and podia. A venetian blind is hung upon a black metal frame at door height, suggesting an office window. This minimalist set is consistent with the pared-down, streamlined plot and dialogue which depend, for their punch, on the direct, physically articulate style of play. Music written for the show and songs in Turkish give a "folk" quality to the production. Small segments of the dialogue are delivered in Turkish.

This brief account of *No Fear* will help us place spectators' remarks on what they consider to be the main purposes of the theatre. We have already noted the MWT's expressed purposes. Looking from on stage as well as off it is crucial, since one of my central questions is whether spectators and practitioners conceive of the theatre in a similar way. In posing this question, I keep well in mind the fact that spectators complete my questionnaires after they have seen a particular kind of production. Whatever the production, it probably reflects to a greater or lesser degree the house style of the company or venue. Or a production may reflect a director's vision or even only her/his habitual way of staging. Thus a particular production may influence how a spectator talks about the purposes of the theatre in general.

These provisos are essential. Nevertheless, my data indicates that spectators' views on the purposes of the theatre as such are not contingent on the production that they have just seen. If influenced by it, their views have been developed, just the same, over time. It seems that how they conceive of the purposes of the theatre is formulated in terms of the *type* of theatre at issue (establishment-mainstream, and so on, as defined above) as well as in relation to their social group, sociocultural values, aspirations, imagination and other factors integral to their existence. What needs to be determined, when these elements are taken into account, is the impact of dominant values on group values; similarly, whether specific types of theatre create values specific to them and - interwoven in the process - also create specific types of audiences whose values are perpetuated by the theatres that they go to. If this is the case, then stage and audiences merely combine to reproduce the values in place. It may be taken as given that different theatre types presuppose and seek out different audiences, those that are thought of as "their" audiences.

The fourth and last type of relevance to this study is bilingual-bicultural theatre, which is here represented by Doppio Teatro's *Tinti di rosso/Red Like the Devil*. Doppio Teatro was founded in Adelaide in 1983 and is still, to my mind, the most important example of a theatre that grows out of a specific ethnic community and aims to return, to that community, the history, cultural particularities, immigrant experiences and present state of affairs which define the community and distinguish it from any other. Since its inception, Doppio has been composed of professional arts workers, each of whose gifts and skills have been absorbed in ensemble creation. The company's emphasis on sharing the whole preparatory process and thus being collectively responsible for the artistic outcome (or "product", as contemporary - and reified - jargon would have it!) goes a long way towards explaining how it became a cohesive unit. This also helps explain how Doppio, although functioning on a shoe-string within the economic as well as ideological confines suffered by all community theatre groups, has succeeded in creating works having the strength, polish and finish normally expected of professional, "high" art and/or mainstream companies. Extremely sophisticated from both a conceptual and artistic point of view, Doppio belied the idea in vogue during the eighties that community theatre was a people's theatre of some sort and, therefore, by definition could not aspire to "real" art. One of the ideological constraints imposed on community theatre, principally from non-community sources, has to do precisely with this kind of image, an image which, by projecting the notion that community theatre is necessarily amateur and, consequently, necessarily of inferior quality, continues to widen the rift between theatre considered to be art, on the one hand (mainstream), and theatre presumed to be a pastime - or, at best, a social service - on the other (community theatre). These remarks are just as relevant for the Melbourne Workers Theatre which, like Doppio, proved that a people's theatre and art were not a contradiction in terms.

Doppio, though fully professional, is community-based and community-oriented insofar as it turns for material, inspiration, legitimation and audiences to Italian neighbourhoods, clubs and associations which generally group people from this or that particular region in Italy. If Italians and Italo-Australians are intended to be "its" audience, first and foremost, Doppio Teatro nevertheless does not turn down invitations from prestigious organizations like the Adelaide Festival or growing ones like the Canberra Festival. *Red Like the Devil* was performed at the Canberra Festival after having been premiered in Loveday in South Australia, where the play is set, and also in Adelaide earlier in 1991. In other words, Doppio does not cultivate a fringe or unofficial "no frills" brand name. Indeed, its appearances at venues thought to attract well-heeled and/or practised spectators of whatever ethnic group bring in members of the Italian community who would probably not have gone there. How it extends audiences for both community and mainstream theatre, merging the boundaries between them, is a measure of Doppio's public importance and success. And its public role is to be seen, as is also the case with the Melbourne Workers Theatre, in how it provides a great social benefit to the community that it targets in the first instance - this being the "service" dimension of its work. The term "service" refers here to a broad, humanitarian conception of democratic access to the theatre rather than to a purely utilitarian, narrow notion of theatre as something fulfilling some bureaucratic function.

However, unlike the Melbourne Workers Theatre, Doppio makes no special claim on the working-class component of its ethnic constituency. Its primary concern is not with a class perspective which, as the MWT shows, cuts across ethnic boundaries, but rather with what could be called an ethnocentric vision. Its principal aim, then, is to articulate the problems of cultural identity experienced by Italians and Italo-Australians and, in doing so, recover the cultural heritage belonging to them that had been attenuated and fragmented through the processes of immigration. Since immigration has had, and continues to have, a similar impact on any immigrant group, whatever its ethnicity, Doppio's ethnocentric focus, while homing in on the Italian community, is by no means a factor of exclusion.

Given its line of vision, it is not surprising that Doppio productions are clustered around several themes: the weight of past history on the present; the struggle experienced by the children of immigrants who wish to affirm their social, cultural and psychological independence from their dispossessed parents; the binding strength of traditions, notably of the rural traditions on which the southern Italians who have emigrated to Australia rely, albeit now in an alien environment which, in addition, does not even attempt to accommodate "foreign" values, customs and behaviours; the cultural stagnation that is a consequence of freezing life in the past and in memory; the difficulties of integration, where pressures to conform with the prevailing norms collide with the incomprehension, resistance or rejection felt on both sides, Anglo/Celts urging adaptation and commitment to the "Aussie" way while denying the channels for entry into it, Italians, meanwhile, afraid to let go of the very thing, "identity", that had assured their survival and was still likely to help them survive. The substance of Doppio plays foregrounds issues of immediate concern to Italians and Italo-Australians. But the company also highlights Italian popular culture, particularly from the south, by using the legends, tales, masks and especially music and songs that are intrinsic to it. By doing so, Doppio demonstrates the beauty of that culture, declares its validity for the arts in Australia, and challenges the negative conceptions and prejudices regarding southern Italians that abound among Anglo/Celts and are current among northern Europeans who have settled in Australia, a small group of northern Italians included in them.

Red Like the Devil draws on all these aspects of Doppio's repertory but concentrates on a little-known facet of the history of Italians in Australia, that is, on their internment during the war when Mussolini's Italy was Britain's enemy and, consequently, also Australia's. Loveday, where the production was first performed, was the site of one of these internment camps. The play tells of Francesco Fantin, an anarchist who was hounded out of Italy by the fascists and who was subsequently put behind barbed wire in Australia along with fascists and communists, all of them deemed indiscriminately to be possible traitors to Australia. Fascists, anarchists and communists are taken by the military authorities running the camp to be one and the same entity, irrespective of the ideological differences irreconcilably separating them. Fantin befriends a communist in the camp who tries to warn him about the foes within - the fascists - and the foes without - the army officers guarding the camp. Although he is wary about stating his political allegiances, Fantin donates money to buy sheepskins to assist the allies fighting in Russia. This fact is discovered by the interned fascists. Realizing that the mounting tensions between him and them are putting his life at risk, Fantin officially asks the camp captain to transfer him to another camp. The captain refuses. Fantin is assassinated by the leader of the fascists.

The production is made up of short scenes, some being flashbacks to the events in Italy leading up to his exile. A poignant scene shows Fantin as a child discovering his mother hiding an anarchist flag. Another shows his mother urging his flight after news has broken that his anarchist friends have been arrested. Marching soldiers singing *Giovinezza*, a fascist hymn, interrupt this scene. Yet another episode in Fantin's past life shows his relationship with Clara, who questions the heroics of men and speaks of the courage of women. Other songs, both folk and political, break up the dialogue and create different time dimensions, the past converging on the present. The chorus of the Hebrew Slaves from *Nabucco* by Verdi "frames" the argument on freedom running right through the production. Sets are simple. A table, a stool, a peeling knife and then, later, Fantin's pot plant sketch out the curiously quasi-domestic environment the internees make for themselves in the camp. Metal sculptures in the shape of picture frames are hung at the back of the stage, the whole suggesting a barbed-wire wall. These are images of war. Metal parrots on the wall represent the type of craft objects internees made when they were not working. They are also signs of the natural environment in which the unnatural camp was built. Lighting is hot - essentially white and red - to denote, like the birds, the semi-desert landscape where Loveday was located. Besides conveying heat, it captures the feeling of loneliness, isolation and desperation for which the barbed-wire wall presented to the spectators' gaze is an apt metaphor. Fantin's memories of the past are, by contrast, swathed in muted spotlights and shadows.

Who Spectators Are and What They Say

Three Sisters

What, then, do the spectators attending such distinctive productions have to say about the purposes of the theatre? Audiences for *Three Sisters* overwhelmingly agree that the theatre's main objective is to entertain people. The words "entertain" and "entertainment" appear 402 times in 551 completed questionnaires. This 551 represents 2% of the total number of viewers for a six-week season. The hierarchy of key words gives us, at 155 times, "education" and its collocations (thus "instruction", "enlightenment", "information", "teaching" and "learning"). The next in line is "stimulation" (56 times) followed by statements on the theatre's purpose of presenting/teaching values, ideas and issues (48 times). The view that the theatre seeks to give pleasure or touch the emotions is not held widely (39 and 15 times respectively). Nor is the idea that it should "interpret life in its many aspects", here quoting a Greek-Jewish Australian. References to "life" or "people's lives" appear 37 times. The notion that the theatre has a cultural purpose appears rarely.

The references to culture that do appear may be summarized pretty well exhaustively by the following: "to tell me what is going on in other cultures, either today or several centuries ago and to make me more Kultural!" (Anglo/Celtic female librarian); "to educate on diverse cultures" (Anglo/Celtic travel consultant who is a woman); "to widen one's horizon culturally" (retired Anglo/Celtic woman); "the theatre is a way to teach culture" (retired Hungarian-Australian woman). Now and then a respondent will note "cultural values", "cultural exchange", "development of culture" (Greek-Australian male manager) or simply say "culture" or string it with "relaxation, leisure" (Franco-Australian male student).

It seems that STC spectators place entertainment above all other purposes even when they combine "entertainment" with other terms, thereby indicating that, in their view, entertainment is not the *sole* purpose of the theatre. Nor is the primacy of entertainment in any way weakened by the following kinds of observations of which, comparatively speaking, there are few: the theatre's purpose is "to stretch the boundaries of our thinking and imagination" (Austrian-Australian), "express new movements in the arts" (Anglo/Celtic-Australian) or "exist for playwrights, actors, directors, etc., to indulge their favourite passion" (also Anglo/Celtic). References like these to the artistic endeavour that the theatre indubitably is occasionally include the compositional elements of stage work. Take, for example, "I enjoy the artistic creation of sets and costumes" (from a clerk in her sixties who notes in her preceding phrase that the purpose of theatre is "to be entertaining"). Or else we have this: [the purpose of the theatre is] "to entertain and to create an illusion of a kind of magic through the spoken or sung word, stage setting and lighting" (a woman in her fifties involved in marketing).

The majority of *Three Sisters* respondents are between the ages of 21 and 50. Most are university educated and are in the upper occupational categories, namely, managers and administrators, and professionals (teachers, doctors, lawyers, and similar liberal professions). Most of them (78%) are from an English-speaking background. Those who are not nevertheless belong to the same social stratum by virtue of their education and occupation. We could probably say, on the basis of this data, that the STC is a mainstream theatre precisely because it plays to comparatively well-educated and well-off audiences, in short, to an established rather than, say, a social-climbing, "new money" middle class. An additional characteristic that helps to define it as mainstream theatre is the orthodox taste of its audiences. This orthodoxy penetrates their discussion of *Three Sisters* as well as their remarks on what they like about STC productions in general and what they would like the company to stage in the future.

The Tempest

Turning now to *The Tempest* where there are 364 respondents who represent, as occurred with *Three Sisters*, 2% of the total number of viewers. This audience also essentially belongs to the upper echelons, give or take some minor discrepancies. There are, for example, more professional people at *The Tempest* and fewer managers and administrators. (Compare 52% professionals and 7.6% managers at *The Tempest* with 47% and 13.2% for the same categories at *Three Sisters*.) There are also more students and fewer clerks at *The Tempest* (16.4% and 5.4% compared with 7.9% and 7.8% at *Three Sisters*). The comparatively strong presence of students under twenty at this production possibly has to do with the fact that *The Tempest* was set that year for the Higher School Certificate. Those not at high school are studying at a university. The great majority of the audience already holds a university degree. Thus, going by their occupational profile combined with their educational one, the spectators answering questionnaires for *The Tempest* could be described as the intelligentsia of the social elite that goes both to Belvoir Street Theatre and the STC. It is probably no coincidence that the theatre cited most by *Tempest* spectators as the one they last attended before coming to see this production is the STC - and the answer was given before the *Three Sisters* season had opened. STC respondents, for their part, cite Belvoir Street Theatre most frequently. Moreover, the intelligentsia of the social elite at Belvoir Street is predominantly Anglo/Celtic (85%). Australians from non-English-speaking backgrounds along with those who do not claim to be Australian in any shape or form (they describe themselves as straight "Dutch", "German", and so on) constitute 13% of the respondents (2% give no answer). At *Three Sisters*, 19% is of non-English-speaking background.

Now, a glance at the key words shows that, once again, "entertainment" tops the list (233 mentions). What is significantly different, however, is that proportionally fewer spectators place "entertainment" first on their list than is the case for *Three Sisters*. And from here stem many more differences. To start with, the notion that entertainment is the main purpose of the theatre is couched in terms that qualify and perhaps even weaken the importance of the notion itself. Take, for instance, this statement by an Anglo/Celtic childcare worker in her twenties: "entertainment firstly, involving issues (current or otherwise)". Or this from a university-educated woman in her thirties who describes her occupation as "mother": "Theatre should stimulate - either aesthetically or intellectually, entertainingly or emotionally". Or take again: "I go primarily for a good night's entertainment, but I also think theatre is a perfect vehicle for bringing social issues to the fore" (analyst-programmer in his fifties). Or again: "To entertain - sometimes to educate - something to lose myself in. Fact, fiction or fantasy" (Anglo/Celtic manager in her forties). These examples are fairly typical of the more elastic and also more articulate train of thought as well as of expression of *Tempest* spectators when compared with those at *Three Sisters*.

The next most striking difference is the arrangement of the key words when they are mapped out according to numerical frequency. *Tempest* spectators strongly believe that the theatre's purpose is to make people aware of social issues. References to this idea and to variants of it are noted 124 times. As we have seen, the idea was voiced relatively infrequently by *Three Sisters* spectators. Which factor helps to distinguish the upper-stratum audience at *The Tempest* from its homologue at *Three Sisters*: the first is more socially oriented and possibly has a more developed social consciousness than the second. Even so, although

Tempest spectators advocate the theatre's *engagement* or social commitment, they do not support didactic theatre. The terms "educate", "enlighten" and "inform", when clustered, are low on the list (39 appearances). So are the opinions that the theatre should "provoke thought" (32 times) or "stimulate the intellect" (8 times). Third in the order of priorities after "entertainment" and "social issues" is the idea that the theatre aims to create an artistic experience for its audiences and give them pleasure. Only 5 spectators refer to how the theatre broadens people's cultural horizons or is part of a culture and, therefore, gives insight into it.

There does not appear to be a pattern of response according to ethnicity. Spectators of non-English-speaking backgrounds reply very much like the Anglo/Celts do. Let us look briefly at the high school and university students, since they form a relatively important group and can be isolated relatively easily for special attention. On the whole, they cover much the same range of ideas and in much the same order of priority as respondents who are older than them. Taking the high school students first. Anglo/Celtic high schoolers do not, as a general rule, elaborate on their thoughts. For this reason the following reply from one of them stands out from the ordinary. She writes: "entertainment, to be aware of social issues and see some real talent and famous plays brought to life by modern actors". And her statements on plays and actors put her in the group of remarks I have noted above which attribute some artistic purpose to the theatre. High schoolers of non-English-speaking background, while generally going into the same areas covered by most spectators - again as I have noted them above - nevertheless differ in how willingly they elaborate upon their ideas (not a feature, as I have already said, of their Anglo/Celtic counterparts). And it is their development of themes that recur across the board that enriches these themes. Take, for example, this from a Swiss-Australian: "I think its purpose is to entertain while making someone aware of social issues. The entertainment value is necessary, I think, to attract the audience". Or again, let us take this from a Polish-Australian high school student: [the purpose of theatre is] "mainly to entertain, but as I see different types of plays etc., I think that they're becoming a main way of communication and education about social issues: they're also bringing different social groups together (i.e. different age groups, etc.)".

University students, whatever their background, tend to echo their juniors in the kind of development of ideas they provide. However, the following reply from a Yugoslav-Australian is quite distinctive. After having alluded to entertainment and social issues, he continues that the purposes of the theatre are to "try to promote Australian culture, initiate and inspire new works from local writers and directors, especially from minorities, e.g. aborigines, migrants, etc".

When we leave the student body and look at the rest of the respondents across all the ethnic groups, we see a fairly consistent pattern of replies. This from a Sri-Lankan university-educated male may be said to cover many of the ideas expressed by *Tempest* spectators as a whole. He states: [the purposes of the theatre are] "educate, stimulate, entertain, raise awareness, challenge, provoke, criticize". A few spectators across the ethnic groups note that the theatre ought to deal with political issues or transmit a political message. But this interest in politics appears almost as rarely as allusions to culture. If anything may be said to distinguish respondents from non-English-speaking backgrounds, it is their referring less than Anglo/Celts to the idea that the theatre sets out to deal with social issues, past or present. A Lebanese-Australian teacher in her fifties states plainly that "plays which focus mainly on social issues often BORE me because the message tends to be negative". An Italian academic could not be more eloquent when he states that the purpose of the theatre is "to be a theatre, i.e. a space where actors perform. All other purposes are welcome and useful and meritorious but are complementary".

Love and Magic in Mamma's Kitchen

A similar observation on how spectators' viewpoints tend to converge on much the same ground irrespective of their ethnic grouping can be made of audiences for *Love and Magic*. Variations offered by non-Anglo/Celts modify the main points made by respondents taken as a whole, Anglo/Celts setting the tone of the replies. But these variations stay within the boundaries set by the majority. What this suggests is that ethnicity or cultural identity as such does not determine spectators' views. As far as this particular sample goes, at least, it would seem that social status - social class, stratum, seam, or what you will - is the dominant factor in shaping what may be called common opinion. And the results for this particular sample, as we shall see, correspond with those for *Three Sisters* and *The Tempest.*

Let us look at *Love and Magic* spectators in order to substantiate these points. We are here dealing with 353 respondents who represent 7% of the total number of viewers over four weeks. The majority (74%) is of

English-speaking background, 65% of them being Anglo/Celtic Australians. Of the remaining 26% composed of non-Anglo/Celts (the percentage significantly higher than for *The Tempest*'s 13%), 10% are Italian or Italo-Australian. The high proportion here of them relative to *The Tempest* (where they are virtually non-existent) must surely be linked to the fact that the production is directed and performed by Italo-Australians, and, moreover, in the legitimating context of Carnivalé. A number of questions arise. Does this mean, for instance, that people of Italian background, Greek background, and so on, who live, and many of whom were born, in Australia are not familiar with Shakespeare? Do they consider him to be foreign, not part of their own culture? And this irrespective of their introduction to Shakespeare in high school? Or does the fact that most casts in most theatres have Anglo/Celtic names suggest to them that the theatre is primarily a matter of Anglo culture and, consequently, for people of English-speaking background? Are they, then, alienated from the theatre? And if alienation is at issue, to what extent is it related to what might be called the ideology of the theatre in Australia, namely, its recourse to conventional Anglo models of performance (which, of course, have long been abandoned by such innovative British companies as Cheek by Jowl and the Théâtre de Complicité)? In addition, to what extent does such an ideology of the theatre anticipate audiences commensurate with these models, thereafter reproducing audiences who are not only especially responsive to them but also expect the models to which they have become accustomed? The question of expectation, as I have just formulated it, leads to the issue of how expectation (or user-demand, or consumer-demand - take your pick of contemporary computer/commercial jargons!) feeds into a vicious circle in which all parties involved in making the theatre a veritable social institution are merely mirror reflections of each other. If it is true that people get the governments they deserve, do they get the theatres they deserve?

All these questions are directly tied to the study of sociostructures and cultural values and viewpoints undertaken by my research as a whole. Whatever, in the final analysis, are the answers to them, the point to notice here is that more than half of the respondents from non-English-speaking backgrounds are in the liberal professions. Half of the Italians and Italo-Australians, when isolated for the purposes of closer investigation, also prove to be professional people. The next largest groups are clerks and students. The breakdown of occupations for Anglo/Celts follows this pattern. The data on social stratification indicates, once again, a relatively homogeneous group cutting across ethnic categories. In other words, no one ethnic group is distinguished by its different class status.

The fact that the occasion is Carnivalé, which is presented as being a people's event, does not change the class picture emerging from the data. There are two respondents from an Italian background who belong to the category of "salespersons and personal service workers" as defined by the Australian Bureau of Statistics. The same, or close on the same, number of people from other backgrounds, Anglo/Celtic included, appear under this particular occupational classification. There are no people of non-Anglo/Celtic background, Italian or otherwise, who fall into the blue-collar categories of "plant and machine operators, and drivers" and "labourers and related workers" devised by the ABS. Which suggests that, although *Love and Magic* was billed under Carnivalé, the supposedly "ethnic" event par excellence, it did not bring out and embrace - or Carnivalé at Belvoir Street Theatre did not do so - the disadvantaged groups *within* the ethnic minorities integral to multicultural Australia. Furthermore, the only people who figure under the two lowest occupational categories of the ABS are people of English-speaking background. There is a grand total of 4 of them out of 262 respondents who are Anglo/Celtic-Australians (229 of them) or come out of another English-speaking background (for example, English, Canadian, New Zealander)! The data unfortunately suggests that the people's festival of Carnivalé in a mainstream theatre, even in a radical-mainstream one, is not for the people.

What is the picture regarding the purposes of the theatre as drawn collectively by our respondents? Not surprisingly - since this also happened in the case of *The Tempest* - the range of observations was wide and required coherent assembly. Once again (perhaps now predictably!) "entertainment" comes out on top (cited 204 times). It is followed by "educate/enlighten/inform" (82 times) which, as you can see from my slashes, I have grouped together for the sake of coherence and manageability (otherwise we would all be lost in a sea of details). This bunch is followed by remarks on how the theatre should provoke thought (65 times), stimulate (36 times), and comment on society, deal with social issues and conditions, and show social change (33 times for the last three put together on society). Then comes the idea that theatre aims to be artistic and creative (31 references). The idea that the theatre wishes to enrich people culturally, celebrate cultural difference or provide a "cultural outlet" (though the respondent quoted does not say for whom) figures 10 times. Minuscule though the association between theatre and culture may be, it certainly compares favourably with *The Tempest* where, for a larger sample, there are a mere 5 allusions to culture.

As happened for the preceding two productions, *Love and Magic* spectators link references to entertainment with other purposes that they assign to the theatre. More often than not, the linkage is with "education" or a variant thereof. The process of linking shows that spectators attribute multiple purposes to the theatre. In addition, it shows how they refine crude terms or terms that are open to crude interpretation. The following words from an Anglo/Celtic university student in her thirties are an excellent example of the two points I am making on the linking process. She says: [the purpose of the theatre is] "entertainment primarily; social challenge/education/thought provoking secondarily (maybe this is what I find entertaining)". Our spectator's parenthesis is worth noticing because, in it, she attempts to understand what she means by "entertainment". Furthermore, her reflections modify the notion of "pure" entertainment or show-biz which has been touted for so long and so noisily by so-called commercial theatre.

Can any conclusion be drawn from the fact that "entertainment" comes swiftly to spectators' minds? Its very frequency may point to the notion's ubiquitous presence in society at large. Thus, whatever its origins, the notion has become hegemonous; consequently, the ideal of being entertained appears to have become part and parcel of general social expectations. The thoughts of an Anglo/Celtic translator are illuminating in this regard. She writes: "I don't think there is a single "main purpose" of theatre. One normally expects theatre to entertain above all else, but it often raises social and/or moral issues and provokes strong emotional feelings. What dominates depends on the play being performed. I did not find *Love and Magic* an entertaining play, but I did find it sad, tragic, and very thought-provoking". This spectator is, of course, absolutely right about the changes of emphasis according to the play "being performed". And what is striking in a mass of data where, without any shadow of a doubt, references to entertainment predominate is that this spectator announces a principle that she holds to be true for her society ("One normally expects").

It is clear that I have begun to construct a "dialogue" between spectators. It could well include the voice of an Italian teacher who states: "I don't know, never thought about it. I go to the theatre possibly for any of these reasons: (a) to be entertained (b) because I know a text and like it (c) to be exposed to a different reality, perspective, frame of reference from mine; to get a new insight". Is it significant, in the context of a discussion about hegemonic expectations, that a spectator who "never thought about" the purposes of the theatre should then proceed to think about entertainment, writing it down first? It may not necessarily be first in her own hierarchy of values. We cannot know from her formulation whether she gives "any of these reasons" priority. But it may be possible to say that she echoes a dominant sentiment precisely because it is so widespread as to appear self-evident and, as it were, be of second nature.

Clearly, detailed responses like the ones quoted above (and they are representative samples) cannot be transposed easily into a numerically hierarchical word order of the kind I have established. The nuances and even richness of perception and conception are lost. Nevertheless, schemata are a reasonable guide to spectators' views concerning the role of the theatre in society. Schemata are not adequate - at least not in hierarchical table form - when it comes to organizing material on spectators' interaction with productions. Here a different kind of methodology is required.

No Fear

With these reflections in mind, though not in the foreground for the immediate task at hand, let us look at the survey of *No Fear*. The first question to ask in the light of the preceding information is whether notions of entertainment predominate in the accounts of spectators for this production. Let us remember that the production was geared specifically to members of the working class, whether blue- or white-collar workers. As we have seen, white-collar workers are a very small part indeed of the audiences discussed up until now. Blue collars, for their part, are as good as non-existent: a paltry 2 out of 551 at *Three Sisters*; 2 out of 364 at *The Tempest*; 4 out of 353 at *Love and Magic*. Audiences for *No Fear* do, indeed, turn out to have a significantly different social base from those at the establishment-mainstream and radical-mainstream theatres at issue.

There are 224 respondents for *No Fear*. A cursory glance at the demographic data (which, to date, is tentative) shows that unskilled as well as skilled workers (the latter including plant and machine operators, and drivers) well and truly outnumber any other occupational category. They constitute 28% of the total 224 respondents. Tradespeople or those who have an ambiguous status in that they have trades skills but are not self-employed (for example, those who give their job description as "electrician") and may well be employed as workers by the railway or in car plants, for example, constitute 25% of the total. My guess is that some of the people who generally correspond to the ABS descriptions for its occupational classification of "tradespersons" belong, strictly speaking, to the category of skilled workers. If this is the case, the percentage noted above for the combined group of skilled and unskilled workers should be higher. Until such time as I am able to resolve this ambiguity, the figures will have to stay as being tentatively devised. Among the remaining categories figure 15% of professionals (for example, union leaders, project officers, writers, and arts workers, the latter including government bureaucrats involved in arts grants, and the like). There is also a fairly significant group of nurses. Prison inmates, who form part of the sample, frequently sabotaged the question on their employment, replying that they were car thieves, bank robbers, drug dealers, and the like, which descriptions could well explain why they were in jail. (They could also well fit, by the way, their regular employment, but are not listed as such in the occupational categories of the Australian Bureau of Statistics!) When replies were straight, prison inmates usually had a trade (for instance, plasterer or motor mechanic) or held down menial jobs (kitchen hand, car cleaner).

Now, when this rather heterogeneous audience is taken as a whole, "entertainment" surprisingly does *not* top the charts by a long shot, as occurs in our previous samples. In fact, it is marginally *behind* the grouping composed of the terms "educate", "enlighten", "learn", "understand" and "inform". Next in line is the idea that theatre "strives to get the message across", an idea well and truly in favour among the nurses in the sample. This might be termed the militantly didactic view of the theatre. Then comes the notion that the theatre seeks to express "thought" or "points of view" or "the contradictions between workers and bosses". Towards the bottom of the list are to be found references to culture (and notably to the opinion that theatre should present other cultures and foster interest in them); to society and social awareness; to the working class as such. Those speaking of the working class state quite firmly that the theatre should help it and should show the struggles and problems of this class. Also in the lower rungs of opinion are reflections on audiences. Here respondents note that the theatre aims to empower, stimulate or involve audiences. Right at the bottom are references to emotions and to the theatre's purpose of telling stories. Emotions fare poorly in all the cases covered by my survey. Story-telling is cited only by spectators at *No Fear* and *Love and Magic*, where it is also at the bottom of the list.

Are there any significant trends marking out any of the groups composing audiences for *No Fear*? Do the Turks and Turkish-Australians, who were targeted specifically by the production, assign purposes to the theatre in culturally-specific ways? Is there, in other words, a discernible cultural influence on their views? The second question, in particular, is extremely difficult and cannot be answered adequately from the limited information available. Still, let us see what indications the data does give us.

Putting it briefly. When the data is examined from the standpoint of occupational categories, it is clear that railway and other blue-collar workers believe as strongly as people classified as professionals that the theatre seeks to deal with "real-life drama", "people's experiences" and "other people's ideas on different issues". "Entertain" and "educate" (along with affiliated terms) appear in both these groups, "entertain" usually preceding the latter. (Thus we might have "entertain and educate". The word order in this sort of coupling does not contradict the fact noted above that, all told, "entertain" is not the term most frequently cited.) Since the few references made to culture are usually made by the (usually) university-educated professionals, an exception to the rule is all the more noticeable. The exception is a moulder working on the railways who states that the purpose of the theatre is "to teach culture". A few references are explicitly made to the unions whose responsibilities, among other related topics, are, after all, the subject matter of the script written for the production. The references come from blue-collar workers. Thus we have this fitter's assistant: "to show the people that everyone should support each other and the unions, and vice versa".

When, on the other hand, the data is viewed from the perspective of ethnic categories, two main groups of remarks have to be made. The first pertains to non-Anglo/Celts in general, who tend to put entertainment in second place in their order of thoughts. Some simply do not mention entertainment at all. The second bloc of remarks concerns the Turkish community in particular. The large majority of respondents from this community are skilled blue-collar workers. A significant group among them is composed of high school students. All attended the public performances that are always given by the MWT. When it comes to seeing how Turks and Turkish-Australians express their views on the purposes of the theatre, they *invariably* stress education, putting it well and truly at the top of their priorities for the theatre. Furthermore, they very rarely refer to entertainment at all, not even as a last possibility. (Anglo/Celts, we have noted, tend to place it second.) The rare mentions of entertainment among respondents of Turkish background come from the high school students among them. The particularity I am noting means that the lexical combinations of Turks and Turkish-Australians take on a very specific character. Time and again these respondents explain that the theatre should "provide people with political and cultural knowledge", "provide messages" or "communicate clear messages", "help the working class with social and cultural issues", or "take up the issues and problems of the people and educate them".

The political underpinnings of the last cluster of observations, which are very typical of the Turkish and Turkish-Australian respondents, emerge fully into the open in other commentaries. Two examples of what may be called political advocacy and highly developed political consciousness will serve to illustrate the point. An electrical welder states that the theatre's purpose is "to form a relationship with the masses; to question and take up their problems; to make them think". A man who simply describes himself as a worker states: "to unite people; to demonstrate the oppression of the people; to show social reality to the oppressed people". All these observations were written in Turkish, which may suggest that these respondents are still uncomfortable about using English - or will use it only when absolutely necessary.

So let us return to the question posed earlier regarding culturally-specific views. Is it possible to say anything relatively conclusive about the social roles attributed to the theatre by people of Turkish background? Do they have a culturally different perspective - different, that is to say, from views expressed by others included in the data for *No Fear*? One thing is clear. No other group vocalizes, so consistently and so strongly, such an unmistakably political - and politicized - viewpoint. It may well have satisfied Brecht, Piscator, Mayakovsky, Tretiakov and similar practitioners of the theatre involved in the great political struggles of the first half of the twentieth century and in which they sought to involve theatre audiences. Once the political dimension of the Turkish respondents, male and female, has been noted (women are by no means politically weaker in their outlook), we still have to come to terms with the question of whether this political dimension is actually a *cultural* trait. Or should we primarily explain the political militancy evident here in terms of the *kind* of immigrants they are? Most of them emigrated for economic reasons. A good number of them are also political refugees. Are they, therefore, primarily distinguished by their sociopolitical experiences, world view and status, their being Turkish rather than, say, Lebanese being of secondary importance? If our answer is in the affirmative, then the notion of ethnicity, of cultural identity per se, must take second place. Or should we, on the other hand, enrich the concept of ethnicity and not define it as a matter of cultural identity pure and simple, but as a matter in which culture is inseparable from politics? In this case, culture would be an all-embracing phenomenon, the political particularities of a given society being integral to its culture. I opt for the second alternative. However, whatever the most appropriate frame of reference regarding "culture" turns out to be, there can be no doubt as to the profound difference between the Turkish minority and the Anglo/Celtic majority culture in respect of the purposes of the theatre.

Red Like the Devil

It is now time to turn to the results of the survey on bilingual-bicultural theatre, the fourth and last type of theatre involved in this study and which is here represented by Doppio Teatro's *Tinti di rosso/Red Like the Devil.* As is clear from my earlier remarks on the company and this production, the broad category of bilingual-bicultural theatre is here illustrated by *Italo-Australian* theatre. It must be remembered that, unlike the Melbourne Workers Theatre, Doppio Teatro does not focus on the working class as such, nor, therefore, on the working-class constituency of the Italian community. I am, of course, including under the general heading of "Italian community" those who describe themselves as Italo-Australian, this description serving the people who have taken out Australian citizenship or whose children were born in Australia.

The survey covers 219 spectators over four performances, which gives us 25% of the total number of viewers of the production. Since we are dealing with a company that aims primarily, though certainly not exclusively, to reach the Italian community, however it is broken down analytically in terms of social class, the ethnic composition of our respondents will be of particular interest to us. Anglo/Celtic-Australians are once again in the majority at 59%. People from other English-speaking backgrounds (New Zealander, English, Canadian, American) form a group at 8%. Australians of non-Anglo/Celtic origins constitute 26% of the total. People belonging to non-English-speaking backgrounds but who do not describe themselves as X-Australian (e.g., Chinese-Australian) make up 5%. The remaining percentage gives no answer. Those whose background is Italian, whether they define themselves as Italo-Australian or Italian (and three Italians show up in the group marked "non-English-speaking background"), constitute 18% of the total number of respondents. This is a much higher percentage than appears for *Love and Magic*, especially when taken in proportion to the total number of respondents for each survey. (Compare 219 respondents for *Red Like the Devil* with 353 for

Love and Magic of whom only 10% are of Italian background.) Given the general pattern emerging from all the data examined up till now, it is not surprising to discover that, once again, "entertainment" comes out on top of the word list. It is cited 75 times, followed, in order of importance, by "educate" and its collocations (46 times), then by the view that the theatre "expresses" (or "explores" or "broadens") ideas (33 times) or "provokes thought" (25 times, variations on the same theme included in the count) and, finally - still in the upper cluster of terms appearing most frequently - by references to how the theatre "communicates", "brings across" or "conveys" ideas, messages, meanings or a moral (24 times). Once again, feelings and emotions are low on the list, though not as low as in some of our earlier cases (17 mentions). The idea that the theatre is connected to "real life" or mirrors or reflects it is also mentioned 17 times. We then have the view that the theatre's purpose is to state messages (13 times), present issues (11 times) and provide social comment or raise social awareness (10 times). References to culture appear less frequently than may, perhaps, have been expected at a bilingual-bicultural event. They occur 10 times and usually allude to how the theatre disseminates or helps create an understanding of different cultures.

Our sample also gives us spectators who are aware of the relationship of actors to audience or of how the theatre aims to "stretch" audiences (8 references to audiences). Once again, as in most cases before this one, references to creativity and art are few and far between (6 times), as are those to actors and artists (also 6 times). We also find a few references to the idea that the theatre's purpose is to show aspects of "the Italian way of life". The spectators who attribute this specific purpose to the theatre either take the question asked of them to refer directly to *Red Like the Devil* (which means that they have misinterpreted the question) or are influenced in the answer they give by this particular production. Story-telling also appears at the bottom of the list, as happened, as we have already seen, for *No Fear* and *Love and Magic*.

All told, then, the respondents for *Red Like the Devil* could be described as being fairly earnest insofar as they place a good deal of value on education, information, instruction, ideas, thought, messages and meanings, all of which terms indicate that they have a cognitive approach to the theatre or see it as a place where statements appealing to their reason are made, generally for their edification. In this respect they are rather like respondents for *The Tempest*, although, as we have also seen, most of the audiences covered by my survey, with the exception of those for *Three Sisters*, tend to stress the educative dimension of the theatre, whether of the fairly "straight" kind, as was the case for *Tempest* spectators (emphasis on learning as such), or of the more militant and more politically oriented kind, as was the case for *No Fear* and particularly for the Turkish respondents in the audience, whatever their gender or age. Furthermore, although respondents for *Red Like the Devil* put entertainment at the top of their list, as occurs everywhere *but* at *No Fear*, the number of times that this term and its off-shoot "entertain" appear in proportion to the total number of respondents is lower than in other cases, except for *No Fear*, where, as we already know, "entertainment" scores second. Viewed from this angle, that is, in terms of proportion, spectators at *Red Like the Devil* give a mitigated first vote to entertainment. Take, for example, the difference implied by a count of 75 for entertainment for 219 respondents for *Red Like the Devil* as distinct from a count of 204 out of 353 respondents for *Love and Magic*. Thus, although numerical measurement is no more than an indication of trends, it adequately points out that what I have called a "mitigated first vote" for entertainment in the case of *Red Like the Devil* makes spectators at this production more like those at *No Fear*. We may, then, be able to conclude, on the basis of this particular piece of data, that audiences for workplace-community theatre are more like those for bilingual-bicultural theatre, which is also community-based, than they are for any other type of theatre.

In the light of this tentative conclusion ("tentative" because it is based on one rather than on several supporting pieces of evidence), it is important to isolate the Italian-community component of the whole audience for special attention. What do we see, in fact, in the 18% of respondents who are Italian or Italo-Australian? The first thing to note is that half of this group is made up of high school students. (Since high schoolers are an important part of the sample audience for *Red Like the Devil*, making up 24% of the sample, it may be worth looking at them in some detail shortly.) The remaining half is primarily made up, on the one hand, of arts workers who are theatre directors, television producers and actors, and, on the other, of teachers, clerks and those who fall into the category of "managers and administrators". The group, then, may be said to fall relatively neatly into a small number of sub-groups, as defined by people's occupations.

This, of course, simplifies the task of coordinating the responses of the Italo-Australian group. Thus, when the high school students are taken in one bunch, what we find is their tendency to see the theatre as a message-communicating medium. Only one of these students refers to entertainment. The arts workers, on the other hand, tend to give a high priority to entertainment, linking the latter to the purposes of stimulation, education, "expanding one's horizons" or "pushing the boundaries of people's experiences". One of the television producers in the sample puts together a whole range of purposes, as follows: "to educate, entertain, enlighten, motivate, provoke, excite, question values, to play with language and ideas". By contrast, one of the managers in the sample narrows the issue down to *Red Like the Devil*, and does so deliberately, unlike those referred to above who appear to have misunderstood the question. She states: "This time - how we Italians were treated; to show others we are just like them". High school students figure prominently among those who directly connect the question regarding the purposes of the theatre to the particular example at hand. Thus we find such observations as "show what Italians were going through at that time" or "make people aware of the difficulties Italians had". Precise interpretations like these of the production itself do not lead our students to extrapolate or abstract from the production to cover the general cross-cultural issues which it also set out to explore. Only one of the respondents in the Italo-Australian group notes the production's underlying cultural project. This person is a teacher in her thirties who states that the purpose of the theatre is "to broaden understanding of both cultures; to give a new culture - Italo-Australian - an identity". Although one of several who connects the "purpose" question specifically to *Red Like the Devil*, she is the only respondent in the 219 sample as a whole who is finely tuned in to the motive force behind Doppio's work, namely, that it is giving voice to *Italo-Australian* culture, which, because it is a hybrid, is indeed a new culture.

The issue of culture is generally taken up by Anglo/Celts, whose main points of reference are well illustrated by the following examples. A university-educated environmental planner states that the theatre's purposes are "transport from daily routine; give meanings, interpretation of society, history, culture - across cultures and within". A theatre administrator in her forties writes: "Ideally, to broaden awareness of other possibilities, ideas - a cultural yardstick! If it entertains *and* awakes/heightens awareness, so much the better". A retired university-educated person (who did not note her/his gender) writes: "To entertain and instruct. Another purpose is to disseminate an understanding of other cultures, e.g. the Russian, French, Greek, etc. classics". By the same token, Anglo/Celts also take up issues to do with art. The words of a technical college-educated houseworker in her sixties eloquently sum up allusions made by others to how the theatre aims to give talented people an outlet for their abilities. She writes: "Entertainment; venue for audience participation;

outlet for skills in acting, stage design, choreography, voice production, musical ability, etc". A designer laconically notes: "To keep middle-class audiences happy, and serious actors/artists serious and hungry". But a theatre worker exclaims: "What a question to ask a practitioner! TO CHANGE LIVES".

Well, if Anglo/Celts are more inclined than Italo-Australians to discuss matters of culture and art, neither ethnic group gives evidence of the acute sociopolitical awareness that distinguishes the Turkish spectators at *No Fear*. As for the high school students in our Canberra audience, they are concerned with how the theatre expresses ideas and emotions, communicates messages, and shows aspects of life - generally "through entertainment", as one of them puts it. There is nothing startlingly different about the viewpoint of Italo-Australian high schoolers from their peers of other ethnic origins, except for the fact that they hardly refer to entertainment at all. Taken as a whole, the group of students, though articulate, tends to echo the points raised by those who are older than them. In other words, they do not stand out as having a different or "alternative" point of view. We are not here faced with a generation gap of any kind.

When we look right across the spectrum provided by my data on the different types of theatre attended by respondents, it is quite clear that the majority view focuses on entertainment. I am including in the majority view the multiple non-Anglo/Celtic groups represented, albeit in a very small way, in my surveys. We have seen how these non-Anglo/Celtic groups - the Turkish group excepted - essentially share the viewpoint of Anglo/Celts. In doing so, they are absorbed, to all intents and purposes, by the majority culture. Furthermore, by not offering a noticeably alternative role to the theatre, they can be said to be sustaining that culture. Given this general picture, what the respondents from the Turkish community seem to throw into relief is just how firmly implanted the notion of entertainment is in the majority culture's conception of the theatre. And the picture holds good despite the shades of meaning attached to the term "entertainment". Perhaps what we should be doing now is seeing whether, today, this scene is peculiar to, unique to, Australia or whether - and where and why - the scene is being replayed elsewhere in the world.

PART IV

PERFORMERS

10

BICULTURAL PERSPECTIVES: INTERVIEWS WITH ITALO-AUSTRALIAN ACTRESSES

What is presented here is a montage constructed from sections of interviews with (in alphabetical order) Rose Clemente, Eva Di Cesare, Laura Lattuada, Lucia Mastrantone, Dina Panozzo and Peta Toppano after they had completed a four-week season of *Love and Magic in Mamma's Kitchen* directed by Teresa Crea. Performances took place at the Belvoir Street Theatre in Sydney in October 1991.

All performers, with the exception of Rose Clemente, were interviewed within several weeks of the end of the show. Interviews were held separately, except for the one with Laura Lattuada and Lucia Mastrantone with whom I spoke together simply because it turned out that way and not for any particular reason. The fact that this was a trialogue will show in how I have fitted the pieces together.

A whole host of circumstances prevented me from catching up with Rose Clemente until early January 1993. Thus my interview with her is like a retrospective gazing upon an experience that the other performers discussed *sur le vif*, while it was still more or less a part of their present. Because it looks backwards, time having ripened some of the thoughts we share in it, I use this interview as something of a coda, as the last fragment in a collage that by its very nature cannot have a conclusion. I hope to have captured its inconclusive quality by splicing the interviews and grouping voices around particular issues. The material, then, does not follow the chronological line of the interviews as such. The exception is my interview with Rose Clemente whose linear development I have kept. However, it is not presented in its entirety, any more than are the other reflections given with such generosity by all. I thank these remarkable actresses for their time and energy.

One performer from *Love and Magic* is missing from this montage. She is Teresa Haremza, a beautiful, immensely gifted Polish singer who was the only non-Italo-Australian in the cast. Although she was not part of the Italo-Australian group of special interest to my research, I would like to have heard her thoughts, the thoughts of an "outsider" in relation to the group of Italo-Australian performers with whom she was working. Once again, as in the case of Rose Clemente, circumstances prevented us from meeting, only in Teresa Haremza's case far more dramatic obstacles were involved.

The last two essays on spectators in this volume give a summary of *Love and Magic* and some brief indications as to how it was directed and performed. Consequently, there is no need to repeat them here. What I would like to point out, however, is that this montage does not concentrate on the production's artistic processes as created by its performers, but focuses on the issues raised by the very existence of the production itself. These issues address the many concerns that link essay to essay and run like a filigree right through the book. At its heart is the premise that theatre is an art as well as and because it is a cultural practice, that is, an activity exercised in a particular social context whose values, fantasies, dreams and fears permeate it, making the theatre a *caisse de résonance*, a sound chamber, like no other inhabited collectively.

Maria Shevtsova: Do you see yourself as an Italo-Australian actress?

Laura Lattuada: When I see another Italo-Australian actor, I find myself saying, "Yes I am an Italo-Australian actor, yes I do that as well, I work in both languages, I am bilingual"; but then when I am talking to Anglos, I just call myself an actor because I resent the fact that they put me in a box - you just do community theatre and it's just about your nationality. That's not just what I want to be. I suppose that's what the market is for me because I've been stereotyped in some ways as being just an Italian, because of my face, the way I look, and so on. But I'd rather just call myself an actor.

MS: Tell me, have you had any difficulties in getting jobs in - let's call it for the moment crudely - "Anglo" theatre?

Lucia Mastrantone: Yes, in mainstream theatre.

MS: Why? What is being said to you?

LM: First of all, the funniest experience that happened was with an agent. I walked into an agent. She looked at me and said, "Lucia Mastrantone, you don't look Italian", and she smiled at me. It was almost like "Maybe we could use you because you don't look Italian". I thought "Fine". She still didn't take me on. Whenever I've worked with mainstream companies, it's tokenistic, it's the exotic thing. It's hard for me to get work in mainstream that does not require an exotic aspect to the show. So therefore it is really limited what people put me in and the amount of work I get.

MS: Does this stereotyping you just mentioned have to do with the fact that you've done five shows with Doppio Teatro and that has somehow marked you as a Doppio actress?

LM: Absolutely, that's the backlash of what's happened because I believed so much in Doppio. I've wanted to work with them and they've taught me a lot. They've made me really proud and made me think "No, I don't want to assimilate; no, this is my style". And yet, because I've been working with them ever since I left drama school, everyone has been saying "No, we won't use Lucia because she's with Doppio. She's a Doppio Teatro actor". There is a backlash that has affected my other roles.

MS: You went to Doppio because you were interested in acting rather than because you were an Italo-Australian actress. What Doppio was doing happened to be part of your culture, so you clicked in very easily. Do you think that Doppio ought to be characterized as Italo-Australian theatre? It's a bilingual theatre, so what do you do with a label that is causing difficulties?

LM: Doppio actually started as a bilingual company. The Italians have been its dominant actors. Because Teresa Crea is Italian, it has actually evolved into an Italian theatre company. But Doppio Teatro means dual theatre in any other language as well. There have been Greek people. There was a German in there at one stage, but they all worked in Italian. The plays were worked in Italian. At times they went into Greek. This was right at the beginning. But Italian has become dominant.

MS: Would you describe Doppio as a community theatre?

LM: Yes I would. In its first stage and even up to about three years ago, it was a community theatre.

MS: In what way?

LM: They'd go to clubs, just like people in the Italian community who go to places rather than get people to come to them. They'd go to schools. Now Teresa wants to educate and sensitize her audience to the fact that you've got to pay for entertainment. You've got to go to the theatre. You've got to make the effort to support this part of your culture. A lot of migrants actually don't go to the theatre very much and she's trying to bring them out of their clubs, out of their houses, out of their schools to the theatre. It's a physical transition.

MS: Do you think this might also be a way of bringing them out, of making them more visible to the community at large, of integrating them into the public generally and, at the same time, educating them to the theatre as an art form?

LM: Yes, and also the fact that they have to pay for something that's not food, like at a "ballo", when you go to the ball. They always ask, when there are ticket prices that say $16, "Do we get food with this? Do we drink?" You say "No, just theatre", and they think "I don't know". The fact that they have to pay more than two dollars to go and be entertained, and to put that back into the migrants' minds. In Italy, they always go out for coffee. They go to the theatre. They go and see the opera. Whereas here, because their soul hasn't been nourished for so long, all they think of is work and eating. I know I'm generalizing, but I'm thinking more of the people who came out very young and have just been working.

MS: Do you think that the performance style of Doppio, from a cultural point of view, is specifically Italian rather than Anglo? How would you actually discuss this great gesturality, the mimicry, the movement in space, the physicality of the acting?

LM: It's definitely got the hand [mano] of the director, who is Italian. Because she would go with what the actors feel and the actors, because they're Italian, express themselves gesturally a lot. And it's also to make people who aren't Italian understand. I don't know if it's Italian. I think it's something that we've created here in Australia. It's something Italo-Australian more than Italian.

MS: My feeling about it is that it has to be big in performance and that it has to be extremely clearly articulated physically, because the gestures and the movements supplement the language that might be missed by some of the audience. They've got to understand through other means, means that are not verbal.

LM: Yes, by visual means and other senses, like hearing, like the rhythm of language.

MS: How do you feel about switching languages all the time?

LM: It's very natural for me. I do it at home all the time because, first of all, my Italian is a dialect. I swap all the time. Even sitting at the dinner table: "Ma, passa me lo burro, passa me lo knife". It's the way I actually speak. It's a real bastardized Italian. It's a real bastardized Neapolitan dialect, if anything. Like "Passa me lo knife", and things like that.

MS: So there is no strain on you and your concentration. What about you, Laura?

LL: The same, basically. We do it in real life. We do it in the car going to work, in the car going home. I think that's what makes it an Italo-Australian piece, the combination or the marriage of the two. I personally think there should be more of it.

MS: Of this kind of theatre?

LL: Absolutely. More of this kind of theatre. And more of the Italian going in and out of *Love and Magic*. I get into a dilemma about whether the use of Italian in this production is token. Because a lot of it repeated stuff that we had already said in English rather than allowing a character to represent a reality. A reality is someone like me and Lucia, sitting in the car going to work, and speaking in Italian and English. That's a reality. You don't get that on stage with the characters. You actually get the repetition of a particular English phrase in Italian so as to cater for the Anglo crowd. So I have a problem with that: Why are we using Italian? The characters that I played in the Melbourne Workers Theatre and the characters Lucia has played in Doppio have been Italo-Australian migrant workers who speak English with an accent and then go into harangues of Italian for reasons that are logically tied. They might get aggressive or they might get emotional or they might get the urge because they can't find the right word to say it in English. So that's a reality, and it works.

We've got the gift of speaking both languages, so it's good that we presented *Love and Magic* in English. A part of me says "Yes, ease them in just a little and then go pow with Italian", and another part says "No, let's just go pow from the beginning". I guess I wanted more dialogue in Italian in *Love and Magic* and not just repetitions or paraphrasing.

MS: Would it work, though, in this play which is *Italian* and not Italo-Australian and which is historically centred? It is situated in Italy and not Australia. The kind of bilingual theatre you are talking about belongs in this country.

LL: I think it's good to challenge audiences. I feel that we could have challenged them even more. What about having the whole play in Italian?

MS to Eva Di Cesare: I saw you in *The Olive Tree* and I know you were also in *Ricordi*, although I saw someone else in the role you took over. Both are Doppio productions. Could you tell me about the difference in experience between *Love and Magic* and your work with Doppio? What differences occur when you have a group that is united in some sense, as Doppio presumably is (goals, training, the fact that it is bilingual and that its members are Italo-Australians who have taken on board their cultural heritage) and a group that is brought together artificially, so to speak, for the purposes of a production, as was the case for *Love and Magic*? Was there a qualitative difference for you as an actress in terms of the work process itself and in terms of the production as an artistic whole?

E Di C: Firstly, on the actor side, I think that all the people at Doppio that I've worked with seem to have come from a similar background. So we're children whose parents are in their fifties, or sixties maybe. We know all the things our parents do which are very funny. In Doppio, we are allowed to work on those things. There I don't feel restricted. I feel that I have permission within Doppio to be as ridiculous as I like, to be as angry as I like, without being hated for being too strong. There was a nurturing of my background. I met people like Lucia and Laura. Our backgrounds are very similar, especially Lucia's and mine - middle class; parents who came here in the forties and fifties, mostly from peasant origin and who have done well for themselves. There is a lot of humour in that background; there is a lot of sadness, and openness. I suppose that *The Olive Tree* allowed me for the first time, as an actress coming out of college, to finally become completely open, able to experience every sort of emotion, without feeling ridiculous for doing it. Whereas at college I placed upon myself a restriction that said: "If you do this, you'll be seen as ridiculous".

MS: Would you be seen as Italian? Did that worry you?

E Di C: I was always seen as Italian. In the first year or so I tried desperately to be a nice Australian, and halfway through second year my teachers at the VCA [Victorian College of the Arts] freely gave me a kick. That's when I started to develop. So Doppio for my first job out of college. There, all the pent-up emotions that I had had for three years came out in *The Olive Tree*. From that point on, I realized it was okay to be like this, but only within Doppio.

MS: Because of the binding threads between you as individual actors, with a very similar cultural context, all resonances shared?

E Di C: Yes, I believe that. It was amazing that this experience came to me at that particular time of my life. I would have been a very frustrated actress by now if I had not worked with Doppio.

MS: What was the difference with *Love and Magic*, given that you were all Italo-Australians bar one?

E Di C: The girls that come from Doppio - and I would include Laura - Lucia, Laura and myself work every day with our background. We talk it. We live it. We always have it in the forefront of our minds. We speak like our parents.

MS: You mix Italian and English. You create that special language called Italo-Australian, like "la fenca" [fence]?

E Di C: Yes, and we perpetuate that. I don't think "Australian". I always think a bit Australian with all the emotional Italian stuff that I feel. I see myself as Italian and I think that Lucia and Laura do as well. When we came to *Love and Magic* - and we've all been in the business three or four years, we're the younger group - we met Peta who's been in the business for twenty years and who had denied her Italianness all her life till this production. We met Dina who doesn't come from our particular background.

MS: Are the three of you Southerners?

E Di C: That's it. Dina is a Northerner, and so is Peta. Rose is a Southerner and she does come from the same background. The parents of Northerners are different, completely different. They are from a different culture. It's a fact that, within *Love and Magic*, we had two cultures.

MS: My question, therefore, is: Given that you were all Italo-*Australian* actresses, why and how was it different?

E Di C: As I said, there is the cultural difference between North and South.

MS: Are you trying to say that the Northerners are more contained, that this is one cultural difference between people from the North and the South of Italy?

E Di C: No. Look at Dina. She's completely the opposite.

MS: So what's the difference?

E Di C: I have a feeling that Northerners see themselves as superior.

MS: They do. They think that the South of Italy is Africa. I've even heard some Northerners say that Rome is in Africa! Come to think of it, I have heard Romans say *Rome* was Africa!

E Di C: I think also that the older actresses - Dina has been in the business for twelve years, and Peta about twenty - came in with the attitude: "We've been in the business that long and we don't do community theatre".

MS: So, you're talking about North/South differences, age differences, experience differences and perception differences when you're talking about someone saying "community theatre" as distinct from "mainstream theatre"? What's the difference between mainstream and community theatre?

E Di C: I don't know. I don't think Doppio is a community theatre. I understand community theatre as people really working together, shaping the whole art work together.

MS: If you, Eva, were sitting in the audience as an Italo-Australian, and you weren't acting but watching, how would you feel about the kinds of gestures used by you all? Are they a mixture of Northern and Southern gestures?

E Di C: Gestures have to mean something to you. They have to come from within, otherwise they become stereotypes. I find the gestures attributed to Italians very embarrassing when they don't come from within. When they do, they're hilarious. They are fantastic, but you have to mean it.

MS: Wertmuller's films rely, of course, on very developed gestures, particularly on those thought to be typically from the South. And this playscript works on the North/South dichotomy, among other things that remind me of her films. Do you think that part of the problem of performing *Love and Magic* was that you had a script with complex shifts in it from pathos to grotesquerie, from the comic to the tragic?

E Di C: I don't think that is a problem. I personally never found it to be a problem as a performer. I did that a lot in *The Olive Tree*, for example, at the funeral, telling my grand-daughter to shut up, which was quite funny; and then suddenly looking at my daughter in the coffin and becoming quite sincerely hysterical. I tried very hard not to parody. I tried very hard to keep to the truth of the character. But I look at my mother: she goes between tragedy, comedy, pathos, hilarity, all in one, in ten minutes.

MS to Peta Toppano: Peta, was this your first experience with a bilingual production? Was it a problem for you?

PT: Yes, terrifying! I'm Italian. My father is Italian - from Udine - but was not born in Italy. He was born in Broken Hill. My grandfather had put in an application before the war to come to Broken Bay because he loved to fish. Mistakenly, he was sent to Broken Hill where he died of asthma, from coal mines. My dad grew up trying desperately to assimilate. He spoke Italian at home - very confused, very torn between the two cultures and consequently didn't wish to speak Italian. He married an Australian woman and only one language was spoken at home; but the Italian sounds were very familiar to me because I grew up around my nonna [grandmother]. I understood a lot but was very inhibited about speaking Italian. Teresa [Crea] wanted me to speak the language, so I worked with Mr. Pitosi from the ABC on my Italian.

MS: How did you feel about recovering these long-lost roots of yours? Did you find a new sense of yourself through this?

PT: Absolutely fabulous. I think it's one of the greatest experiences of my life. Also being with a group of girls, in that dressing-room, where I never had to censor what I said. I never had to put a pressure cooker lid on my head to stop any anger. If you wanted to get angry in that dressing-room, you got angry. There was no censoring, no bullshit. It was like being six sisters and you just said what you said, you did what you did. The shared experiences were amazing. We all had fathers who were very volatile and mothers who were very frightened. It was a kind of shared history, a shared culture, a shared life that bonded us together. Not like anything I've ever done before. Because I've always been the odd man out in a company.

MS: Are you suggesting that you've not ever really been amalgamated with a group before, no matter where you acted, in regional films or on stage or whatever?

PT: I always do feel like that, except in a mini-series that I did where there were other Italians in the cast. I was working mostly with Italian boys. There was a lot of swearing and carrying on. I found that with them I could be myself, and the Australians made a very strong dividing line between us and them. There was also a Polish girl on our team. She was the other foreigner. But in other television roles where I had to be an Australian, I always felt I wasn't true to myself. Something was wrong. It didn't ring true.

MS: It's a real problem, I think, this whole question of cross-cultural work and of being true to your cultural sense of yourself. Even if you don't have a language, you absorb all the cultural coding. You absorb the behaviour patterns. Some of it is genetic too, but you absorb it in the environment you live in so that it becomes part of you almost unconsciously.

PT: That's right. If I had a fight with my husband who's English, terribly terribly British, I would go "What are you talking about?" and he would say "Why are you shaking your hands at me like that? Stop being so Italian!" I was never quite sure of what I was. Now I know. I am Italian first and foremost, that's what I am.

MS: I find it fascinating that you have made this journey and come to a sense of yourself as being Italian, fundamentally, it seems, by working through this production.

PT: Absolutely. I tried to explain it clumsily to Teresa and I think she probably knew. I never had a chance to tell her properly what a difference it has made to my life. Not that there was ever a skeleton in the closet, not that I ever denied it, although I used to as a child at school. I'd say, "I'm not Italian". Many things happened to me when I was a child, but I remember being on a school bus and being hit from behind - I was about eight years old, in the sixties - by one of those little boys: "Your father retreated in the war you bloody wog". I didn't know what he was talking about. I asked Mum: "What did Daddy do during the war? Did he retreat?" I just thought I was the same as all the other kids, but I wasn't. I was small. I was dark. I had curly hair. I had hair on my arms.

MS: What do you think of this particular attempt on Teresa's part to create a bilingual theatre? You know she does it in Doppio and this is really the first non-Doppio production she's made for a place like the Belvoir Street Theatre. How is it for you who are working on the stage in two languages and having to come to grips with a new form of theatre?

PT: I panicked initially because I said to her - and I think I offended her by saying it: "Teresa, I can't do this. We're not playing to an Italian audience. Perhaps in Adelaide you were playing to a more Italian audience, in factories, in clubs, and so on, where there were large Italian communities. But here in Sydney, we're going to be playing mostly to English-speaking people". I said, "We're going to confuse them. I can't say a line in Italian and then just go and say a line in English", and she said, "It works, trust me". I said, "Maybe it worked in Adelaide, but it won't work here". She said, "It will work, just trust me; you don't trust me". I said, "I'm sorry, I just feel so ill at ease doing this". But she said, "Just do it". Every time I tried to analyze: "Just do it Peta". Looking back on it, I think it worked very well. Some people, in fact many people, said they felt a bit lost. Did you find that in your questionnaires?

MS: They say it in the questionnaires. Not many, but they do say it.

PT: They got confused, or they thought they missed something, or they didn't hear something correctly.

MS: Isn't it curious though, Peta, because what Teresa did was to have what was said in Italian paraphrased in English so that, in fact, if they had been listening to the English carefully, they wouldn't have felt that they had missed something.

PT: It seems that even in English it's a hard play to follow.

MS: Do you feel that the use of Italian in the production, which, I believe, was about 15%, might lend itself to charges of tokenism?

PT: No, I believe that Teresa did it with immense integrity.

MS: Were you at any stage worried that the acting style, this declamatory, rhetorical style right through the production might degenerate into stereotypes of women, particularly stereotypes of Italian women as, perhaps, Anglo/Celtic spectators might conceive of them?

PT: I've got aunties who behave like that. You put a bunch of Italian women together and they're crazy. Have you ever seen a gathering of Italian women at a wedding or a party? They all scream and yell. I remember at our family gatherings everybody yelling over the top of each other to be heard.

MS: I want to ask you about this: One of the questions in my questionnaire asked people how they saw the director's perspective in this production. I gave them a choice: "Anglo-Australian, Italian, Other". This was followed by "Please specify" and "Any further comments?". A number of them said "feminist". They didn't say "Italian" or anything else. They didn't give it an ethnic interpretation. They took it out of the ethnic context and talked about its feminist view. How would you answer that question? Did you see it from a cultural perspective?

PT: Yes, I saw it from a cultural perspective.

MS: Would you describe it as Italian, as Southern rather than Northern?

PT: Yes, I would. I wouldn't describe it as feminist. Feminist because it had women, but they certainly were not what you call "feminist". It's a very complex play socially and politically, speaking two languages, the fact that we are dealing with religion, witchcraft, fascism. It's like opening Pandora's box. Leonarda [the principal character, played by PT] was living in contradictions all the time: catholicism and witchcraft, talking to Caterina and talking to God. There are so many things we haven't dealt with yet and even Teresa said, "If only we were touring, we would think a few things over". But I wasn't dissatisfied. It was thrilling. It put me in touch with my culture again. Yet the question of geography, politics and many other issues needed dealing with, I thought. If only we had had six weeks of rehearsal time [instead of four]. I needed that exploratory time just to be able to make mistakes and get up and try something else. We did an enormous amount of improvisation. We did a lot of movements, of washing - miming washing - where I would have liked a lot more work on the text.

MS to Dina Panozzo: How did you feel about switching from Italian to English?

DP: I thought that it was extremely useful and creative because as soon as we got into our own tongue - and we all had different degrees of speaking our own tongue - it gave us this wonderful licence to be in a larger world. If you start making different sounds as an acting instrument, you are obviously opening other doors and necessarily going into other areas. Your body then has the freedom to tell the story of the sound, so the dimension is much larger. Then, those Italian sounds fit back into your English, so that your English is heightened too. I think that only about 15% of the audience had problems with the Italian. It was just a flavour. So I think it would be extremely exciting to use many more foreign languages. It could also give the whole Australian society a little feeling for speaking languages. We are very lazy here because the English language is the foremost in the world, and anywhere we go in the world we expect people to speak English. That's a great shame. For your brain to operate in different sounds necessarily makes your emotional equipment change, experiment, expand. It's a fantastic exercise. Making different sounds allows you a lot of freedom to transform your body in a bigger way.

MS: You said you would like to see more foreign languages being used in the theatre here in Australia. There are lots of community theatres doing this now. There are Arab-Australian productions, Spanish-Australian productions, of course Italo-Australian productions with Doppio, and so on. Can this kind of theatre succeed on the so-called mainstage or is it confined or doomed in some way, right from the start, to the so-called "multicultural" community stage?

DP: I think at the moment it is. I said I was pleased to be in this play because it's historical, and it is because it went to Upstairs Belvoir Street under the umbrella of Carnivalé. Even though I said that it was mainstream, it's not quite. Nonetheless, it's an enormous move ahead. This is an "off Broadway" kind of situation here in Sydney. In Melbourne we have Jean-Pierre Mignon and he uses a lot of different nationalities in his productions. He's a terrific person.

MS: He doesn't use French in his productions, only English. He doesn't want to.

DP: I know, and I wish he would. I think that now it's becoming fashionable to want to hear other languages. It's called multiculturalism. I hope, please God, that it's not just a fashion: last year the Greeks, this year the Italians, and next year the Asians. I really have a very strong feeling that that's not what it is and I'll tell you why. People like myself in our mid-thirties are the first ones to be educated in terms of migrants. I am now an adult artist and I am qualified and I speak up and people are letting me speak up. So the industry is changing. It can't go on being boring. It has to open its doors. It has to have colour. Mind you, it's highly suspicious because it plays with trends and fashion all the time. But you're not fashion if you know how to think. I have very strong feelings that my generation - not only Italians - is moving into positions of power.

MS: You're becoming visible and audible.

DP: Absolutely, and I am not giving it up, not after what we've been through. While I will continue to collaborate with my own race, I will not do it on the fringes. We - mainly the Italians and the Greeks - have got our foot in mainstream and we will even enter much more fully. But we've got to be people with vision and ideas. This year, for instance, marks the beginning for me of actually telling the truth about what I like and don't like, even in my own race. I don't like clubs. As a serious artist with a serious professional training who happens to be an Italo-Australian, I am ready to debate anyone on any level. What we must do is start to create, not just wait for jobs. I've collaborated on a short film with a fellow Italian. I've gone out to get the money. I've got to create a development grant, go for an Australian performing grant from the Australia Council. I don't know how to write. English is still my second language. I do not construct English very well, but this doesn't stop me because I am an ideas person. So I've got money to hire a co-writer who is an Anglo/Saxon and a dramaturge. I will create because it's very important that people like myself in my generation now start to move into positions of creative decision-making. Otherwise it *is* just fashion, and who wants to live here at that level?

MS: The creative decision-making may mean that you will all collectively decide to go bilingual or monolingual as it suits the piece.

DP: Absolutely. It should be as rich as this country actually is. Compared to the other two English-speaking territories: England, for instance, is not in any way integrated; it is not Europe at all. But when I go and visit my Italian relations in Chicago, they are so American. They want to be Americans. Every race that goes to America is American. Australia has a wonderful, unique identity, highly sophisticated, very complex. But we present a face to the world that is totally unsophisticated: Ginger Megs, Paul Hogan. I don't know how to solve this problem. We live in a society where you're very proud to be your own race - Italian - and you're very proud to be an Australian. So this is a truly integrated country in racial terms and we've got to bring it now into the face of the arts which represent society.

MS: Can we dream together for a moment, Dina, and say it is possible that in the future, in ten, twenty years, we might see highly capable, beautiful, artistically refined companies working on the Australian stage and actually working two languages consistently, at the STC, at the MTC?

DP: I think it has to come. The state of a country in a recession is very sad, but there is always great introspection when a struggle develops in a country. If we've been extremely lazy in a magnificent country and got ourselves into a state like this, there is a lot of introspection to be done. I know because I'm an artist and I'm going to starve through this. There's going to be an extraordinary amount of searching about values. People have to be rigorous about their thinking, why they exist, who their next-door neighbour is, what they really feel, where they want to go and how they want to live. I think this is the time for all this moving forward. In times like this, smaller bodies of people rear their heads and come into the mainstream. If you look at the boards of the STC, all the names are Anglo/Saxon names. It has to change. People were highly excited by *Love and Magic* during this phase of Sydney theatre because it's fresh, because it's got hope for the future. We have to find inspiration to live. I really think that theatre is in a terrible state and has been for a while in that we wait for festivals to feed us, like the Adelaide Festival. We want to be fed with imported material and we've got theatre in this country.

Going back to your initial question, I think that it can't not happen, speaking in different languages. Though I am a bit scared about the notion of the world as a global village, because then specific languages disappear, which is happening in Italy. I speak an old Venetian dialect and nobody has heard of it, even there. Only the old folks speak it. I was thinking of the Italian clubs in Australia, for instance. When people like my mother are gone, those clubs won't exist because I won't be patronizing them any more. It's a very sad thing, so it's really up to my generation to decide to maintain something because we want a society that is heterogeneous, multicultural. So there are lots of forces against us just in terms of the global village idea. But for the first time, I see around me in this country people of different cultures actually dealing with their culture on a vocal, artistic level.

MS to Lucia Mastrantone and Laura Lattuada: Do you think that more theatre in Australia of this kind - Italo-Australian, Greek-Australian, Russian-Australian, and so on - would eventually change the form and shape of theatre in Australia?

LM: Absolutely. The Whatever-Australian has filtered through to mainstream, has filtered through to a lot of community theatres. They are all picking up multiculturalism, and yet what makes me furious is that they do not use the real thing. For example, a theatre company in Adelaide did a piece about Thailand and they used Anglo actors, which is shocking.

LL: I think it would be okay for Anglos to play migrants if the balance was there, if the ethnic actors could play the Anglo roles as well. But the balance isn't there because whenever we get sent for a casting, it's the Greek girl, the Italian girl, the German girl. We're never sent for the blond girl. Multiculturalism is very much in vogue now, and has been for the past five or maybe even ten years.

LM: I think it's wrong to use Anglos for playing others because there are a lot of ethnic, multicultural actors out of work.

LL: But that's being as racist as they are. You shouldn't say, "They're Anglo and can't play a Greek". If you're an actor, you've got the skill to play anyone and anything. If they give the job to an Anglo to play a migrant, why not create a balance? But they don't. Just recently they got an Anglo-Australian to play an Aboriginal on television. Why give him the job when there is Ernie Dingo out of work?

LM: That's why I think non-Anglos should get first preference. I don't think it's racist at all. When someone has got the singing skills and the acrobatic skills and is Greek, why give the job to someone who is not Greek and has acrobatic and singing skills? Anglos can do any of the Anglo parts. Why go to them when their spectrum of work is so much larger than ours? You can't fight the system by being outside the system. I think that what companies like Doppio and actors like us have to do is get a mainstream profile.

MS: So that you are *actors*.

LM: So that we are actors. By working in small companies you work outside the system and people put you down as community theatre: "That's a nice small-budget company". Our budgets are always really minuscule compared to the State Theatre Companies. Maybe we could do huge productions of Pirandello using Italian actors or ethnic actors and ask for big money.

MS: Do you think there is an assumption that community theatre actors are not professionals?

LL: Yes, of course, that assumption is made constantly. That's why they are always considered to be fringe actors. Our stuff is art, and it is different.

MS: What was the difference, for you, between working in *Love and Magic* and the Melbourne Workers Theatre?

LL: There are marked differences. One, this play is performed in a theatre. The MWT's policy is to perform in workplaces during lunch time for the workers. Two, this is a given script. Like Doppio, MWT develops your own thoughts as an actor. You're employed to be a researcher-cum-writer-cum-interviewer and collectively devise the script so that you devise the character you're playing. You have a say in the music too, which is more than what happened here. This is a historical piece. Then there is the use of language: the MWT not only employs actors of Italian origin, but also of Turkish, Greek or Macedonian origin. It has a Mediterranean flavour rather than just one culture.

MS: What about performing styles, ways of acting, ways of projecting?

LL: I think that if you have performed for MWT or Doppio or any company like them, little as they may be, you can perform anywhere. The kind of venues we have performed in, and I don't want to sound like a martyr - it's a real credit to any actor. You're not miked. People are getting their lunch. I really think it's great now that I look back. You're singing a song and a little old lady walks by with her tray and drops her fork in the middle of your ballad and you're still singing. Or it's an L-shaped canteen with shocking acoustics. You can forget about real sets, the props or the band. You just set up anywhere and I think being flexible and adaptable and having really good improvisation skills are paramount, are an asset, a credit to any performer who works with that.

MS: And the concentration and the control of what you're doing.

LL: You don't have that here. You have an educated audience who have paid, who sit there. They can hear a pin drop when they go to the theatre. They don't do that when you perform in Melbourne Workers Theatre. There are four Greek men down at the end of the table who don't want to know what you're on about. Then you sing a Greek song and their heads pop out and they begin to smile and you think, "I've won". You have to be brave because we've had people tell us where to go: "Get out of here, bloody wogs, what are you doing here?" It hasn't been publicized enough, all those kinds of things, the real put-down things. Or again, "Melbourne Workers Theatre, who are they?" "You're not professional" - that kind of attitude to community theatre.

MS: Would you say that the MWT was a phenomenal training ground for you?

LL: Absolutely. I was a bit offended actually, because one of the company's past writers said to me: "It was an apprenticeship for you, a stepping stone". Maybe it was an apprenticeship. Maybe it was a stepping stone. It doesn't mean I never want to work with the MWT again. I do. I agree with their politics. I agree with what they write about. I'd like to write a play for the MWT and be in it. I think the MWT should be commercial.

MS: What do you mean by commercial?

LL: I mean mainstream. Everyone should know about it, like Doppio, like Spike Lee films.

MS: I wouldn't use the word "commercial" here. Commercial means money. I would talk about being well-known, being visible.

LL: Being commercial wouldn't necessarily mean losing its authenticity, if it's not for the purpose of keeping bums on seats. No, I just mean it to be better known, more exposed and more recognized so that some of the people who go and see the STC and the MTC go and see MWT plays.

MS: How did you create your role in *Love and Magic*? What did you bring to it that was really yours?

LL: I think a lot of the idiosyncrasies of the character actually came later, in front of an audience. I think that it's true for most actors. You work off an audience. You do something, and they laugh. I think that I probably brought some physical qualities to the character that perhaps another actor might not have. And the comedy came out bouncing off the person I was working with, that is, Lucia. Mind you, we didn't know each other from a bar of soap. Nor had we worked with each other before. But there was a chemistry there that just went. There were two things that Teresa really pushed for for the characters: their sexuality and vulgarity. I think she wanted the sexuality to represent the fascist era. I think that if we had played the two gossips stereotypically, they wouldn't have had these qualities. They would have just been talking like that over the fence. We did a bit of research about fascism - the relevance of the war, young boys being sent off to war, about how you condemn a woman for killing three of her friends in order to save her son when you, the patriarchal system, have sent off millions of Italian boys to fight in the war, about how everything was controlled. The gossips were almost like: "We've got our eye on you. We know what's happening". They represent the political power of the time. I bribed one of the gossips to come on my side and tell the diva [Virginia, played by Dina Panozzo] that she was an idiot. That kind of bribery also reflects fascism. I don't think the fascist quality of the two gossips really comes out.

Dina Panozzo: As far as Virginia is concerned, I had to tread a very fine line. I had to keep that edge there, pathos and being ridiculous, because these women were ridiculous and life is ridiculous, and Wertmuller does say that. That's how she makes you laugh. It's black and savage. But when you lean too often towards the grotesque, the vulgar and the ridiculous, you lose the truth, I think. I had to keep the edge of the pathos finely tuned so that I could lean towards the ridiculous but always keep the truth that although Virginia was a failed diva, she may very well not have failed. This play is about the lost souls of Mussolini's Italy.

MS: Would you have liked the social and political elements to have been worked through the production more so that the audience could understand better that this was Mussolini's Italy, that there were very specific pressures on these women, that there were specific kinds of values attached to the climate in which they lived?

DP: The answer is "Yes", but I feel that it's easier to set a world like that in film. Obviously Wertmuller found that too. Crea is the vision-shaper in this. It's absolutely valid that she took up the notion of woman as witch, woman as power, sexuality, children and merged it with religion and superstition, with the old savagery and the paganism behind it; the fact that women can work in those dark murky corners of their conscious and subconscious. I think it was fantastic because it was a more psychological piece than perhaps had been originally written. But given that we are talking about what world it was in, I definitely think that world did not come out.

MS: That's exactly my feeling. Wertmuller places this world very clearly. It wasn't fourteenth-century or nineteenth-century Italy. Now, I wanted to ask you how it felt to work with an all-female cast and whether this is the first time you've done it?

DP: No, at the beginning of the year I did a Steven Sewell piece. A two-hander, just two women. I have done a couple of things with just two women, but never with seven. I truly loved it because, besides being all women, they were all Italo-Australians except for Teresa Haremza who is a Pole. So we had a lot in common, given our background; and we were able to compare notes about our past. Because, as a migrant in this industry, you start out first of all in the fifties and sixties as a leper and then you become exotic, which is very fashionable lately. Then you become an artist. Meeting Italo-Australian actresses was like home, like being with a whole bunch of sisters, even though we are very different women. But we had the same stories, the same histories, the same terrible and amazing things happened to us. In the case of Peta, for instance, who is probably the least connected to her Italianness, the play was what I called "the getting of Italian". It was wonderful for Toppano. For me it was truly rewarding working with my fellow Italo-Australians at a level of great expertise and in that kind of prestigious position.

MS: Was it because it allowed you to look more closely at your own cultural parameters because you shared them, or was it also because it allowed you to explore your own artistic potential?

DP: This is the hardest question because it's one I haven't resolved. I think that what was most important was being in touch with my background, although I imagined it was going to be the other way around. I imagined that because I had an Italian script with Italian fellow artists I would be Italian finally in my art. That's *not* what happened. What happened to me was a naturalness about myself which I very rarely bring into my work because I'm still trying to understand language codes. I still have a language problem. I'm articulate, but I know I have a language problem because I've done this piece now and I know how I reacted in the past to other casts. For example, working in other casts, I've always been the Italian. By and large they've been Anglo/Saxon casts in television, theatre or film. I found myself relying on my Italianness a little in a predominantly Anglo/Saxon cast or trying very hard to be of the flavour of the whole cast.

MS: How do you define "the flavour"?

DP: Not being as natural as I was with these girls. Our dressing-room was as bad as a male football dressing-room. We talked about everything - bodily fluids, private parts, children, food, love, sex, in great detail. It was ordinary talk, covering all the basics. We were able to freely show off our Italianness and be as wonderful or as terrible or as ugly as we felt, and know the rest of the group would find it infinitely delicious to deal with each other at that level. So, working in other casts, I was always the weird one because I would come in and talk about the experience of love-making for the week-end or how I was sick. When I talked about that in other casts, I was suddenly over the top. They would say, "She's so Italian, so passionate". The people in Florence are very cold and detached compared to the way we peasant migrant Italians have acted in the world. I am from Veneto in Northern Italy. Lots of Italians who migrated during the twenties were Northern Italian. But in the fifties, the mountain people from Veneto and the Calabresi were the poorest ones. We were all thrown together here in Australia and we hated one another. In this cast, we had Siciliane, Napolitane, Turinese and Venete and we're really different. It was beautiful to have that subtle difference between Italians amongst us. So I could refine my identity even further - the *type* of Italian I am in relation to Australia.

MS: Did all this vitality, warmth, openness and frankness in the dressing-room carry over into the way you worked together, into how you performed together?

DP: I think that all of us actually believed it was very important that we didn't go for the clichéd Italian. I think it was consistently a problem because in trying so hard not to be over the top we were held back or held ourselves back to a degree. I know that for myself, at the beginning, I went a bit cute, a bit small with it, because I've always been very exuberant, very "Italian" in most of my work. I'm always a passionate actress. So the question is: "Is she passionate because she's Italian, or is she passionate because she's passionate?" I've never worked that one out. So I think that in the fear of being too big - we wanted to do subtle work, work that challenged the notion of a clichéd Italian who makes a lot of noise and throws her arms around - we had to deal with the dilemma of being too small. We were trying to get an elegant, subtle, intelligent Italian which is not the face of Italians in Australia. Actually, I think that what we were always grappling with was just an acting style. In fact, you just act with the power you have, with the words and with the vision that you were directed by.

MS: Two questions. One is going to be on what you think of the acting style or styles, and the other is about the shaping vision.

DP: I think that Crea's strength is the poetry, the beauty. Where I like savage, dangerous and uncomfortable work, Teresa's style was lyrical, poetic, very beautiful pictures, like a film. She wanted ensemble work very much because there were different levels of experience among us, and very different processes. There were community theatre girls. There were the Melbourne girls. There was the Polish girl. There was Peta with her weight as an actress with lots of film experience, me, Rose, and so on. She was trying to get us all to work at a gentle pace. I thought it was "undangerous". I thought we weren't taking risks, that we were not inventing. I have enormous power as an actress; why wasn't I bringing it to the fore? What Teresa was trying to do was to deal with the play delicately. It's not a delicate play. She also dealt with it in very modern terms in casting Peta, a beautiful woman, an attractive energy, instead of casting someone with a few teeth missing and grey hair, a seventies version of a witch. This brought the play into a much more elegant area, on a very modern level. I think that was most definitely the style of the play. Then it would burst out into the grotesque, in the way Teresa set up the fascists. I think she has massive vision, and it's her own.

MS: Can you say a few more words about what you mean by modern? Why is Peta modern?

DP: For one, Wertmuller writes very modern dialogues. The jokes are really contemporary. Then, Peta's massive television and film experience makes her work quite subtle and intimate. That is very much the eighties and the nineties. It's a very filmic style. Also, to have a beautiful woman portray someone who is wretched and half-crazy, who has given up the world of men and is outside of society, adds a lot of power to the piece. (When I say beauty, I mean a soft, seductive, warm kind of energy that is very beautiful. It's certainly not ugly. I don't think Peta could be ugly.) You couldn't not find the woman attractive. Once you're attracted to a person who murders and chops up three people, there is a huge dilemma. Then you start asking questions and you're forced to go and search for why she did these things. Whereas if the woman was crazy with shaved hair, black teeth, really ugly and spitting out curses - which is really how it was written in fact - then you would think, "She's a crazy. It has nothing to do with my life because I am not a crazy and I know no one like that". Whereas having Peta, having her beauty, you are seduced into really being attracted to this woman. There you are watching the profile of a murderess. So it's like a piece of modern film. In retrospect, I understand what Teresa went through much better now because that's how she got the whole picture, by keeping us full of our dignity, not making us crazy over-the-top Italian women, with strange histories, where an Australian audience could go "Lovely Italians, they're so wild and mad". No, Teresa presented these creatures with lots of pathos, simple truths.

MS: Back to the question of acting styles. Would you describe the style of performances from all of you as extremely physical, declamatory, rhetorical, gestural? How would you describe it?

DP: Etched in space. Very stylized. Certainly not declamatory. I would say it was heavily gestural. I would say the gestural in this play had to do with the choreographed, physical meaning of the story. My character, for instance, holds her chest very high, breathes lightly and speaks in a high, broken, husky voice because I found it through the truth of the character. In smaller roles, you must make statements in your physical body because you don't have the words. So on stage, when you are not speaking, you must fill the picture out with the physical gesture. You must have the truth in your body so that the audience can read something in your body, the sadness, the dreaming, the longing. For instance, in my role, if I wasn't singing, I was holding some physical shape. So I found the production like a musical, physically choreographed and vocally choreographed. I don't know what that style is. I would say it's a highly stylized piece of work.

MS: Does this have anything to do with what might be conceived of as an Italian culture in acting?

DP: Most definitely. I would say that everything I've seen in the past, the great actors I admire, especially the ones in Italy, are highly stylized. Nobody falls into flabby naturalism. Italians have a great need to communicate. They need to be involved. It's a very active and energetic race.

MS: But this is where the stereotypes come from.

DP: With Italian actors, reality is heightened and they have no problems in showing it. Not declaiming it and not over the top, which is what happens in this country and insinuates that you are not telling the truth.

MS: Let's go back to my previous question. How did all this openness and exuberance in the dressing-room and also the showing carry over into how you acted together? Do you feel that one of the things that helped you all in this production was that you all understood this showing, this very gestural and articulate form of acting where even the body in repose is saying something?

DP: I believed it was very simple for us all to bring this highly articulate style onto the stage. I found this so easy that I was wondering what could make the production difficult. In this play we walked on as ourselves because it is our second nature - or our first - to be articulate and tell it as it is from the heart, and shape it because of the great sense of pathos in all of us. I wasn't asked to do anything else: just stay still and be quiet and not work too hard. This was very difficult for me because I had always worked very hard not to be Italian. Suddenly I'm asked not to work hard because I've got everything. It was very confusing for me as an artist. Now that I have talked it through with you I agree that all of that went onto the stage. It was very simple to walk on, strike a pose and people would understand it so clearly!

MS: Do I understand correctly that you are making here an implicit comparison between what happened with you all in *Love and Magic* as distinct from what might be called the dominant or the usual way of performing on the Australian stage?

DP: Most definitely. In this piece, we always tried to work against the idea of "pick a style". We said, "Let's do the roles. Let's not think about the fact that it's Italian. Let's not go for the Italian in them". We understood instinctively the gestures of these women. These women are our mothers. We had no problem with yelling. Nobody had a problem with high emotions. Australian audiences who came to see us were so excited all the time, much more than we were. We felt so comfortable with gestures that our mothers did, finding none of it unusual.

Peta Toppano: I don't have a terribly retentive line-learning mind, so I worked very hard. I am used to working with intentions behind every line. I wanted to play an action on every line like you would in a normal play. But the way it was written, it was sort of what you'd call "stream of consciousness". I would be thinking of one thing and Leonarda would snap straight into something else and then something else again. I hadn't read too much about Leonarda. I bought a book on serial killings. I bought a book on witchcraft. The one thing that I hung on to was *Seven Beauties*. I kept playing the film over and over again. I'd come back from rehearsals and I'd say: "I've got to try and understand her. I've got to understand the grotesque in her, the humour, the rapid changes from humour to darkness". I watched the film over and over again with great intensity and enormous commitment and I started to realize it was terribly funny. I started to latch on to things about Leonarda that made me laugh, sections of the play that were tragically, grotesquely humorous.

I wanted to bring out Leonarda's kindness, nurturing, love not madness. I wanted madness to be the under-belly of it, but I wanted the audience to leave feeling that maybe she did do the right thing, like the speech at the end: "Alright, judge me. I'll pay, but there are millions of boys dying like dogs out there. Mothers' sons in Greece, in Africa, in Russia, being killed. If making me the scapegoat gives you a clear conscience, go ahead". What did these women have? One had cancer. The other one had no future. They were living in a village. I wanted the audience to believe she was sending them to a better place, and I wanted her to be like an angel.

MS: Is this the first time that you have worked in an all-woman cast?

PT: No, I have many times. I did a musical with twenty-one women. I've just done something for SBS called *Piccolo Mondo* with three women. I've worked about four times with an all-woman cast.

MS: Did this one differ from the other all-woman casts you have worked with?

PT: This one did because we were all Italian. It was a unique experience.

MS: And generally, when you work with an all-woman cast, is it very different from working with a mixed cast?

PT: I wouldn't want to make a habit of it! It's nice to have men around. But there isn't any kind of sexual tension. You are who and what you are, and you bring your talent and your integrity and your mind and your body to the job. You don't try and impress anybody. You don't try to be anything you're not. Women behave very differently around men, even in this enlightened age of ours. If there is a man there, women modify their behaviour. So we didn't have to go through any of that stuff and that's very refreshing. Women in groups together are very strong. That was a formidable group. I just felt very proud to be part of that team.

MS: Can we come back to the question of bilingual theatre. I wanted to ask you whether you feel that this kind of theatre can become mainstream theatre, or is it doomed to being small community theatre, confined to clubs and other associations but not necessarily able to work on the mainstage?

PT: I would love to see it done on the mainstage. I would love to see Chekhov partly in Russian and partly in English. If theatre is good, it's good. I saw plays in France, all in French, that just blew me away. I speak some French, but a lot of it I didn't understand. Yet I was still left with my jaw on the ground. Good acting is good acting.

MS to Rose Clemente: What I am really interested in understanding - and I've posed this question in various ways to all the Italo-Australian performers in *Love and Magic* - is how it felt for you, as an Italo-Australian woman who is a professional actress, to work in a production that had only one performer who wasn't Italo-Australian. What was that like for you from a professional point of view? Can you remember what the discomforts were, the joys or the queries or the doubts?

RC: There were many doubts. Initially there was the euphoria that we all felt: here was a group of seven Italian women doing it together, a play by an Italian woman, directed by an Italian woman, six Italian actresses. One thing I definitely learned from it is that I don't think that coming from the same ethnic background is very important in the end. I think that people who have the same artistic spirit, regardless of the culture they come from, are the people who should be working together. It has more to do with something that comes from the soul, a value system, a political ideology that fits with another group of people. They become your source of inspiration. They become the lake into which you dip constantly to refresh yourself, to inspire yourself. I think I've learned that much from *Love and Magic*. I've learned that just because you come from the same ethnic background, it doesn't necessarily mean that you're going to work well together. There was an unspoken assumption that because we came from the same ethnic background and because we were women it was going to be extraordinary. This experience clarified something for me. It actually got rid of a myth, the myth that because we are Italian, because we are women, it's going to be fabulous working together. It made me ask myself what makes good theatre. It's got nothing to do with gender and it's got nothing to do with ethnic background. It's got to do with soul, for me, because if I don't resonate with somebody on a spiritual level, it's no good. We can't create together. It's the stuff that makes theatre that we find very hard to talk about because there is not really a language for it. It's the soul of theatre that counts in the end. It's the spirit in which something is done. It's not for political reasons. It's because this piece must be done. It must be spoken. That's what makes great theatre for me. It's not: "It's now time to use more women in the arts", or "It's now time to use more wogs in the arts". That's a very sound political reason for getting more Italians and more women working in the theatre. Of course, the equality of opportunity needs to be there. But I have to go back and find out what it is that inspires me, what ignites my soul to want to communicate something to other people and I have to be true to that, not true to the correct politics of the time. It's a very fortunate time for me at the moment. I am a woman and I am Italian and that's good. The Australia Council likes that at the moment and so do a lot of people.

MS: Is it really being put into practice, this kind of *positive* affirmative action?

RC: I think that it is still pretty much tokenistic, but there are more women working as directors. There are more people from non-English-speaking backgrounds working in mainstage. This is happening slowly, but it's happening. I think it's very fashionable to be a wog at the moment.

MS: Are you saying that it has become part of official policy? So, officially, the Australia Council is thinking about wogs much more. Is that what you mean by "fashionable"?

RC: Yes, it's in. It's now legal. Places like the Sydney Theatre Company are actually being pressured by the Australia Council to hire women, to hire wogs "because if you don't, we might take your money away from you". So it's quite good for me politically to be who I am in 1993, being an Italian woman working in the theatre.

MS: We agree that this kind of affirmative action is necessary. Now, what's the snag?

RC: The snag is that it still feels like I am being told that now I must create *this* kind of theatre because I represent *this* kind of artist. There is a part of me that goes: "Hang on, don't tell me now that I have to create theatre about the immigrant experience because it makes you feel happy, makes you feel comfortable and makes you think that you're putting your money where your mouth is in terms of women and in terms of multicultural artists in this country". I feel like saying: "I come from a different place. I come as a whole person here. I've got a mind. I've got emotions and I've got a spirit and that spirit may want to speak in a commedia dell'arte or a Chekhovian-style piece or in anything. But don't tell me that now I have to get out there and be this passionate Italian woman artist". I have people in high places saying "Express your Italian passion more" and I feel like we are still being dictated to, but just in a different way. This is what I mean by "fashionable".

MS: When you talk about how you feel pressure being placed upon you to be an Italo-Australian performer - is it because of the way official people, bureaucrats, and so on, ask you to do things, or the kinds of letters they write to you or the kinds of offers they make to you? Where do you get the feeling from?

RC: I get it from the things they say. Once you've done something like *A Little Like Drowning*, you feel pressure to do more of that kind of theatre. I don't always want to be directing plays written by Italian people about the Italian experience.

MS: Tell me about *A Little Like Drowning*.

RC: It's basically about cross-cultural love. It's about an Italian man who has lived in England most of his life and whose family is quite wealthy. He goes to Italy, marries a village girl, brings her back to England with him; but because he's been assimilated into the English culture - she's a very naive Italian village girl - their lives just don't fit together. He wants to be a part of Britain. He wants to be a real Englishman, so he falls in love with an English woman. He leaves his wife and his two kids and he remains forever in a cultural limbo not belonging to his Italian family, not really belonging to his English family. He's just caught in this cross-cultural love. Anthony Minghella who wrote the film *Truly, Madly, Deeply* wrote the play. He is a fantastic playwright. He's Italo-English. His family come from the Isle of Wight. It's like a tribute to our parents for the group of us who got it together under the name of Teatar di Migma. There was Christina Totos, Rosie Lalevich, Dina Panozzo, and Nicolas Papadimitriou. It spoke very strongly about all sorts of issues that our parents must have faced when they came to Australia. In a sense, we wanted to do something that was a tribute to that generation of Italian migrants who had undergone great hardship, not just the physical hardship but a lot of emotional, psychological, sociological hardship, all sorts of terrible stress. The play really highlighted these things for us. So we thought our first piece out of Teatar di Migma should do something that was a tribute to the older generation. Now we are talking about experience from a second-generation perspective.

MS: Rose, there's a whole hidden story in what you're saying. Who proposed to do *A Little Like Drowning*? Did you? Did you have to go and seek a grant from the Australia Council?

RC: Yes, yes, we did and they willingly gave us that grant because the material was appropriate.

MS: And you felt that it was appropriate for you to do it, or you wouldn't have done it?

RC: Absolutely, I was passionate about it. We all were.

MS: But what you're saying is that you don't want this to be the only kind of theatre you do.

RC: That's right, the same as I don't want *Love and Magic* to be the only kind of theatre that I do, either. When it was over, a lot of people said that it was fantastic. They really meant "It was fantastic to see you Italian women out there doing this" without talking about the work. That's what hurts me because nobody was really that interested in talking about what the play was about, what it was trying to say, what it was trying to communicate. There was very little debate in that area. Okay, I accept that it's a part of Australian culture. We don't do very much after we go and see a play. It's not how our culture works. But the emphasis was on the Italian women doing this piece at Belvoir Street and wasn't that wonderful. I wanted the focus to be on my work.

MS: But you see, this is possibly the problem. Perhaps that sort of social statement is necessary as a preliminary statement. But the rest should then follow.

RC: And it will follow.

MS: The rest that you're talking about is the aesthetic, where the social and the aesthetic go hand in hand and it isn't just the social separated from the aesthetic. Is that what you're talking about?

RC: Thank you for putting it so precisely. That's exactly what I am trying to say.

MS: I want to come back to a statement you made earlier about being with these Italo-Australian performers, with an Italo-Australian director, in an Italian play, using Italian - about 15-20% - but all this not being what you thought it would be. How did you think it would be, you, Rosalba Clemente?

RC: I have to talk about it as a performer and as an actress inside it. I thought it would be extraordinarily liberating. I thought I would find a dimension in my work that I hadn't tapped before. That's what I was hoping for.

MS: Which dimension? Liberating in what sense?

RC: This is interesting because I thought I would somehow connect with my Italianness more fully in the work because I would be speaking the language, because I would be working with women who understood me. So I wouldn't have to be afraid of the power and of the difference of my work, which has always been a problem for me. People have never known what to do with me: "Rosalba is wonderful, but what do we do with her? Where do we cast her? What do we put her in?"

MS: And now that she's done *Phèdre/Phedra*, where do we put her?

RC: And I thought it wouldn't be an issue with these women, and indeed it wasn't. We were all there. We were all Italian. We all dived in but I felt really repressed. I'll try and answer why. I found speaking Italian for 20% of the time very difficult. It felt very artificial. I felt I was doing it so that the Italians would understand some and the Australians would understand some too, and that's really fabulous. But apart from that one reason, I was never clear as to the other reasons why we were actually doing it. Again it comes back to me as: "Are we simply making a political statement here?" and that's not enough for me.

MS: Didn't you discuss this with Teresa or the other women? Wasn't it something you discussed together?

RC: No, that was part of the problem. We did not talk enough. We had four weeks of rehearsal. Teresa was away for one of those four weeks because she had to be at the Australia Council. We had singing to worry about. We had dancing to worry about. We had a very complex piece that was quite fragmented, not linear in any sense, totally fascinating. We really talked enough about what the piece was about, so I don't think that was the fundamental problem. We never got around to talking about why we were doing it in two languages. It really did feel like we were doing it for the few Italians who came - because there weren't that many of them. That was incredibly disappointing for me.

MS: What or who in you was repressed?

RC: It could have been the part I was playing, Faustina, who was very repressed, the total opposite of Phedra. I was a mouse and I loved doing it. So maybe it had partly to do with the part. She was obviously the most repressed of all the characters in many ways. This has to be taken into consideration because, as an artist, you take on the psyche of the character you play. I'll say that to qualify the rest of what I'm saying. I also felt that many of us were still in conflict about being Italians, Italo-Australians, as individuals.

MS: As individuals or as individual performers? Do we separate the individual and the performer or do we put them together?

RC: We can't separate them. We put them together. Many of us were still trying to work out what it even means to be Italian. There were some who felt more Australian than Italian, others who felt more Italian than Australian, that "incredibly passionate" sort of stuff. There were some women who were dealing with the beauty myth, women who were dealing with not being beautiful enough, women who were bringing to it all their female personal agendas as well as the ethnic background like: "I come from this particular background. I am a working-class Italian. You're an Italian who comes from a very rich background". There were all of those chasms to bridge too.

MS: You had a whole class problem between you.

RC: Exactly. I can't tell you how complex it was, and it was terribly frustrating because of everybody's expectations that there would be immediate understanding, immediate knowledge of who the others were. As a result, the work would be explosive because we wouldn't have to cross the bridge of getting to know the other people.

MS: And you wouldn't have to cross the bridge of being one Italo-Australian woman in a cast where everyone else is something else and they understand certain things that you don't or they feel certain things that you don't because, after all, you are partly Italian. Somewhere, there is something Italian in you that has survived.

RC: Very well put, yes absolutely.

MS: So you thought those kinds of barriers would fall completely and there would be a wonderful understanding and a symbiotic, harmonious relationship - which didn't happen? Did it have to do with professional competition and cultural difference too, because of the North/South division? After all, Northern Italy is very different from Southern Italy.

RC: Yes, all of that. On a level out there, people pick up those vibes, what's being created on that stage, in that empty space, for one or two hours. It actually has much more impact than we even understand as performers and as directors. It goes inside people in a way that I don't think we understand. What people carry out with them is not just a critique of the piece. They carry it inside them. So we are responsible to the people we work with. We must nurture them and safeguard their psyche while we're working with them because we are doing such phenomenally vulnerable work.

MS: Is it because you were not fundamentally united by a common cause? If you had been Italo-Australian performers absolutely convinced and committed to specific ideals and principles that were social and aesthetic at the same time, perhaps these stresses could have been avoided. So was it the lack of common objectives, the fact that there hadn't been enough talking, the fact that the reasons why you were performing together and performing in Italian and English had not been discussed enough and therefore you could not weld your ideas together as one?

RC: That's a very interesting point. It's pretty close to what happened because it seemed to me that everybody was coming from a very individual perspective and they were all there for their own needs. There was the umbrella of "This is an important historical event in Australian theatre", but we weren't sitting as a group underneath that umbrella. We were actually just skirting around the edges, coming in every now and again and coming out, but we weren't underneath it together all the time and holding the umbrella up so that the days when it rained we were under there saying "You hold it for a minute; I'll hold it for a minute", protecting each other. Teresa had come from a place where she had created Doppio Teatro. She had pulled people in who really wanted to be there. She was clear about what she was doing there and suddenly in this kind of mainstream context where she expected the same kind of commitment as her actors from Doppio she didn't get it. People were interested in what this would do for their career, and rightly so. We mainstream performers - and I move in and out of that boundary - can be absolutely dreadful because we're out there, day in and day out, not knowing when the next job will come, and we come in with all that agenda behind us going: "I'll need this. This has to do something for my career". I wish I'd had more time with the women. I wish we'd had two weeks of work-shopping and then a month of going away and a month of coming back to it or something like that. It just felt so terribly rushed and confused; Teresa wasn't there for a week. We had so many people in the room when we were working, which was very distracting. You talked about competition. In a way the competition was heightened because we weren't different.

MS: I've never thought of that, Rose. It never dawned on me. So you *weren't* different from each other and that's what created the stress and fear?

RC: Yes. I worked with much less fear when I did Phedra. I didn't feel I had as much to prove when I was doing Phedra. I knew that I was the right person for that role. I knew that I was chosen for the difference, whereas with *Love and Magic* I was chosen for the sameness and that was so new it was terrifying. Suddenly I was there with all these women who were the same as me and somehow we had to make ourselves different. To shine, to be seen, to be visible became so much more difficult. We were all wogs, but we were all women too, and let that not be a secondary thing. Women have a lot to learn about being with women. Until we can be with one another in all sorts of situations, until we can learn to be non-competitive with one another, how can we hope for men to change? That was one of the saddest things for me. It wasn't even so much the Italian factor. We were women and I expected it to be a sisterhood and it wasn't. I've been let down by sisterhood before. I still believe in it. I'm still a feminist and I will never let go of those ideals because they're ideals. One day it will happen. But you can't attach yourself to any kind of "ism" in this world. That's where my expectations have slackened off. Feminism isn't going to fix it, nor is communism, nor is any kind of "ism". "Isms" are out as far as I'm concerned at the moment because the more I'm alive and operative in the world the more I realize that it's to do with me, to do with healing myself, and no "ism" is going to make anything right. In an ideal sense, feminism should have been operating in that rehearsal room, but it didn't. We were so damaged by our families, by our migrancy, by the profession, by being women in the profession which is such an oppressive thing to be, by having to look right. Even Peta, who is such a beautiful woman, had so many issues around beauty. It was amazing getting to know her. We were both reading *The Beauty Myth* at the same time when we were doing that show. People come to creative experiences so damaged in so many ways.

MS: How was she damaged by the beauty myth? Did she think she had to be beautiful no matter what?

RC: Yes, and it was very difficult for her to deal with it within her work. She worked so hard - and I really admired her for it - to make herself ugly in that role. She cut her hair. She ripped her dress. She did all those things because she was terrified that people were going to criticize her for being too beautiful. It's the sort of thing she's had to live with all her life, just as I've had to live with being too fat and too hairy all my life. Equally as painful, equally as distressing, but that's a little bridge we built between us, a little bridge of understanding and I wish we could all have built more of those. How do artists get into that rehearsal room and work with an intrinsic respect for one another and put the personal stuff aside and just focus on the work? How do you do that? It's so rare for it to happen, but when it does you really feel the possibility of humanity at work.

MS: Let's go back to the question of the "me" you were talking about: no "ism" but "me". What does this do for the whole idea that theatre is an art but is part of a big framework we call a culture? How do the "me" and the culture connect? Can it all be reduced to a purely personal level? Would you really, even after an experience of this kind, say that my Italian culture has got nothing to do with this "me"?

RC: No, of course not, because it's part of me. But I have to heal that part of me as well; that part of me has been damaged. I have to understand it much more deeply, much more profoundly, because I realized during *Love and Magic* that I wasn't as in touch with my Italian background as I thought I was. In fact, I was still in lots of denial and lots of pain about it, and I think a lot of the women were.

MS: Don't damage, pain and denial pose a lot of problems for the whole issue of so-called multicultural theatre?

RC: I actually think that all this stuff - and we were dealing with it backstage - was the real truth that needed to be spoken on stage. Maybe it was. I don't know because I wasn't outside watching. What do you think?

MS: No. At least I couldn't see it, which shows what consummate artists you all are. What does it make of multicultural theatre? It's an official decree these days. It's an attempt to redress the balance, an ethnic affirmative action and we agree in principle that it's necessary and important. This whole discussion between us points again to the problematical nature of multicultural theatre. I think it's problematical because one of its main assumptions - and it's right - is that ethnicity or so-called ethnic identity or something to do with a particular culture should be preserved, developed and extended so that it stops being in a ghetto and stops becoming wooden. You're a Southern Italian. You know perfectly well what I'm talking about - wooden attitudes, wooden values; it's dead and gone five hundred years ago, fifty years ago, but it still survives in people's memories, and memory and reality contradict each other. A Southern Italian goes back to Italy to her or his village and discovers that it has moved on. It has moved on to the contemporary world, and that same Southern Italian is still living fifty years back: she or he is an anachronism. So there is myth and reality, memory and reality all tied up together. There has to be some sense of evolution, of going forward, and it's socially and artistically important to ask this question about this new type of theatre. It's probably very important to create the theatre of Italo-Australians, French-Australians, Russian-Australians, Greek-Australians or whatever, a theatre that emerges from a particular group of people and allows the artist - you, for example - who has emerged from this group to flourish and grow. I think there's got to be some sort of support structure that allows a minority culture to grow.

But what's the problem? One of the problems seems to me to be, first of all, that you can't create art by decree. It has to come out of those people and those artists wishing to affirm something about their histories. This doesn't mean that you don't share all sorts of difficulties, on stage or off, with non-Italo-Australians or non-whatever-performers. But there are some difficulties - we might agree - that are unique to you, if only because you are known as wogs, if only because you have lived the experience of being alienated in some way and you've had to fight your way back from the margins. There is probably another difficulty. This uniqueness and individuality must be held together, but you become token figures in that you are forced, as artists, to conform to an image of Italo-Australians, or whatever, that holds sway outside the theatre, in society. You may feel this uniqueness from the inside, but it may not give you enough elasticity, enough elbow-room to develop artistically. And unless you can develop artistically, you cannot grasp social reality firmly.

RC: We are tackling something very difficult here. I don't think there are any easy answers. We are searching for answers.

MS: We agree that there is a problem with multicultural theatre and multiculturalism in general. Where are the problems? Where do they lie? We agree that it is important to give space and voice to performers who are not of Anglo background, who do have a different sense of the world because their cultures of origin and even of actuality are different. They have to live with *that* as performers too. You, Rosa, as a dark-haired Italian, will inevitably be typecast by some agent, at some stage. It's going to happen all the time. Someone is going to look at you and say: "I can't have her as Juliet. She's too dark", or "I can't have an Italo-Australian as Hamlet. He looks too small". It poses a problem artistically, but how do you get out of it without reducing artistic aspirations to a very narrow notion of "multiculturalism" which has the worst features of "ethnism", of some kind of notion of ethnic "essence" or ethnic "purity"? Then there is the problem of how so-called multicultural theatre keeps being pushed either into community theatre or what we might pejoratively call folklore, but it hasn't been absorbed into the mainstream yet.

RC: Yet *Love and Magic* was an attempt to do that, and so was *A Little Like Drowning*. It was one of the reasons we went Upstairs Belvoir. Our aim was not to create another piece of "Downstairs" but to say: "This can also happen on a bigger scale". And yet, somehow, it sat very uncomfortably in there. It didn't feel right because, as with *Love and Magic*, who came to see *A Little Like Drowning*? Mainly theatre people. In fact, more theatre people came to see *A Little Like Drowning* than Italians, even more than for *Love and Magic*. We've proved one point and we've lost something else here. I think Doppio's most successful piece was *Ricordi*, a wonderful piece of work. It spoke very strongly not just to the Italian audiences in Adelaide but, when it came to the Wharf, it spoke very very strongly here too.

MS: It was an extraordinary piece. The whole issue of multiculturalism and of mainstream as distinct from community theatre is an extremely problematical and difficult area. I would hate to think that "multicultural" theatre belongs exclusively in community theatre. I say this because I have argued for years that so-called "ethnic" theatre should not stay in the margin implied by the term "community" theatre but should move into the mainstream, move into what is, after all, the arena of art; not be seen as folklore, but be seen as art. If we define the mainstream as the place of dominant art forms, then that's where I've always thought it should be. But maybe it can't survive there too well yet.

RC: I think at the moment we don't know. Perhaps it does need to stay at its source for a prolonged period of time, only making little forays out into the mainstream, to test the water out there and then go back to its origins. We're at the embryonic stage. The whole notion of multiculturalism is still so young.

MS: We were talking earlier about the problem of a common cause, of defined common purposes or objectives. I've been wondering for a long time whether a bilingual, bicultural theatre of the kind that's emerging from Doppio isn't creating a new type of theatre, and what the future of this type of theatre will be. Where will it live? Will it live in a new space all of its own that is neither community nor mainstream? What do you think of the idea that a group of performers from minority cultures can get together, work out a common perspective and common purposes and then create this new type of theatre? It could be new not only in terms of its content - content alone does not make newness - but new in terms of performance style, the structure of performance, the kind of understanding and communication between performers that using several languages ideally implies, and amalgamating several cultures in some way, at least having them come together in some sort of coherent fashion; and have them make some sort of social impact. Is it possible to create this new type of theatre?

RC: All the things you are talking about are the things that Teatar di Migma has spoken about as being part of its artistic agenda for the future. After doing *A Little Like Drowning*, we wanted to extend in all sorts of ways, cross all sorts of boundaries, create a new form, create new styles, create a new language, cross-fertilize different art forms, bring together movement and music and language. But we don't have a shared vision strong enough to hold us and to drive us. There is no one in the group who's willing to take it on and make it their life's work, which is the kind of commitment it would require.